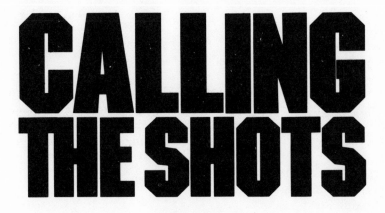

CALLING THE SHOTS

—

*Memoirs
of an
NHL Referee*

—

BRUCE HOOD

With MURRAY TOWNSEND

Stoddart

First published in 1988 by
Stoddart Publishing Co. Limited
34 Lesmill Road
Toronto, Canada
M3B 2T6

CANADIAN CATALOGUING IN PUBLICATION DATA

Hood, Bruce
  Calling the shots

ISBN 0-7737-2209-2

1. Hood, Bruce.   2. National Hockey League — Biography.
3. Hockey — Canada — Biography.
4. Sports officiating — Biography.
I. Townsend, Murray.   II. Title.

GV848.5.H66A3 1988   796.96'23'0924   C88-094448-X

DESIGN: Brant Cowie/ArtPlus Limited
TYPE OUTPUT: Tony Gordon Limited

Printed and bound in the United States

To
Joanne
Randy
Kevin
Marilyn
Cleo
who were always there

Hockey referees and officials

All those armchair referees out there

Special thanks to Barb Blair, Howard Berger, my son, Kevin, Tanya Long, Bill Hushion, Greg Cable, Don Loney and Donald G. Bastian, without whose help and support this book would never have made it.

Contents

Preface

When I meet people and they ask me about my former occupation, one thing is clear — they all want to know what the world of officiating is *really* like.

Depending on the story I tell from my twenty-six years of refereeing in the minors and the NHL, sometimes they laugh, sometimes they're surprised and sometimes they just shake their head in wonder. But they're interested. How did you become a referee? How did you handle all the abuse? Who were the easiest coaches, players and general managers to deal with? Who were the toughest players? Why would someone ever *want* to become a referee? Did you ever make a call you knew was wrong? Were you ever at the point where you thought it wasn't worth it anymore? What's the best thing about being a referee?

It's difficult for fans to relate to a referee. When a call goes against their team, they blame the referee. When a call goes with their team, the referee is just doing his job.

While they may not relate to the referee directly, it's important to note that we're all referees at heart. And that's part of what makes watching sports so much fun.

When a controversial play is replayed two or three times, from different camera angles, viewers are deciding for themselves. For that moment they forget the decision already made and become the referee. By the end of the third replay, they've made their own calls.

Of course, armchair referees do have a few advantages. They don't have to make decisions in a split-second, catch up to seven flights a week to get to the games, read a critique of their work in the newspapers the next day or call the shots while people are yelling at them.

But don't worry. I'll tell you what refereeing is really like. And it shouldn't affect your status as armchair referee. In fact, I think by the end of the book you might be a little better at it.

BRUCE HOOD
Milton, Ontario

CALLING THE SHOTS

THE WILDEST NIGHT
OF ALL

*All I could do was stand by the boards and shake my head
— a referee's nightmare come to life.*

I HAD OFFICIATED in more than 1,000 games, so there
was nothing particularly special about this one. To me it was
just another night at the arena. I had seen just about everything by this time and anything new would have been a
surprise.

I would be surprised that night . . .

I was aware of the tension in the air. To the players and the
fans it was not just a hockey game, it was war — the Battle of
Quebec. April 20, 1984 — Good Friday, of all days — the sixth
game of the Adams Division finals between the Nordiques
and the Canadiens. Montreal was ahead 3-2 in games and
with a win would head into the conference finals.

The rivalry between these two teams is among the fiercest
in all of sport, and seemed destined to be so from the first
time they met. I know, because I was there doing that first
game after Quebec had joined the league with the other WHA
teams. When the siren sounded in the Quebec Colisée on October 28, 1979, the Nordiques had beaten the Canadiens 5-4
and the noise level was deafening — louder than anything I
had heard in any arena for any game. The place was shaking!
I had showered and dressed and was going to find a cab
when I walked through the corridor an hour after the game

and realized three-quarters of the crowd was still there! I was stunned. They were singing songs, chanting and dancing in the aisles. I couldn't believe it!

Nothing had happened since to diminish the enthusiasm generated by a meeting between these two teams. I stepped out onto the ice to the usual chorus of boos, confident that I was in control. The emotion generated by the fans wouldn't faze me. At least for the game itself, I was prepared.

I had met with the series supervisor, John McCauley, and the linesmen, John D'Amico and Bob Hodges, to discuss the series to date and what we might expect from the two teams for game six. The first two games had featured a lot of hand-to-hand combat, but then both teams had settled down for games three, four and five. They had been playing fire-wagon hockey at a fever pitch and there had not been a single fight in those last three games. McCauley had seen all the games in the series and indicated that there were no brewing hostilities, or scores to settle. We all agreed there was no reason to expect the teams to play any differently — there was too much at stake now.

Things went pretty well according to plan for the first period and most of the second. There were a few fights, but for the most part both teams stuck to hockey.

Just as the second period was about to end, the puck trickled towards the left of Montreal goalie Steve Penney and Montreal forward Guy Carbonneau sprawled on his stomach to keep it away from Quebec's Dale Hunter. Hunter was going too fast to avoid Carbonneau and fell on top of him just as the siren sounded to end the period. I expected nothing further to develop and bent forward to pick up a loose stick at the other side of the net. When I looked up, I saw the makings of the wildest night in my NHL career.

As Hunter was getting to his knees he gave Carbonneau a little push on the back of his head. Dale was famous for doing things like that; he'd give a guy a little cheap shot after the whistle and then give the referee an innocent look as if the whole thing had been an accident. In that particular situation his actions didn't warrant a penalty. I assumed he would just get off Carbonneau and the teams would go straight to their dressing rooms. Even when all the other players started coming onto the ice, I figured at the most there might be a little pushing and shoving. And that may very well have been the case had it not been for Chris Nilan.

In my eighteen years as a referee in the NHL there were few players I had less respect for than Nilan. He would take advantage of every situation, giving other players a little shot after the whistle or mouthing off to intimidate them. The thing that bothered me most was that he obviously had little or no respect for other players around the league. Most guys will fight and then go their separate ways, but Nilan would belittle his opponents; he would taunt them or push his glove in their faces, trying to make them react. Many times he would fight for no reason at all.

Despite his attitude there were times he was almost funny. Some of the things he would come up with . . . I'd kick him out of a game and he'd holler at me and call me all kinds of names. Then he'd skate by with a silly grin on his face and say something like, "Aw well, I didn't feel like playing any more tonight anyway." He sure was a piece of work.

As the Montreal and Quebec players tugged at each other — no one was throwing any punches yet — I skated over and warned everyone to cool off and separate. With one period remaining in the most important game of the season for both teams, an incident of this type seemed senseless. To everyone, that is, but Nilan.

While I was warning the players to calm down, Nilan came around from the right side, grabbed Quebec defenseman Randy Moller and sucker-punched him in the face with his left hand. There goes the cheap-shot artist again, I figured. I thought of Moller as a clean, honest player and couldn't understand why Nilan was picking on him. Until then I had thought cooler heads were going to prevail, but that punch had the same effect as lighting a dynamite fuse — everyone else lost control. It acted as a license for the other players to start letting out their frustrations and tensions, and the war was on. Nilan and Moller fell to the ice in back of the net and everyone else piled in along the back boards.

Montreal's backup goalie, Richard Sevigny, was trying to pull a Quebec player away from the pile when the Nordiques' backup, Clint Malarchuk, came over and grabbed him from behind. The two goalies separated and started fighting in the corner to my left. I couldn't believe it! What were they so upset about? They weren't even in the game! All the other players paired off but no one else was fighting. I was trying to keep an eye on everything that was going on, but I concentrated on the main bout between Nilan and Moller, who were rolling on the ice below me.

Just as things were beginning to settle down I heard the crowd roar and looked up to see Mario Tremblay and Peter Stastny throwing punches in front of the net. I didn't see who'd started the fight but knew right then I would have to eject both from the game. The rules state that if a second fight starts while a first one is in progress, the second pair receive Game Misconducts. Montreal's John Chabot and Quebec's Andre Dore moved over to help their teammates and John D'Amico jumped in and tried to pry Tremblay and Stastny apart.

It was mayhem. The crowd was going wild. The players were going wild. And there was nothing I could do about it. My job was to keep control, but the players weren't in the mood at that point to listen to my opinions of how they should play the game. There was nothing I could have done to defuse it ahead of time either, because nothing had happened to warn me of an outbreak of this kind. It was crazy and I didn't know when it was going to stop. I think if I'd taken the players aside, one by one, each would have said, "I don't want any part of this. I want to go to the dressing room and rest up for the next period." But no one wanted to be the first to back off.

As Stastny and Tremblay were being separated, Moller and Nilan were breaking away from the pile and getting to their feet in the corner. Moller was absolutely incensed. Who could blame him? He had a terrible cut on his forehead from Nilan's sucker-punch and was bleeding profusely. Bob Hodges tried to keep them apart but it was no use. Moller was trying desperately to free his right hand and Nilan was doing his best to keep Moller pinned against the corner glass. Hodges finally managed to pull Nilan away but then Moller, left unattended, circled around and tried to get back at Nilan. That's when I decided to go in and help out, even though my job was to stand back and observe the situation. I grabbed Moller by the back of his sweater and told him to calm down.

Meanwhile, over at the far boards, Stastny and Tremblay had gotten to their feet and were tugging at each other. Behind them, Louis Sleigher and Jean Hamel were also pushing and shoving furiously. Everyone else was still paired off. After Moller and Nilan had finally settled down, Hodges went over to try and break up those dumb goalies, who were still sparring with each other near the boards.

I then skated over to the far corner where D'Amico was trying to pry Sleigher and Hamel apart. Then Tremblay, of all players, came over from the pileup in front of the net and tried to act as peacemaker. Unfortunately, what he did led to another full-scale brawl. He distracted Hamel, and Sleigher, with an opening, pulled back his left arm and corked him over the right eye. Hamel didn't see it coming and hit the ice like a fallen oak tree, out cold. Right then I felt another war coming on. Tremblay bent down to see if he could help Hamel, and D'Amico wisely grabbed Sleigher and marched him to the Quebec dressing room.

The Montreal trainer and team doctor rushed onto the ice to assist Hamel, who was lying on his stomach and seemed to be bleeding from his mouth. Again the players began to converge in front of the net. I had long since reached the end of my rope. I skated over and told everyone to get the hell off the ice and to the dressing rooms. I think they were ready for a rest because they listened to me and went their separate ways. The brawl was finally over, but the officials' work had just begun.

We went to the officials' dressing room to sort out the entire mess and dish out appropriate penalties in time for the third period. The overcrowded scene in our room during the intermission would later be the source of a lot of criticism and controversy. The confusion also spawned a blatant oversight that would lead to a second, more unruly outbreak when the teams returned to the ice.

In the room along with D'Amico, Hodges and myself were Andy van Hellemond, the standby referee; Wayne Bonney, the standby linesman; Joe Lamantia, Stan Boshier and Peter Smeaton, the off-ice officiating crew from Toronto; John Mc-

Cauley; Scotty Morrison, vice-president of officiating; and the
NHL's executive vice-president, Brian O'Neill. Al Wiseman,
the league's security director was at the door. It was quite a
scene.

I went over the whole episode from beginning to end with
the linesmen. Van Hellemond helped us out quite a bit, as he
had written down everything that he'd noticed from his seat
in the stands. Bonney was also doing his best to help get
things straightened out. O'Neill told us to get the whole
thing resolved as quickly as possible so we could prevent the
third period from being delayed, and then left. I couldn't
help but think his priorities were a little mixed up.

I assessed a double minor for roughing to Dale Hunter and
a minor for roughing to Carbonneau. I gave the two backup
goalies five minutes each for fighting. I gave Nilan a major
penalty for fighting, a second major, a ten-minute misconduct
for continuing to fight and a game misconduct. I sure didn't
need that troublemaker around anymore. Moller received a
major for fighting plus a misconduct for continuing. I had to
give Stastny and Tremblay majors and game misconducts. I
also threw Sleigher out of the game and gave Hamel a two-
minute roughing penalty. I passed the information on to the
off-ice officials so they could record the penalties on their
sheets.

Finally we got everything settled. Everyone left the room
and I had enough time to splash some water on my face and
drink a Coke. Then I took a deep breath and went back out
onto the ice. As it happened, I would soon wish I had never
set foot outside the relative calm of our dressing room.

Upon returning to the ice I summoned the two team captains — Bob Gainey of Montreal and Mario Marois of Quebec
— to the penalty box area and began explaining the penalty
situation. The Habs' public-relations director, Claude
Mouton, who handles the P.A. chores during games, was busy
announcing all the penalties from the second-period incident.
When he announced Nilan's game misconduct, the Montreal
player skated over to me and naively asked why he was
being sent to the showers.

I looked up and after a moment's hesitation realized that
there had been a screwup. Nilan had been tossed out of the

game after the brawl and wasn't supposed to be back on the ice for the start of the third period. Then I looked around and saw Sleigher, Stastny and Tremblay out there. No one had informed the teams which players had been ejected from the game!

As the teams were skating around in their respective ends, Moller stopped near the Montreal bench and started challenging Nilan, who was being led off the ice on my direction. As soon as I saw this, I rushed over and warned Moller to cut it out. But he kept calling Nilan every filthy name under the sun. After warning him a second time, I gave him a game misconduct and told him to get off the ice. While I was waving at him to go to the dressing room, Tony McKegney came over and started pleading with me, practically begging me to give Moller a second chance. But Moller had still not regained his cool and I felt he would serve no useful purpose on the ice.

Quebec's coach, Michel Bergeron, was incensed when he heard the announcement that Peter Stastny was out of the game but he was smart enough to grab Moller at the bench and keep him there. Tremblay skated past Moller and yelled something at him that made him even angrier.

A moment later, Montreal's Mark Hunter stopped at the center red line near the Quebec bench, yelled something at Sleigher and dropped his gloves. I couldn't believe it! I didn't need this! Not again! All the players rushed over and Wally Weir of Quebec and Mike McPhee of the Canadiens emerged from the pile throwing punches.

Dale Hunter grabbed Richard Sevigny, then Clint Malarchuk moved in and pulled Sevigny away. John Chabot went over and pushed Hunter. After a few seconds, Hodges separated Weir and McPhee. The situation seemed to be settling down again when Mark Hunter skated towards Sleigher in the corner. It was obvious the Habs had cooked up a plan during the intermission to get back at Sleigher for punching Hamel — they were doing everything possible to surround him. I was between Hunter and Sleigher, trying desperately to keep them at arm's length. Wilf Paiement of Quebec came over and grabbed Hunter's stick. Hunter was trying to swing it at Sleigher, who was obviously frightened and was doing his best to duck behind D'Amico.

Sevigny rushed in to get at Hunter and once again it seemed like everyone was going at it. Malarchuk, Chris Chelios, Alain Cote, Bobby Smith, Andre Savard, Mario Tremblay, Michel Goulet — all of them were involved to some degree. Hodges and D'Amico had done a good job separating the main combatants but they couldn't be everywhere at once.

Mark Hunter decided he still wanted to get Sleigher and went after him again, shaking off his brother, Dale. He circled around in back of Sleigher, who was now being held by D'Amico. Dale was just about to grab Sleigher when Tremblay came flying through the air and tackled him to the ice. This triggered a quick and violent chain reaction: Andre Dore jumped on top of Tremblay and began punching him in the back of the head. Rick LaPointe and Chris Chelios then leaped in and the whole pile of players went crashing to the ice in front of the Quebec bench.

All I could do was stand by the boards and shake my head — a referee's nightmare come to life!

Dore and Tremblay got up and continued punching. Then they fell to the ice again, with Tremblay on top. Peter Stastny, standing by himself in front of the bench, calmly peeled off his gloves, then skated over to the fight scene, bent down and started punching Tremblay in the back. And they say Europeans never fight! Guy Lafleur pulled himself free of J.F. Sauve and managed to yank Stastny off Tremblay.

The other players matched up again. Dale Hunter took over from Stastny and started pummeling Tremblay. Then Mark Hunter skated in from behind and jumped his brother. His brother! Hodges went down to break them up. "Will it ever end?" I asked myself.

Thankfully, once Hodges separated the Hunters, all of the fighting seemed to stop.

After this further delay of twenty minutes, I assessed game misconduct penalties to Weir and Dale Hunter of Quebec, and McPhee and Mark Hunter of Montreal. I also threw the two backup goalies out of the game. With order restored, it was once again time to play hockey.

Lost in all the turmoil was the fact that the Nordiques still had a 1-0 lead and had to maintain that advantage to avoid elimination. Their prospects appeared better when, two minutes into the third period, Goulet stripped the puck from Larry Robinson inside the Montreal blue line and walked in alone to beat Steve Penney with a backhand deke. The Forum audience sagged after that play, but it didn't discourage the Canadiens. Steve Shutt popped one in on a slapshot at 6:23 and scored again three minutes later. The crowd came back to life.

Weakened defensively by the ejections of Moller and Weir, Quebec never recovered from Shutt's two quick scores. Attacking the Nordiques' net in waves, the Canadiens blitzed goalie Dan Bouchard with a three-goal outburst in a 2:14 span late in the period to build an insurmountable 5-2 advantage. As the Forum shook with noise, the Nordiques managed one last gasp — Wilf Paiement blew a slapshot past Penney at 16:51 — but the game and the series ended with Montreal's electrifying comeback. The remaining players on each side shook hands at center ice — as if nothing had happened — and the Canadiens left to prepare for their semifinal series with the New York Islanders.

THERE WAS MUCH excitement and exhilaration around the Forum as the game ended, but my thoughts were on the incidents that had taken place. The game was over but I knew there would be a lot of finger-pointing at whomever had slipped up in allowing the ejected players to return to the ice. I couldn't believe that someone — anyone — had not informed the teams.

A number of factors led to the oversight. First of all, someone had pressed the buzzer that told the teams to return to the ice, before either team had been informed of the ejections. There had already been a long delay beyond the normal fifteen-minute intermission, so why someone decided to press it at that time, I don't know. Second, in a situation like that, each team would usually send someone to the officials' dressing room to find out what penalties had been assessed and relay the information to the coaches. It hadn't happened.

Perhaps I should have designated someone to visit the two dressing rooms with the penalty information, but I had enough on my mind just getting the penalties sorted out. There were a lot of people in that room and when I went out onto the ice for the third period I assumed someone else had done it, most likely the series supervisor — John McCauley — or even Scotty Morrison, who had been busy taking notes the whole time.

McCauley later told me he had intended to visit the dressing rooms but was accosted outside the officials' room by the forceful president of the Nordiques, Marcel Aubut, who was quite upset. By the time he got away from Aubut, the teams were already heading back onto the ice and he didn't have time to inform them. That would have been a valid reason had he related it that way in the newspaper the next day. Instead, he passed much of the blame onto me.

To be fair, it wasn't as if this sort of thing occurred often. It had never happened to me and there was no precedent to guide the principals involved. If it happened now, you can bet the first thing to be considered would be making sure ejected players didn't return to the ice.

If Scotty Morrison had thought it was his job to take care of it, he would have done it in a second. The same thing goes for the other people that were there.

One of the off-ice officials, "Banana Joe" Lamantia, made a valid point to me later. "Bruce, can you imagine *me* going to the dressing rooms, knocking on the doors and commanding the ejected players to get undressed? They'd tell me to fuck off so fast, I wouldn't know what hit me!"

In fact, Scotty was quoted in the newspaper the next day as saying that from then on it would be up to the off-ice officials to get the information from the referee and relay it to the coaches.

That was fine, because the teams would have to respect that ruling as well as the off-ice official who told them. Even if the players didn't know who the officials were — as in Joe's case, because he was from a neutral site — they would know that the information was coming from an off-ice official and that they would have to abide by what was told them or face the consequences from the league.

A column by Michael Farber on the front page of the *Montreal Gazette* sports section the next day was titled

"Forum brawl disgraced game," and in it was a mug shot of me, underneath which was written:

BRUCE HOOD BOTCHED THE JOB
Shame on you Bruce Hood. Hood, the referee, blew it. He was as effective as the U.S. peace-keeping force in Beirut. He let an already messy situation degenerate into what literally became a battle of brother against brother . . .

"It was a mistake," McCauley said. "The teams were on the ice before they should have been. Everyone's to blame, the referee, the minor officials. But, in fairness to the people in this room" — McCauley pointed to the officials' dressing room — "they weren't told that the teams had gone back onto the ice."

I felt like I had handled that game as best I could and as professionally as possible from beginning to end. If my bosses wanted to blame me for the incident as far as the public was concerned, that was okay. I didn't expect otherwise and I didn't react. I had the opportunity the next day when I was interviewed by Brian Williams of CBC's Sportsweekend, but I didn't lay the blame off. I had learned over the years that the attitude of the league brass was to let the officials take the heat while they said nothing. Now, at least, I can set the record straight.

Despite all the turmoil an interesting thing stood out in my mind. While the second incident was taking place at the start of the third period, Claude Mouton kept announcing the penalties from the first incident. Right over top of all the punching and crowd noise, there he was still announcing away. It just seemed so damned ridiculous. But that's the kind of night it was.

A LUCKY BREAK

Bev Hamilton once told me that I should always call a game's first penalty against the home team, to set the standard and to show that I was the boss and would not be intimidated by the hometown crowd.

WHAT KIND OF PERSON would choose a profession in which they suffer abuse night after night, are rarely appreciated and know they're doing a good job when nobody notices them? The answer is simple: nobody plans on that type of career. You won't often find "referee" on a young person's list of career aspirations, and it certainly wasn't on mine. Like most Canadian youngsters my dream was to play in the National Hockey League. Becoming a referee was the farthest thing from my mind and it was only by chance that it happened.

On March 14, 1936, I was welcomed into the world by Hazel and Melvin Hood. I was their second son. My brother, Murray, had been born five years earlier, and my sister, Marina, fifteen months before me. Freelton, Ontario, a small village about fifty miles west of Toronto, was home for the first three months of my life, before we moved to nearby Campbellville to continue the family farming tradition. Mom and Dad had both grown up on farms in the Freelton area and farming had been our way of life for generations, most notably on my mother's side. Her grandparents once owned the rich farmland in Campbellville where Mohawk Raceway — one of North America's premier standardbred horse-racing tracks — now stands.

Once we had settled into our new home, my first public appearance was not long in coming. Only six months after I was born, Mom and Dad decided to enter me in a baby contest at the fall county fair in Milton. I was a plump little guy and pretty healthy looking, I guess, so Mom and Dad dressed me up in the best dress they could buy and off we went.

I'm glad this story never got out during my refereeing days, even though all babies were dressed this way back then. Some of the guys I sent to the penalty box just wouldn't have understood; no doubt they would have reminded me between curse words that I had once worn a dress.

I was up against about ten other babies from the area and I won! They pinned a little red ribbon on me and handed Mom and Dad a check for four dollars, which went a long way back then. A full meal at a restaurant cost about thirty cents, so it was a decent prize. Mom still recalls with pride how everyone stopped and congratulated them as we made our way through the fair after the contest.

Small towns are good that way and Campbellville certainly qualified. I can remember lying in bed as a boy and counting each and every person who lived there — about 175 people. Now that's small.

Small or not, Campbellville was a great place in which to grow up and there was always lots to do. Summertime activities revolved around the baseball diamond and the pond in the center of the village, where we swam and fished. In the winter, once the pond had frozen over, we spent most of our time on the ice.

My buddies—Bob Lush, Brian Moore, Russ Hurren, Cliffe Bill, Jack Roberts—and I used to watch with envy as my brother Murray and his chums—John Bousfield, Stan Henderson, Ron Roberts (he later played hockey at Michigan University and is a friend of John Ziegler)—played hockey on the pond. Other guys would come in from the country off the farms to join the games, which made the pond the busiest spot in the village every winter day after school and on weekends.

As part of the younger group, we didn't always get to play. When they did let us there was usually a catch — they needed somebody to stand in net or some extra bodies to clean off a patch of ice. We didn't care. All that mattered was playing and we felt like big shots when we were included with the older guys.

They were well aware of this and missed few chances to take advantage. It definitely wasn't from them that I learned the concept of fair play that would be so necessary for refereeing. Once our school, Public School #10 — a one-room schoolhouse that accommodated grades one through eight — was to play a game against P.S. #6. The younger guys were designated to lug the equipment four miles down the road to their pond, using the big sleigh our family owned. That may not sound so difficult, but there was one problem: several stretches of road weren't covered with snow, and pulling that sleigh with the heavy equipment over bare pavement was exhausting. About halfway there our energy was spent and our desire had just about disappeared.

The older guys had gone ahead of us to the other school and were now coming back up the road to meet us. Not to help us, but to give us some good news: the pond P.S. #6 used was slushy and we would have to play the game on our own pond. We were ecstatic because we hadn't been looking forward to lugging all that equipment back home four miles after the game. We wouldn't have been able to walk by then. But that was about as big a favor as they ever did for us. We were always getting stuck with the dirty jobs, but the chance to participate usually made up for it.

I started out wearing strap-on blades. Having an older brother did have its good points because I used to get his hand-me-down skates, although they were always a couple of sizes too big. I never had any other equipment in those days. We wrapped old magazines around our legs in case we got whacked with a stick or hit with a puck, and those were our shin guards.

Real rubber pucks were hard to come by and we'd have to improvise, especially before the ice got hard, when we had to play on the road. There were still a lot of horse-and-buggy units around town, and often we would have a choice of frozen horse "doughnuts" to shoot around the street. The goalies were never too thrilled with having to stop a chunk of poop but it was better than nothing. Even my older sister,

Marina, who always wanted to play goal for us, wouldn't have volunteered to stop those pucks. Not that it really mattered anyway because it was strictly no girls allowed.

Campbellville was a close-knit community but still afforded plenty of chances to make mischief. Our village stood at the top of the Niagara Escarpment, a long, slow climb for the old steam-engine trains coming west from Toronto. By the time they reached Campbellville, the cars would be moving at a snail's pace — only two or three miles an hour — an open invitation to fun-loving kids. We'd walk down the track, hop a ladder on the side of a freight car and ride along for a while. The tracks curved through the village and around the pond, so neither the engineer at the front nor the trainman in the caboose could see us. It was all great fun, and pretty daring, until I got caught one summer evening.

Mom was out walking with a neighbor when she happened to spot me riding on one of the freight cars. I could tell from the look on her face that she wasn't too pleased and I got kind of scared. She didn't say too much. I ran right home and went off to bed.

Mom got home about twenty minutes later and came into my room. I was lying there, pretending to be asleep, when she suddenly pulled back the covers and gave me a whack on my behind that nearly sent me through the ceiling. I learned my lesson that day. I vowed to make sure she was far away before doing any more train-hopping.

I was no angel while growing up but some of my friends were a lot worse. Jack Roberts was a prankster and a real little devil. What a guy he was. In later years, he was a fabulous left-handed baseball pitcher who led Campbellville to several championship victories in the early fifties. But to me he's also memorable for his wacky stunts around the village and in school.

Our teacher, Emma McDowell, used to read to us every day after lunch. Instead of sitting at her desk near the front of the room, she would take the book and wander up and down the aisles while reading. Most of us would sit and listen silently. Not Jack.

He would get down on his hands and knees, follow slowly and quietly behind Mrs. McDowell as she was reading the book and start peeking up her dress. We'd do our best, for Jack's sake, to keep from bursting out laughing and were always on the edge of our seats wondering if he would ever get caught.

Sure enough, one day, Mrs. McDowell suddenly changed direction and began to back up, almost falling over Jack. We were all in shock when she turned around and found him at her feet, looking up. She started to reprimand him but Jack was a quick thinker and claimed he was only on the floor looking for his pencil. It was the worst excuse you'll ever hear, but somehow he got away with it.

If that wasn't daring enough, other times he would sneak up to the front of the classroom while the teacher was writing on the board with her back turned. He'd open her desk drawer, pull out the strap and take it back to his seat.

Jack also taught us how to get free oranges and apples. A big truck used to deliver fruit to Cramps' General Store and, generous souls that we were, we would always be on hand to offer our assistance in carrying the fruit cartons inside. By the time we had finished our pockets would be stuffed with freebies. We knew it wasn't right but justified it by considering it payment for the work we did.

Jack was always around to help me get in trouble but I could manage on my own when I had to. I remember one autumn when the ice started to form early. I was walking home from Sunday school with a couple of chums when we decided to see how strong the ice was on the pond. It was okay so we decided to try the ice on one of the other ponds — which wasn't necessarily logical because that ice was affected by an open area that never froze, where the water flowed under the railroad tracks. We decided to test just how far out we could go.

I moved slowly along the patch of ice until all of a sudden it gave way. Splash! There I was, all spiffed up in my Sunday best and up to my armpits in water. Worse was the realization that we were scheduled to visit my grandparents as soon as I got home. I mulled that over for a while, considering possible punishments while I tried to drip-dry in the cold.

When I got home I sneaked quietly into the house, opened the door on the coal-burning stove in the kitchen and sat there drying off. Dad had often warned me to stay away from that part of the pond and would have tanned me pretty good if he'd found out what happened.

I guess I wasn't all that bad most of the time, as kids go. My mother remembers me as "a real good boy who had respect for his elders." She rarely had to spank me and found that a good scolding, either from herself or Dad, would suffice as punishment.

I'm a sensitive person, probably a carry-over from my childhood. When I was old enough to be told about the baby contest, my parents teased me, saying they had entered me in a livestock contest, and I got pretty upset. Another time my cousin Betty, who had been boarding with us, decided to dress me up for Halloween. I don't remember the costume but it was hilarious, and when Mom and Dad saw me they cracked up. I started crying, went to my room and refused to go out trick-or-treating.

I was also a very determined child. I was only about seven or eight when I decided to go after school to meet my dad while he was working. Part of his job was to go from farm to farm and do the threshing for the other farmers. I thought he was headed to my grandfather's place, about ten miles away. I started hiking that way and had gone about three miles before a friend out in the country called my mother to tell her that I had just walked past their house. She sent her daughter with a bicycle to get me or I would have kept walking until I made it. It turns out that Dad had not gone to my grandfather's, but to a farm only a mile and a half from the village.

When I was older and we had moved to Milton, Mom and Dad decided to take a holiday up north for a few days and arranged for me to stay at our next-door neighbor's — the McPhails. Little did they know that I was planning the same holiday. They dropped me off at the McPhails' and about ten minutes later started out for the north country. They drove around the block and when they got to the stop sign they couldn't believe their eyes: there I was, standing on the corner with a little travel bag draped over my shoulder. I was all set to go with them and they took me. I think they knew they would have broken my heart if they had dropped me back at the neighbors'.

Another childhood incident sticks out because I almost lost my head over it. My brother Murray was cutting some wood in the backyard with an ax one day and I was sitting on the ground, watching. On one of his swings, he accidentally caught the ax in the clothesline above him. He yanked at the line and brought the ax right down on my head. There was a piece of wood stuck on the blade or it could have been the end of me. Still, I was bleeding plenty enough and was rushed to a doctor, who stitched me up.

WHEN I WAS eleven years old my father was offered a position with the P.L. Robertson Manufacturing Company, seven miles away in Milton. My brother Murray had moved there one year before to work in the bank, and now the rest of us packed up and moved, too. This company, the first to manufacture the socket-head screw, was considered the place to work in the area back then. For Dad to get a job in the big town was quite a step for the family.

Milton, about thirty-five miles west of Toronto, was quite a bit larger than Campbellville. When we first settled there in 1947, some 4,000 people lived in the town and on its outskirts. Its population was less than 8,000 as late as 1976. Since then Milton has become part of the Region of Halton; it has swallowed up Campbellville and now has about 33,000 people, a desirable place for those who don't want to live in a big city but want to be close. Mom and Dad still live there, as do my wife, Joanne, and me.

Milton has several links with professional hockey. The first was Enio Sclisizzi, who worked his way up through the local minors and went on to play in the NHL. Sclisizzi was born in 1925 and played eighty-one National League games with Detroit and Chicago, but spent most of his career in the minors. A forward, he scored a total of twelve NHL goals, his best season being 1948-49 when he counted nine goals and seventeen points in fifty games with Detroit. He made a lot of people in Milton very proud and still resides in the town.

The most recent pride of Milton is John Tonelli, who helped the New York Islanders win four straight Stanley Cups between 1980 and 1983, and won the Most Valuable Player award in the 1984 Canada Cup tournament. He went on to play left wing for the Calgary Flames and signed to play with Los Angeles for the 1988-89 season. His boyhood teammate, Mike Kaszycki, played for a few years on the Islanders before going on to join Washington and later Toronto. Rick Bourbonnais, who played with St. Louis for three years, lived in Milton for a while and his family still does. Tom Martin, who played a few NHL games for the Toronto Maple Leafs and three seasons in the WHA, moved to Milton while playing for the Toronto Toros. Martin also coached the Toronto Marlies in the Ontario Hockey League and the Milton Junior B team. He is still active coaching minor hockey in Milton. Darren Eliot, a goaltender with the Detroit chain who also played with Los Angeles, was born in Hamilton but moved to Milton as a teenager. Peter McDuffe, who played goal briefly with the Rangers and St. Louis in the seventies, was born in Milton and played all his minor hockey there. My good friend and former working partner, Leon Stickle — one of the top NHL linesmen — is also from Milton. Leon now lives in Mount Forest, a smaller community several miles to the northwest.

Mike Kaszycki's parents recall attending a game in which four people from Milton were on the ice at the same time — John Tonelli and Mike Kaszycki were playing for the Islanders, I was refereeing and Leon Stickle was one of the linesmen. Considering the size of the town, that was quite a feat!

Moving into Milton changed things drastically for Murray and me; it meant we could play hockey in an arena. Imagine, playing inside boards, with a roof overhead . . . All arenas in those days had natural ice and the quality of the ice surface depended entirely on how cold it was outside. Sometimes that could create misery. I remember walking to the rink one Saturday when it was fairly warm out and seeing the rink covered with water. Our game had to be postponed and I was so disappointed I ran all the way home with tears in my eyes. Playing hockey was easily the highlight of each week for many of us when we were young.

A big event in my young life was the day Murray bought me my first new pair of skates. I was overjoyed when he came into the house with them. Unfortunately, the same old problem arose. They were a bit large — by about three sizes.

Murray said not to worry, that I would eventually grow into them. I couldn't help but wonder, happy though I was, when I was going to get a pair of skates that fit me.

WHEN I WAS fifteen I left school and went to work in Toronto for a company that installed intercom systems. It was no big deal back then leaving school at such a young age. Most kids fifteen and sixteen went into the work force and my job with the intercom company offered me a chance to get out and see the big city and find out what it was like living away from home. Stan Henderson, born and raised in Campbellville, was working for the company and got me the job. We shared an apartment.

Eighteen months later I returned to Milton to become a partner with Murray in the town's ice-delivery business. We purchased the ice company from Art Higgins, who was also the manager of the Milton arena.

Ice delivery flourished during the summer. There were many refrigerators and freezers back then, but many homes had iceboxes. Three times a week I would hoist the twenty-five- or fifty-pound blocks of ice up to my shoulders and make deliveries to local homes. On Saturdays I would deliver up to two-and-a-half tons of the stuff. I would put the blocks in the top of the ice boxes and that would keep the food cool for a couple of days.

The ice was manufactured by the arena's refrigeration system and I learned a lot about its mechanics by working around the arena with Higgins during the winter months. Years earlier, in 1949, when the arena went from natural to artificial ice, I had helped wheel in sand to put between the pipes for the refrigerator system. Ice has always played a part in my life. As kids we used to take pieces of ice off the back of the ice truck when it came to Campbellville, to suck on. Later I made ice at the arena, delivered ice as a business and eventually skated on it for a living.

Even with the advent of artificial ice there was no such thing as a Zamboni machine to clean it. We had four or five rink rats who went out and scraped the ice with shovels and tossed the snow out the side of the arena. To flood the ice we used pull carts. Still, that was an improvement over the natural ice that we could only flood once a day, with a big hose.

I STARTED DATING my wife-to-be, Joanne Tufford, a sixteen-year-old native of Milton, shortly after I returned from my job in Toronto. Joanne and I had known each other from the time I first moved to Milton, and had gone to public and high school together. She used to play tennis all the time at the courts on Main Street, so I always knew where to find her. We ended up getting married a few years after we started dating. We had three children in three consecutive years — Randy, Kevin and Marilyn.

Besides working in ice delivery and dating Joanne, I also kept busy playing Juvenile hockey in Milton, as well as some Junior with the nearby Georgetown Cotton Kings.

My Juvenile coach was Lorne "Dooney" Evans. Once he set a rule down, he meant it. I learned some valuable lessons the hard way. He told me that if I didn't stop taking stupid penalties, he'd bench me. I got more dumb penalties and sure enough, I sat on the bench for a while. Another rule was that if we missed the early morning practices we didn't play in the next game. I missed one, showed up at the next game with my equipment and was told I wouldn't be playing.

Eventually I got a tryout with the Milton Pontiacs Intermediate club. They were the big deal in town. The Pontiacs played every Friday night and packed the arena for every game. The goal of most young guys growing up in Milton at that time was to be good enough to make that team.

I wasn't a good puck handler, but somehow I made the team. I was a big, awkward defenseman who knew how to bump people around. I used my elbows a lot and knew all the dirty tricks, which came in handy as a referee later — I knew what to look for. In one exhibition game, after receiving a fighting major, I went after the referee and bumped him a little. I received a misconduct. Immediately after my temper tantrum I realized how ridiculous it was for me to behave that way. Later I apologized to him.

Although we lived fairly close to Toronto, we had very little contact with the NHL. Pro hockey was a pipe dream for most of us, not something we considered seriously. There was no such thing then as television, so our only link with the NHL was Foster Hewitt's Saturday-night radio broadcast from Maple Leaf Gardens. Also, the Toronto papers would come to town and fill us in a little bit more on the Leafs.

I didn't visit Maple Leaf Gardens until I was twenty-three years old. It was during the 1959-60 season and I was already working in the Ontario Hockey Association as a linesman. One night Al Salmon, a fellow official from Burlington, phoned me and said he had a couple of tickets for the next Leaf game, on Wednesday against Chicago. It was one of the biggest thrills of my life. I don't recall watching much of the game. I spent most of the evening staring up at the enormous ceiling and looking around at the massive number of seats. I'd never been inside anything that huge.

When I wasn't playing for the Intermediates I spent a lot of time at the Milton arena. Art Higgins had made me assistant arena manager in the winter and I would spell him off a bit and do chores like cleaning up the arena, sweeping out the stands and painting the lines on the ice.

I was at the rink one Monday night when a local league, the Junior Farmers Hockey League, made up of farm boys from the surrounding area, realized they were short a referee. Bill Boyd, the head referee, approached me and asked if I would officiate the game with him. A chap named Bruce Marshall was supposed to be there but couldn't make it because he had to baby-sit. I figured, why not?, and went over to Marshall's house to borrow his whistle. I wore a plain, tan-colored sweater, worked the game and was surprised to find that I enjoyed it. They asked me if I would come out again the following week, which I agreed to, as long as it didn't interfere with my Intermediate games. I was almost always available and it quickly turned into a weekly thing.

I had no idea at that point that it would turn into a profession. My chief interest still was playing defense on Friday nights with the Pontiacs. An incident in one of those games would alter my attitude.

I went to take a shot from the blue line on the power play when one of my opponents came out to check me and knocked me over backwards. He fell on top of me and my left ankle caught underneath me. I had torn every ligament in my ankle and was told I wouldn't be able to play for two months. I was devastated.

While I was healing, my doctor told me I should stop playing hockey. He said I had a wife to look after and another serious injury to my ankle could really be damaging. Although he made a lot of sense I knew there was no way I would stay away from the team once my injury healed. Hockey was still too important to me.

Then one night, just before I was about to return to play, Bill Boyd got struck in the face by a puck during one of our Friday-night home games and was severely cut. Back then the OHA would assign a referee from a neutral site and the local team would provide a linesman. That night it was Boyd. I was well enough to skate again, so they came to me because of my experience in the Monday-night league, and asked if I would be the linesman for the remainder of the game. I obliged and again enjoyed it.

Bill wasn't able to work the following week either, and then he decided he didn't want to do it at all anymore. Would I be interested in taking his place? The next thing I knew I was the local linesman instead of the local defenseman. To me it was a compromise with my doctor, giving me the chance to be stay involved in hockey at much lower risk. Plus I got paid.

I worked hard at becoming a good official and learned a lot from the referees in the league. Joe Sadler and Stan Boshier, who came out from Toronto, were two of the refs. Both are now off-ice officials in NHL games at Maple Leaf Gardens — Sadler a goal judge and Boshier the penalty timekeeper.

When I was growing up a number of people contributed to my increasing attraction to the world of officiating. Cliff Houston, Dave Brush and Arnold McDuffe refereed games in Milton and worked hard organizing minor hockey. I admired the work they did. When they were out on the ice officiating, there was no disputing who was in charge. It might seem strange to have referees as boyhood idols, but they were positive influences because of the amount of respect they commanded.

If, as is often the case in minor hockey today, they had been constantly abused verbally, their role wouldn't have been as attractive to me and my life could have taken a completely different turn.

Two other men I admired in a similar way were Bev Hamilton of Burlington and Bill Divorski of Guelph, both of whom had long minor-league officiating careers in Ontario. Bill's son, Paul, is one of the good, young, up-and-coming officials on the NHL staff.

Bev Hamilton told me once that I should always call a game's first penalty against the home team, to set the standard and to show that I was boss and would not be intimidated by the hometown crowd. So that's why Bev had always stuck it to us right off the bat when I was with the Intermediates!

Meanwhile, other leagues started calling on me to referee their games. I handled some minor games in town on Tuesday nights and a Wednesday after-school league. Then a Thursday-night industrial league got in touch with me. I also helped out with minor hockey games on Saturday mornings.

The work was enjoyable, and besides, helped out financially. I didn't get paid much — about eight or ten dollars a game (excluding minor hockey, for which there was no pay) — but I was married and Randy had already been born so those few extra dollars came in handy. I was also writing a sports column for the *Canadian Champion*, the local Milton paper, often covering the games I was officiating. There was never any criticism of the refereeing!

When I was twenty-two Art Higgins left the arena and I became manager. The arena board got me to write exams for my refrigeration operator's certificate. The whole thing was easy to adapt to because Art had been a great teacher. I became the first full-time arena manager Milton ever had. In previous years, they would hire someone only for the winter months. They paid me $6,000 for that year — big money in those days — and I worked seven days a week.

I also kept officiating, which enabled me to earn a little extra. Naturally, both jobs kept me away from home almost all the time. All three of our children had been born by then and it kept Joanne a lot busier than she deserved to be. But God bless her, she did a wonderful job of raising our family while I was running around trying to make money.

THE FIRST MAJOR breakthrough in my officiating career happened in early 1962, just before my twenty-sixth birthday. One Sunday morning I got a call from Pat Patterson, referee-in-chief of the OHA, and he gave me an assignment as a fill-in linesman for a Toronto Marlboro Junior game at Maple Leaf Gardens. The regular linesman had been injured. So I got to fill in for one of those Sunday afternoon doubleheaders that were so popular at the Gardens back then. Both the Marlboros and St. Michael's would play games and the place would be sold out each week.

The Marlies were playing the St. Catharines Teepees. "Banana Joe" Lamantia was the penalty timekeeper for Junior games back then (he's now the timekeeper for the Maple Leaf games). I was standing in front of the penalty box, doing my job, when he leaned over the glass and yelled at me to get out of his way. "You're too god-damned tall," he barked. "I can't see the play!" I turned around and stared at him in disbelief, but I sure as heck moved.

Pat Stapleton, a defenseman who went on to have so many fine years in Chicago, was playing for the Teepees that day and I remember he skated over to pick up some pennies that had been thrown onto the ice. He then came and handed them to me and said, "Here, maybe this can help you buy some glasses." He said it with a good-natured grin on his face. It didn't bother me. In fact it was such a thrill just to have a player talk to me at that level that I didn't care what he said.

After the game at the Gardens I started to get regular assignments in Junior A as a linesman.

While my officiating career began to skyrocket, a major conflict developed with the arena board in Milton. I was still holding my seven-day-a-week job as arena manager, and the more OHA assignments I accepted, the more I was pulled away from my regular work. I would be refereeing a game somewhere when I really should have been in the arena running things. This happened several times, though I would always designate someone else to look after the place for a few hours while I was gone. Then I would rush back to the arena after the game and check things out. Usually there was no problem.

I tried my best to ensure that the arena board wouldn't find out about my absence each week and it worked pretty well until a local Hamilton station (CHCH TV) started televising Red Wing Junior A games from the Hamilton Forum on Thursday nights. One Friday morning I got a call from a board member who had seen me on TV the night before, and he wasn't too pleased. The arena board called me in and told me I had a job to do at night and I couldn't continue running around as an official. They said I had to make up my mind which one I wanted to do.

I was so involved in officiating, lapping up the excitement and challenge, the choice wasn't difficult. In one quick stab at a compromise, I told the arena board it wasn't fair that I was working seven days and seven nights per week and that they should allow me to continue my job as an official by bringing someone else in for the arena part-time.

They didn't like my suggestion at all so I handed in my notice even though I didn't have anything definite yet in officiating. But I knew exactly what I wanted to do. I had to see how far I could go with it. I never would have been able to forgive myself if I didn't take the opportunity to go after my goal.

At the end of the 1961-62 season I really hit the big time when I worked as a linesman in the Memorial Cup Junior A championship between the Hamilton Red Wings and Edmonton Oil Kings. The series was played in Hamilton and Guelph and I worked one game in each city. Apart from the thrill and satisfaction of being considered competent enough to be given such a prestigious assignment, I will always remember that play-off series because of a bad toothache. Earlier in the season I had arranged to have a wisdom tooth removed during the week of the Memorial Cup, simply because I never thought I'd still be working that late into the month of May. The night after having it out, I was scheduled to work the Cup game in Guelph. The socket was still bleeding and very sore, but nothing was going to keep me from making that game. The dentist packed the area with gauze to stop the bleeding and it hurt like hell, but I still managed to work.

Also memorable in that Cup were the carryings-on of Howie Young, a former Oil King defenseman who had just completed his first season in the NHL with Detroit. Howie already had a reputation as a real shit-disturber. During one of the games, he positioned himself about five rows in back of the Red Wing bench and hassled Hamilton coach Eddie Bush all night long. He wouldn't get off his case — sitting up there with his ten-gallon hat exchanging barbs with Bush, no slouch himself in giving out verbal shots.

IMPRESSED I SUPPOSE with my work as a Junior A linesman and my reputation around Ontario as a decent hockey referee, the NHL contacted me before the 1962-63 season and offered me a tryout. I was more than a little excited!

Bill Hanley — the secretary-manager of the OHA then and one of the finest men I ever met in hockey — was asked each summer by NHL referee-in-chief Carl Voss to recommend any good officiating prospects. That autumn Voss auditioned nine candidates from across Canada and said he was going to hire two of us. Art Casterton, Tom Smith, Bob Nadin and I were the four from Ontario. I was pretty pumped up about the whole thing because I never dreamed I'd get a shot at the big time that quickly, if ever.

The nine of us went to Toronto and had a meeting with Voss, who said we were going to work several American Hockey League exhibition games. He split us up into groups of three and told us we'd each referee one period and, the other two periods, work the lines. Back then many of the AHL teams trained in Ontario with their NHL affiliates. I worked a game in Hamilton and one in St. Catharines. I felt pretty good about my performance but when the final decision came down, Voss had chosen Casterton and Tom Smith. He wanted Nadin, but Nadin was making a lot of money as a schoolteacher in Toronto at the time and didn't think the NHL job was a sound proposition financially. He went on to become a very distinguished referee in the OHA junior and senior ranks and is now the referee-in-chief of the Canadian Amateur Hockey Association, as well as our country's officiating representative in international hockey.

In those days officials hired by the NHL started in the minors at rock-bottom salaries with no guarantee of advancement.   With the average starting salary at $5,000, real dedication was required to reach the NHL.

Carl Voss recommended I get some more refereeing experience and suggested I try the International Hockey League. He phoned IHL president Andy Mulligan, who lived in Toledo, Ohio. Mulligan, in turn, got in touch with me. He said that Voss had spoken highly of me. Would I be interested in refereeing games in his league? My answer goes without saying.

At the start of the 1962-63 season Mulligan phoned to say he was sending me my first assignment — a three-games-in-four-nights excursion to Fort Wayne, Muskegon and Port Huron. I would receive thirty-five dollars a game and twelve dollars *per diem*, plus mileage.

It wasn't a lot, even then. I had a home and a family to raise, but it seemed like the right thing to do and it was what I wanted.

I was so psyched up for that first trip that I packed just about every piece of clothing I owned. I threw it all in the back of my car and away I went. It was the first time I had been in the United States, not counting the times I had gone to Buffalo to sample some American beer. The five-hour drive to Fort Wayne seemed to take forever, I was so anxious to get there.

I arrived on Monday evening and drove right to the arena even though I wasn't scheduled to work until the following night. It was pretty exciting to think that I was there to referee a hockey game. As I looked at the arena I thought, "Well Bruce, there it is — give it your best shot and if you succeed, it'll be wonderful; if you don't, you'll be back in Milton and better off for the experience."

The following night I worked my first game as a professional. There was one memorable incident, when I called a delay-of-game penalty on St. Paul goalie Jacques Marcotte.

Fort Wayne scored on the power play. When I got back to center ice to drop the puck the Fort Wayne centerman — Len Thornson — asked if I would be refereeing in the league the whole year. I said I hoped so.

He said, "I sure hope you do because we need some good strong officiating in this league and I think you're the guy who can provide that."

I felt good about that, even if it was from a player whose team had just scored on the power play.

I was on my way!

UP TO THE MINORS

*I skated back towards center ice and when I got there,
some guy in the stands picked up a couple of folding
chairs and heaved them over the screen.*

THERE WERE PLENTY of nights in the minor leagues
when I would have had good reason to pack my bags and go
home. But I was there to do a job. Even when it seemed like
all the people in the arena had lost their sanity, quitting was
still the farthest thing from my mind. I was there to do the
best I could and learn as much as possible. The minor leagues
were stepping-stones and the proving grounds. If I did the
job well, I would — I hoped — get my chance at the big time.

If ever there was a test for a young official, the International
League was. The league wasn't officially recognized as professional at that time, but for all intents and purposes it was.

In 1962-63 the league consisted of only six teams in two
divisions: Fort Wayne, Muskegon and Port Huron in the East,
and Omaha, St. Paul and Minneapolis in the West.

I would usually work one division for a while and then move
over to the other. The East division teams were within four to
seven hours' driving time of Milton so I almost always took my
car. For games in the West I flew to the first city, took the bus or
train between games and then flew home.

There were considerable distances between some of the
cities, which made for a lot of back-to-back games. Teams
that went into Omaha often played on consecutive nights and

teams that arrived in Minnesota would sometimes play three consecutive nights. They might go into St. Paul on a Friday, to Minneapolis on Saturday and then head back to St. Paul for Sunday.

The problem with back-to-back games was that bad blood could, and often did, spill over into the next night. Experience taught me that if a ruckus broke out in the first game, it would be followed by a hell-raiser in the second.

And ruckuses weren't hard to come by. There was some good hockey, but there seemed to be some major incident just about every night.

One evening brawls in two different cities made headlines. I was refereeing a game in Fort Wayne between the Komets and Muskegon when fighting incited a bench-clearing free-for-all. I called fifty-one penalty minutes just in that one incident and dished out nineteen minors, seven majors and three misconducts over the whole game. But my night was routine compared with that of my buddy, Morley Meyers, from Winnipeg.

He was doing a game at the St. Paul Auditorium between the Saints and the Omaha Knights. Dick Bouchard of St. Paul was battling it out with Ted Lebioda of Omaha when Lebioda's teammate, John Bailey, left the penalty box to join the fight. He struck Bouchard on the back of his head, knocking him down and causing a wild riot.

A group of irate fans actually swarmed onto the ice and chased Bailey back into the penalty box! And Lebioda received a cut when a fan belted him on the head with an air horn. Somehow, order was finally restored but Morley had to suspend the game with fifteen seconds left on the clock and St. Paul ahead, 3-1.

Lebioda and Bailey were almost always in the middle of any Omaha altercation. One game story called it a surprise when the two of them went a whole game without a single penalty. That was a difficult feat for Lebioda, especially. Once, his wrist in a cast, he had a fight with Wayne Freitag of Fort Wayne. The players picked up their own sticks and gloves after a fight in those days, and as Freitag bent down to get his stick, Lebioda smashed him on the side of the head with his cast, knocking him out cold.

I called IHL commissioner Andy Mulligan about it but he didn't seem too concerned. The two teams were playing back-to-back games and I told Andy that it was going to be a tough situation. If Lebioda was there, I said, I didn't particularly want to be. I received a telegram at my hotel in Omaha the next day, saying that Lebioda had been suspended for one game.

Another time in Omaha a fight broke out late in the game between the Ted Lebioda and Ivan Prediger of the Fort Wayne Komets. When Prediger sat down in the penalty box someone threw an egg and hit him in the back. A few seconds later a cherry bomb exploded at center ice. And then a couple of fans got into such a wild fight in the corner seats that most of the players went over to watch.

With the fans being so hostile in most arenas, there might have been a temptation, for some referees, to make things easier on the home team. That was not my way of officiating, however, and there were many nights when my decisions disturbed the crowd.

My first run-in with a fan happened at the Allen County War Memorial Arena in Fort Wayne. I was skating off the ice at the end of the rink when this fellow kicked me and then ran off towards the exit. The police tore after the guy and caught up to him several blocks down the street. About fifteen minutes later a cop knocked on the door of our dressing room and told me he was going to press charges against the fan. Just another routine night, I told myself.

Omaha definitely had the nuttiest fans in the IHL. The Knights played their home games in the Ak-Sar-Ben Coliseum (Ak-Sar-Ben is Nebraska spelled backwards) on the state fairgrounds. Our dressing room was off the main lobby and we often had to fight through a crowd of rowdy fans on the way to safety. A few years later, after Omaha had moved to the Central Hockey League, I did a game there against Minneapolis that I'll never forget.

The teams had a pretty good rivalry going and there were a lot of penalties that night. Minneapolis was leading 2-1 late in the game and the Knights were a man short. With two minutes left, an Omaha defenseman, Noel Picard, hauled off and punched a Minneapolis player in the mouth. I gave him a minor, which put Omaha at a two-man disadvantage, and the fans went nuts.

They started throwing all kinds of debris on the ice and I had to call out the rink attendants to clean up the mess. Popcorn boxes, squashed beer cups and programs kept flying down towards me and I finally went over to the P.A. announcer and told him to announce that if the shower of garbage didn't stop, I was going to call the game.

I skated back towards center ice and when I got there, some guy in the stands picked up a couple of folding chairs and heaved them over the screen.

That was the clincher. I skated right over and told the announcer that the game was over. I wasn't fooling around — I meant what I said and Minneapolis had the victory, 2-1.

That didn't sit too well with the Omaha fans and they were not in a good mood as I skated towards the gate to leave the ice. Thankfully, three policemen were waiting there to help me and I wedged myself between them for the trip to the dressing room. Just as we were about to enter the lobby, a fan in the balcony above us with pretty good aim threw a cup full of beer and it splashed all over us. Beer-throwing was a favorite pastime of the fans at Ak-Sar-Ben.

I left the arena that night taking no chances, a skate in my hand until I got safely into a cab.

Even the Omaha media used to zero in on the fights. Game stories often led with blow-by-blow accounts of the rough stuff. The actual game information, like who scored and so on, was often buried towards the bottom of the story. One Saturday night, the Knights and Minneapolis Bruins played to a 2-2 draw in a Central League game I officiated. The next Monday afternoon, in the Omaha *World-Herald*, the game story read as follows:

KNIGHTS, BRUINS, TIE IN RIOTOUS PUCK FRAY
The wildest fight on — and off the ice — climaxed Omaha's uphill scrap to salvage a 2-2 tie with the burly Minneapolis Bruins at Ak-Sar-Ben Coliseum Saturday night.

The partisan throng of 4,045 had hardly recovered from the climactic tying goal by Claude Larose when Mount Vesuvius erupted.

And what an eruption.

The Knights, plagued and tormented all evening by the crunching blocks of Harry Sinden's invaders, finally had their fill of indignities.

So, every Knight on the ice doffed his gloves and paired off with a Bruin. So many man-to-man slugfests were in progress, the fans witnessed a three-ring circus.

Only 48 seconds remained when the donnybrook broke loose, but 20 minutes were needed to quiet the combatants. And, still, it wasn't over.

Moe Bartoli, who always pesters the Knights, was escorted to the dressing room door by two burly men in blue.

And, who met him at the door, swinging from the floor?

Barclay Plager, the broken-ribbed Knight, who had been banished to the dressing room only moments before. His shirt was torn off, revealing yards of tape around his midriff, and extra policemen were needed to separate the battlers. Referee Bruce Hood doled out 48 minutes in penalties.

Only then did the story go on to explain what happened to produce the 2-2 tie.

The type of incidents reported in that newspaper article took place — if not in Omaha then somewhere else — almost nightly, and this ten years before the Philadelphia Flyers and the so-called "goon era" of pro hockey.

TRAVEL FOR ME in the IHL was an exercise in thrift. I got eight cents a mile going from point A to point B, regardless of how I was traveling. To save a few dollars from my expenses, I would try to take the most economical means of transport. I worked it out that bus travel cost me an average of three and a half cents a mile, while train travel was four and a half cents and flying was eight cents. So to save a few bucks, I would take the bus as often as I could and try to travel overnight to save on hotel bills.

For example, I'd be scheduled for a Friday-night game in Minneapolis and a Saturday-night game in Omaha. I would fly to Minneapolis from wherever I was and stay there until Friday. I would check out of my hotel before the game and store my luggage in the arena. After the game, I'd take a cab to the bus station and the overnight bus to Omaha, getting there at about six-thirty in the morning. That way I'd save about $6.50 for one night's lodging. When you only make thirty-five dollars a game, every nickel you can save is extra money to take home.

Other times I would finish up back-to-back games in Minneapolis and St. Paul and then take the overnight train from St. Paul to Chicago. I'd get off at one of the suburban stations, make my way to the airport and fly home. That cut the cost of the flight and saved me hotel charges.

I had lots of time to kill between games — I'd average about three games for every seven-day road trip — and traveling the slower ways gave me a chance to see some of the countryside.

My most vivid off-ice memories from those days are of the times I spent in Minnesota. I always stayed at the old Capri Hotel in downtown St. Paul. The rooms were only six dollars a day but you had to fight like hell to get one that had a TV set. A typical day's expenses in the early sixties — hotel, three meals, cab fare and tips — would run between twelve and fifteen dollars. I could order a full-course dinner for $1.40 and a quarter tip was considered generous.

A lot of older people stayed at the Capri and many of them lived there on a permanent basis. One day after lunch I decided to sit in the lobby for a few minutes and read the paper. I glanced at the front page for a couple of seconds and then I looked up and saw an elderly gentleman staring at me. He wasn't saying anything and I figured he was just old and had nothing better to do. So I went back to reading. About two minutes later, I looked up again and he was still standing there, fidgeting nervously.

As it turned out, I happened to be sitting in *his* seat. All of the old chaps who regularly stayed at the hotel had their own little place in the lobby and I soon found out that a couple of seats over by the front entrance were for transients like me.

Every so often, though, it would be fun to sit in the reserved seats and get some of the old guys agitated. They would stand there with angry looks on their faces, waving their arms at me. Nothing ever changed at that place. I'd be there for a two- or-three-day period, then come back a month or so later, and it was like I had never left. The same people were sitting in the same seats, doing the same things.

I spent many of my off days in St. Paul around the corner from the Capri at the Ace movie theatre. I could sit there all afternoon and watch three movies for fifty cents.

There was an old railway car diner downtown that made great bacon and eggs and I passed a lot of time there as well. After the bars closed, the diner turned into a hangout. I would spend hours chatting with the chef and watching him go through his various maneuvers. Nobody could flip an egg like that guy.

Sometimes I would head over to a strip joint in that same block and watch some of the antics. Till that time, I hadn't realized that women actually made money by getting up on stage and taking off their clothes — quite an awakening for a small-town guy.

The St. Paul Auditorium held about 8,000 fans and they'd come close to filling the place for weekend games. The arena was only a couple of blocks from the Capri. Ordinarily I would have a little snooze in the afternoon and then head over to the rink about ninety minutes before the eight p.m. game time. One day I woke up around five o'clock and decided to read for a while before going to the arena. I wound up dozing off again. The next thing I knew, it was a quarter to eight! I had fifteen minutes to get over to the rink and drop the puck. I jumped out of bed and got dressed in my officiating gear and hustled over to the auditorium with my skates tucked under my arm.

When I got to the arena, both teams were out on the ice and the national anthem was being played. I sprinted to the dressing room and when I opened the door, the two linesmen were sitting in a corner, panic written all over their faces. The IHL used local linesmen, so the poor guys had no way of knowing if I was even in the Twin Cities!

When I told them what had happened and started frantically tying my skates, they both laughed like hell. We all hurried out. As we were walking through the corridor towards the ice, I looked across the way at the off-ice officials, who had not seen me yet. They were nervously shrugging their shoulders and probably wondering how they were going to have a game without a referee. I went over to get the puck and they were all sweaty. "Jesus, where were you?" one of them asked. I had no time to explain because the game was already a few minutes late. But we got things going. The incident cured me of lying around late in the afternoon on game day.

The only other time I was late for a game was in Fort Wayne on a Sunday afternoon. I was getting a ride from Port Huron where I had done a Saturday-night game, with a friend from Detroit, and I figured he knew how much time it would take. We ran into some traffic problems. Listening to the pre-game show on WOWO radio, we could see we weren't going to make it in time. I started getting dressed in the car.

The announcer said, "We'll be right back for the anthem and the start of the game," and then broke for a commercial.

I said, "Oh no you won't. You can't start the game without me."

We were still about six or eight blocks from the arena when the announcer came back on and said the start of the game was going to be delayed because the referee hadn't arrived. We pulled up to the arena, and I jumped out of the car with my skates in my hand and ran to the dressing room. They had about 9,000 people there that afternoon for a big promotion, and the game was being televised. Fifteen minutes after the scheduled start, the game got under way.

AFTER MY SEASON of training in the International League I was offered an NHL contract by Carl Voss. Carl had sent me letters indicating he was receiving good reports on my work and hinting that I might be added to the NHL staff for the 1963-64 season. When the Central Hockey League was formed over the summer, that clinched it.

The first letter Carl sent was in March 1963 and it asked me to refrain from making any commitments for the following season. His second letter, in early June, still contained nothing definite but informed me that the Eastern Professional Hockey League had ceased operations and that the NHL clubs were trying to organize a replacement league in the American Midwest. Finally, in July, he wrote to ask if I was interested in joining the NHL staff. It seemed an odd question. Of course I was, and I wrote an immediate reply.

I didn't hear from Carl again until the end of August, just three weeks before training camps opened. The letter of August 24, 1963, read as follows:

Dear Bruce:

I am enclosing your NHL contract (worth $5,000) for the 1963-64 season. Inasmuch as this is your first experience with one of our contracts, please feel free to have it examined by your lawyer or other trusted advisor. If there is anything you do not understand about it or wish explained, just telephone me collect.

We would like you to sign, and have witnessed, the "original" copy and return same to NHL Headquarters as soon as possible. Retain the duplicate copy for your records. I will be in touch with you in a few weeks as regards to exhibition game assignments and our pre-season meeting.

Sincerely Yours,

Carl P. Voss

Naturally I was thrilled about the contract. That year Carl had a staff of nine full-time officials. The referees were Frank Udvari, Vern Buffey, John Ashley, Art Skov and Bill Friday. The linesmen were George Hayes, Neil Armstrong, Matt Pavelich and Ron Wicks. On Saturday or Sunday nights, when there was a full slate of three games (remember, the NHL still only had six teams), the league would fill out the staff with part-time linesmen. They were known as "weekend commandos."

My first professional hockey assignment (the IHL was considered amateur in those days) took me to Hershey,Pennsylvania — "Chocolate Town, U.S.A." — for a game between the Hershey Bears and the Providence Reds on Saturday, October 12, 1963. I got a ride from Milton to Hamilton late Friday afternoon and took a bus from Hamilton to Buffalo. Then I rode the overnight sleeper train from Buffalo to Harrisburg, Pennsylvania, and caught a bus from Harrisburg to Hershey early the next morning. The entire trip took about thirteen hours.

This being my first-ever visit to Hershey I made sure to tour the famous chocolate factory that afternoon. It was fascinating to walk through the place and see all the vats of chocolate being stirred and prepared. Even the light standards in town are in the shape of Hershey candy bars.

I stayed at the Cocoa Inn on the main corner of town and had to go through the fairgrounds to get to Hersheypark Arena. Walking into that arena, with all its years of minor-league hockey history, was an exciting moment for me. I refereed my first game before a full house without any incidents of note. After the game, I got a ride back to Harrisburg and caught the overnight train to Buffalo.

The next night I did a game between the Buffalo Bisons and Baltimore Clippers. My parents drove down from Milton to watch me and give me a ride home. Working in the Memorial Auditorium for the first time was no less exciting.

ONCE BACK HOME I could reflect on my first two AHL assignments. Refereeing in professional hockey truly was a dream come true. I had that whole week off and started to feel restless around Wednesday. All I could think about was my next assignment — a weekend doubleheader in Pittsburgh and Rochester. I was counting the hours.

Carl Voss suggested I take Joanne with me on that trip to give her an idea what the business of big-league officiating was all about. That sounded like a pretty good idea, so we packed up the car and left on Friday afternoon. In those days, before the advent of superhighways, the drive from Milton to Pittsburgh was a long one. After about seven hours — the last part through incredibly bad pot-holed streets — we pulled up to the Penn-Sheraton Hotel. The next morning we did some shopping and looked over downtown Pittsburgh, which was beginning to change from a grimy steeltown to the bright, modern city it is today.

That night, during the game between the Quebec Aces and Pittsburgh Hornets, I had my first official run-in with a general manager. I left the ice after the first period and was walking to my dressing room when a squat little man with glasses came running up and really laid into me.

"God-damned Junior referee," he growled. "What the hell are you doing out there?"

I looked at the man and wondered who the heck he was. He looked like one of the arena workers. Turns out it was Baz Bastien, the Hornets' general manager.

The Hornets' dressing room was just around the corner from the referees' room and that meeting with Bastien was an omen of things to come. Any time someone wanted to tell the referee what he thought, he could wait outside that room and lay into him all he wanted.

Jack Price and Bob Ferons were the local linesmen during that game and they suggested Joanne and I join them and their wives for a drink afterwards. We ended up in a club that was hosting a pretty wild shindig and we joined right in with the crowd. We didn't get back to the hotel until the wee hours of the morning.

The next day we made a five-hour trip to Rochester. If Joanne had been anticipating a glamorous road trip, she surely had different ideas by now. I could sense that she was looking forward to getting home later that night — and staying there — but we still had a few hectic moments ahead of us before returning to Milton.

That night in Rochester I made an instinctive decision that helped shape my entire future as a referee. Fred Glover was a player-coach for Cleveland and was one of the most fiery competitors in all of hockey. He was also a miserable son of a bitch when he was on the ice. Although I had heard a lot about him through the years, we had never formally met. Our first exchange was less than cordial.

The AHL employed local, part-time linesmen for its games and some of the guys weren't very good. Still, they were legitimate officials trying to do a decent job and they had to be respected. One of the fellows I worked with that night, Ed House, happened to be a very competent linesman, but Glover spent the whole night hassling him.

"For Chrissakes, open your eyes and get in the game, you asshole!" he yelled. Fred wouldn't get off his case and I finally skated by and told him to pipe down.

"Keep your mouth shut and mind your own fucking business," he snapped back at me.

His reply caught me off guard. Without even thinking, I spun around and gave him a ten-minute misconduct. After skating a few strides towards the penalty box with the Rochester fans cheering my decision, I thought to myself, "Holy shit, I just gave Fred Glover a misconduct!"

I could almost hear him thinking, "Who the hell is this rookie sending me off the ice for ten minutes?"

But after tossing a few more barbs in my direction, he went straight to the box and the game continued.

After the game, in the quiet of the dressing room, I speculated on the call. Although I personally felt my decision on Glover had been correct, I wondered if perhaps I had overstepped my boundaries so early in my career. Maybe I had shown too much authority. When Joanne and I left for the three-hour drive back to Milton I had a lot on my mind. We were both anxious to get home.

The next morning I was having breakfast around ten-thirty when the phone rang. Joanne answered and said it was Carl Voss. I walked over to the phone thinking that Carl had heard about the Fred Glover incident and I was in for it.

"How'd your weekend go, Bruce?" he asked.

Taking advantage of his cheery tone I figured I might as well play it to the hilt and sound enthusiastic.

"Oh, great, Carl, just great," I gushed. "The games were real good and the whole thing was a great experience. I was impressed with the cities and the arenas and I really enjoyed the drives. In fact, so did Joanne."

I was beginning to think maybe he was just calling to see how things were, so my heart sank when he said, "I heard you gave Fred Glover a misconduct last night."

I figured, okay, this is it. Glover has complained to Carl and I'm going to catch hell.

"Yes sir, I did give him a misconduct penalty," I replied, bracing for his assault.

"Well, I think that's great, Bruce," he said. "Congratulations. It's the best start you could have made in this league, giving a guy like Fred a misconduct and showing him you're not going to stand for any of his bullshit. Way to go."

I couldn't believe it! There I was, all ready to be chewed out for standing up against one of the most renowned veterans in the AHL, and Carl congratulates me! Until then I hadn't been sure exactly how Carl wanted me to officiate, whether I should take that kind of abuse and let it roll off my back or call the game the way I felt most comfortable. That call from Carl was one of the biggest inspirations of my career. It gave me the confidence I needed to go out and work in the fashion that had made me successful in the International League the previous year. From that day on I gained a reputation as one of the stricter officials in professional hockey. There were some players and management people who resented my style, but it worked, and it worked well.

CLIMBING THE LADDER

Finally, the screen buckled under the weight and folded back onto the ice, taking seven or eight players crashing down with it.

CARL VOSS OFTEN TALKED to us about trying our best to save a few dollars while on the road. Since I'd practiced that routine quite regularly the year before, it really wasn't a problem. Many times I would arrive in a city by train or bus and find out that the hotel was only a few blocks away. So instead of finding a cab, I'd pick up my suitcase and take a little hike through town. It was a good way to get some exercise and it meant more dollars in my own pocket. I used to stumble across all kinds of ways to save money and any way I could do it was fine with me.

On my third road trip of that first AHL season — a three-game excursion to Hershey, Springfield and Quebec — I went to Hershey for a Wednesday-night game and then on Thursday morning I flew to Boston, where I had some anxious moments after landing at Logan airport.

We used to carry just one suitcase with us on the road and it contained both our personal effects and our officiating gear. As a result, it was quite large and we always had to check it at the luggage counter before boarding the plane. Nowadays, a referee travels with a garment bag for his personal stuff and a separate case for his officiating gear. To avoid losing them, referees carry both on board, a league requirement.

After landing in Boston that day, I went down to the luggage area to claim my suitcase and it wasn't there. So I waited and waited and finally realized that it might have gotten lost somewhere along the way. I went to see the representative from Allegheny Airlines and he told me that all the luggage from my flight was already off the plane. After pleading with the guy to check one more time, he finally agreed to go back on the plane and look. Sure enough, he returned a few minutes later with my suitcase in hand. But it was slightly damaged and I wanted it fixed.

In the interests of good customer relations, he hustled off to write me up a pretty healthy claim. It turned out that the repairs only cost me two dollars. I don't recall exactly how much the rep gave me but it was enough to fix my old suitcase and buy a new one, with a few bucks left over for personal expenses. Like Carl used to say, saving bits of money here and there was important for a minor-league referee.

I took the train from Boston to Springfield the next afternoon and worked a Saturday game between the Springfield Indians and Providence Reds. Both the Indians and the Springfield Civic Center were owned and operated at that time by the infamous Eddie Shore. Once a great defenseman in the NHL, his tactics as an owner became legendary throughout the hockey world.

There would be twenty-four or twenty-five players on the Indians' roster and Eddie would dress eighteen for each game. The remaining six or seven guys would blow up balloons, make popcorn and sell programs before the game, and then sit right behind the bench during the action. They were Eddie's "Black Aces."

Other well-known stories told of how Eddie tied a goaltender to the net during practice so he wouldn't flop down to his knees, and how he rigorously worked out with his players, despite suffering four near-fatal heart attacks.

Eddie also had a reputation for being incredibly cheap, and it was well-deserved. He would rarely wait more than a minute after the final buzzer to shut off the arena lights, forcing many fans to feel their way up the aisles to get out of the place. In the time it took the linesmen and me to shower and dress, even the lights in the corridor would be turned out. On many nights we had to slither our way along the wall to find the exit.

Immediately after the game in Springfield that night, it was back to the train station for an overnight ride to Montreal. I arrived early in the morning and then took another train to Quebec City. Teams usually played in Quebec two consecutive games because the city was so far away from the other towns in the AHL. Games often were played on Tuesday and Thursday nights, which meant that a referee would spend the better part of three days in the city. Those occasions were some of the loneliest times of my life.

I stayed at the old St-Louis Hotel, feeling like I was the only person for miles who spoke any English. The rooms in the hotel had no TV, and if I wanted to use a bathroom I had to go to the end of the hall. To top it off, the place was as cold as the Arctic inside. I would have to put blankets over the window to keep out the icy wind, and I almost always slept in my flannel hockey underwear. I had nowhere to go and nothing to do. Even the newspapers were in French.

Thank God there was one restaurant in town, called the Café de la Paix, where the owners spoke some English. It was on a little side street a short walk from the hotel. The people who ran the place were very big hockey fans. I would go there and spend hours talking to them.

The fans in the Quebec Colisée were something to see. I remember a French guy screaming at me one night. He obviously spoke very little English but he knew enough to keep yelling, "Hey Hood, you fuckerrr." I finally decided to look up, and there was this well-dressed gentleman sitting beside an elegant-looking lady. I just shook my head and figured the fellow probably didn't realize how strong a swearword he was using in English. He thought it was all fun and games.

Some Colisée fans did more than shout obscenities. Once I was standing by the penalty box relaying a Quebec penalty to the timekeeper when a fan sitting behind the bench flicked a lit cigarette at my face. In another game, I was skating up the boards near center ice when some guy in the front row stood up and took a punch at me. When the play stopped, I went over and asked an usher to remove him from the arena. He wouldn't listen to me. Finally, Doug Harvey, the Quebec player-coach, skated over and demanded that the usher throw the guy out. He listened to Harvey.

The fans in Quebec used to love throwing stuff on the ice. In one afternoon play-off game the Aces were playing it rough against Baltimore so I called quite a few penalties against them and the fans got pretty upset. They littered the ice so badly that I had to blow my whistle while the play was in progress and summon the maintenance crew to clear the debris. While I was standing over by the boards, waiting for them to clean the ice, I looked up just in time to see an object flying at me from a long way up in the stands. I turned my head and it hit me on the outside of my eye, cutting me. When I looked down, there was a solid-silver cigarette lighter at my feet. Another typical night.

Probably the shabbiest rink I ever worked in was the old arena in Providence, Rhode Island. The dressing room was always a filthy mess. The shower was old and only spouted a trickle of water, and the floors, which were cold and cracked wooden racks, were always covered with a layer of slime. And it was the same thing, week after week, and year after year. It was also the only rink in which the doors from the players benches opened *outward* onto the ice. A number of times I would be going full tilt up the boards only to be flattened during a line change.

Linesmen in the AHL were usually former players and were hired by the home team. Chuck Scherza was one of the guys they used in Providence and another one was Art Leseur, the biggest official I ever saw. Leseur must have been six feet four and 320 pounds. He'd go into a scuffle and the players would say, "Alright, that's enough, this guy's bigger than all of us." He couldn't skate that fast but he sure as hell had everyone's respect.

JOANNE MADE very few trips with me after that initial one, but one year during the Christmas break I took the whole family on a five-game job.

We all piled into the car on a Friday morning and drove to Rochester for an evening game. From there we went to Springfield for a Saturday game, and to Providence for a

Sunday game. I had Monday off, so we enjoyed a leisurely drive down to Baltimore, where I worked a game on Tuesday night. Wednesday, it was on to Hershey. We ended the trip with an eight-hour overnight drive back to Milton to make sure we would be home for a New Year's Eve party the next day.

During the game in Baltimore, Joanne and the kids were sitting up in the stands when some guy really started getting on my case. My son, Randy, who was about nine years old, didn't like the abuse I was taking, so he turned around and said to the guy, "You shut up, that's my Dad out there!" Instead of making some crack back at him, the guy actually got a big kick out of it and began chatting with my whole family. By the third period they were great friends. When Joanne told me the story, I seriously considered taking Randy on all my trips to keep the fans off my back.

That same trip we ran into severe blizzard conditions. It was so bad driving home from Hershey that a tractor trailer jackknifed in front of us on the state highway. That scared the daylights out of me and I was pretty concerned about my family's safety the rest of the way home. We finally arrived in Milton around six-thirty in the morning. It was sure a treat to get into our own beds, as tired and exhausted as we were.

EACH CITY provided a new experience, a new lesson or another crazy night.

Cleveland was another prominent AHL city in the early sixties. The Barons played their games downtown in the old Cleveland Arena and used to pack them in most nights. When Cleveland became part of the NHL in 1976, they had trouble drawing fans. The new Richfield Coliseum was a beautiful building but it was just too long a drive away.

The Cleveland Arena had chicken wire surrounding the ice surface. It wasn't pulled together very tightly so it had a lot of bounce to it. Whenever I jumped onto the boards to avoid play, I ended up virtually leaning into the first three rows of seats. I was like a human slingshot. Often the spectators would push on the area by my rear end and catapult me out onto the ice.

Fred Glover and his brother, Howie, were the big shots in Cleveland at that time. After my run-in with Fred in Rochester, he was no treat to deal with, but compared with his brother he was much more of a professional. Howie was the type of guy who always made smart-ass remarks and I never had too much respect for him. One night when I was working a game between the Barons and Buffalo, Howie was wearing a football-type helmet with a single bar across its mouth area to protect his jaw, which he'd broken. There was a scuffle in front of the net and a Buffalo defenseman grabbed Howie by that bar. Fred was standing beside me, hollering for me to give the guy a penalty. Helmets were a rarity in those days and I couldn't think of any punishment for face-masking—and at that point I didn't really care to. I looked at the Buffalo player and sort of wished he would give the bar on Howie's helmet a good yank.

Our dressing room was separated from the visitors' room by only a thin plywood partition. The players knew we could hear just about everything that went on next door and they'd use the opportunity to voice their opinions on the officiating. One referee got so mad he actually gave the visitors a bench penalty to start the next period. Usually, though, we tried our best to relax and ignore the comments.

We stayed at the old Auditorium Hotel in Cleveland, right on the shore of Lake Erie, next door to the giant Municipal Stadium. With the winds whipping off the lake, it felt like the coldest spot in the entire country, and I used to stay inside most of the time. I remember getting ready to drive to Buffalo one Sunday morning when it was twenty degrees below zero outside, yet thousands of fans were pouring into the stadium for a National Football League game. I couldn't believe people would actually sit through those biting winds for four hours.

IN 1964-65, MY SECOND season under contract to the NHL, I began officiating games in the old Western Hockey League. There were six teams in the WHL that year, spread up and down the west coast: the Vancouver Canucks, Victoria Maple Leafs, Seattle Totems, Portland Buckaroos, San Francisco Seals and Los Angeles Blades. Each club had a working agreement with one of the six NHL teams.

The caliber of play in the WHL wasn't quite as good as in the American and Central leagues. The teams were manned primarily by NHL players who had grown too slow for the big time, and by others who were not good enough to make it in the first place. Many years later, when the World Hockey Association was formed, a number of old Western League vets got their chance to play at a higher level of professional hockey and cash some of the big paychecks the WHA was throwing around. I was happy for a lot of those guys, who had roughed it out in the minors for many years, with virtually nothing to show for it. They deserved a break.

Al Leader was president of the WHL back then and one of the finest gentlemen I ever met. The league offices were maintained in Seattle. Murray Costello, current president of the Canadian Amateur Hockey Association, was Al's assistant.

I started the 1964-65 season by flying from Toronto to San Francisco and working a full month on the west coast. It's funny to look back at my travel expenses from that era. The airfare to San Francisco only cost $157.55. Today it could cost more than $800. Plane fare from Vancouver to Seattle was only $7.50, and now it costs almost three times that amount to go by bus. Hotel rates ranged from seven dollars a night for the higher-class ones to three dollars for an average room. A fancy dinner cost around $3.50 and occasionally I'd splurge and leave the waiter a thirty-five-cent tip. My expense total for the entire trip (October 8-31), including transportation, hotels and meals, was only $504.10.

Each city in the Western League offered something unique and I enjoyed walking around and taking in the sights during my time off between games. I always looked forward to working in San Francisco. The Seals played their games in the Cow Palace, an old barn-shaped arena at the south end of town. One of the wildest brawls I have ever seen broke out there in a game between the Seals and Portland. I saved the game story from the *San Francisco Examiner* the next day. It provides a very apt description of what took place.

It was slaughter on Geneva Avenue last night, as the Seals took an unprecedented second victory in a row from Portland, in a game featured by a full-scale player riot in which every player in sight became embroiled on the ice, on the fences, in the penalty box and in the stands.

The score of 4-2 was almost an afterthought and the 6,881 Cow Palace customers will never remember it, but they'll never forget the wild melee that erupted toward the close of the second period.

Some of those same spectators have wounds this morning as a result of either being innocent bystanders or foolish participants.

It all began at 18:26 of the middle stanza, when Jean Picard and Buckaroo Larry Leach were thumbed to the penalty box. Picard shoved the lanky center and Leach retaliated with a right cross to the jaw. They tangled amidst the spectators, fell to the floor, and both enemy benches swarmed across the ice to get a piece of the action.

The game erupted into what was the wildest free-for-all—with fans included—in the Seals' four-year history at the Cow Palace.

Before it was over, players on both sides swarmed around the penalty box, climbed the wire fences, were beating sticks over unidentified players' heads, and the one policeman who patrols the sin-bin was swamped by bodies.

Those who couldn't get in, climbed the wire screen, using sticks to batter the unprotected heads of rivals and over-zealous spectators. The original antagonists were soon out of sight in the milling, and brush-fire brawls flared on the fringe of the main event.

The screens soon folded from the weight of those who attempted to scale them and the lone policeman who usually keeps peace in the penalty box was completely helpless. Many minutes later, he was joined by two aides but they couldn't handle the group of fighters.

After the brawl subsided momentarily, it erupted again, and a lone fan on the ice tried to join in, only to be pinned to the rink by a Portland player.

The sum total of it all was 14 minutes in the box for each original antagonist and referee Bruce Hood cooled things off by sending both teams to the dressing room with 1:34 remaining in the period.

My reaction was similar to that of the cop in the penalty box: sheer helplessness. What the hell could I do with all those players and fans?

All referees were absolutely thrilled when, a few years later, pro arenas started installing glass around the boards. It offered far better protection for people on and off the ice, and was a hell of a lot more difficult for players and fans to climb.

The league really wanted to clamp down on unsportsman-like conduct that season, especially when it came to players talking back to the officials, and I had to enforce the new standard about ten seconds into my first assignment of the season, while in San Francisco. Just after the opening face-off, there was a pileup along the side boards and I blew my whistle to stop play. Perhaps thinking that I had reacted too quickly, one of the San Francisco players spun around and said, "What the hell was that for?"

I instinctively put my hands on my hips and gave the guy a misconduct penalty. The players all looked at me in surprise and it even surprised me. But it was one of the most important decisions I ever made in that league because it showed them that yapping out of line was not going to be a part of the game that year. It was my first season in the WHL and they had to realize right from the start that I intended to uphold the league's new standard. From that moment on, I received a very high level of respect from most players in the league.

San Francisco was such a great place to visit that the hockey games often seemed like an intrusion. There was an endless variety of things to do and see in the Bay area, and I tried to fit them all in during my brief visits. Riding the cable cars was always a lot of fun. Walking to Fishermans' Wharf and Chinatown was always one of my favorite activities in the daytime. I also enjoyed the boat cruises that went along the bay, around Alcatraz and under the Golden Gate Bridge. Sometimes, I would tour the Napa Valley vineyards and do a little wine sampling, other times I was content just to sit on a sidewalk bench and watch the different folks stroll by along Market Street.

Throughout the winter months, weather conditions along the west coast were often diverse and unpredictable. It could be sunny and beautiful in Los Angeles, snowing like crazy in northern California and raining cats and dogs in the Oregon-Washington corridor.

I worked a Sunday night in the Cow Palace in San Francisco one time and had to be in Portland for Tuesday night and in Seattle for Thursday. I had noticed an advertisement in the San Francisco newspaper for one of those car delivery outfits, and it happened to be just around the corner from my hotel. With a couple of days off, I figured it would be nice to drive, so I walked over to the office and made a thirty-five-dollar deposit for a car they wanted delivered to Tacoma, Washington, which butts Seattle.

On my way to Portland for the Tuesday game, I encountered some severe flooding. It was the aftermath of one of the worst storms of the year and things were a mess. Bridges were washed out at various places and at one point the army was ferrying cars across the river.

I checked into a motel for the night and in the morning continued on my way. I was now able to see the destruction caused by the flooding much clearer. Debris had been deposited along the shores of the rivers and included everything from trees to cars to parts of buildings. I had marked out a town on my map in which to have breakfast and when I arrived, nothing was there. The houses were completely washed away and all that remained were the foundations of two or three buildings and some gas pipes sticking up from the ground. Other than that, the entire area was completely covered in mud. The roads were still passable, however, and I was able to get to Portland.

Experiences like that made me look forward to working in southern California, one place where I never had to worry about weather conditions. Every time I visited Los Angeles to officiate a hockey game, it was like having an all-expenses-paid vacation. At times we'd be accused of still being on vacation when the game started, but actually, once we headed to the arena it was all business. Those long trips were a lot less agonizing when I could look forward to relaxing by the pool.

The Blades played their home games in the Los Angeles Sports Arena, across the road from the famous L.A.

Coliseum. It was the only indoor arena in Los Angeles until 1967, when Canadian-born businessman Jack Kent Cooke built the Forum, in Inglewood, for his NHL expansion team. The new arena wasn't completed until December of that year, so the Kings had to play some of their early home games in the Sports Arena while the Forum was being finished.

The Sports Arena was one of the nicer buildings in the league. It was big and spacious, and the seats were all covered in a corduroy material that was quite comfortable for the fans.

One time I was alternating a string of games in Los Angeles with another ref, Lloyd Gilmour, and I went to the Sports Arena to watch one of his games.

Earlier that day we had gotten a directive from Scotty Morrison — who had taken over as referee-in-chief from Carl Voss — telling us to be more demonstrative when making penalty calls. Apparently our signals were lacking enthusiasm and he wanted us to show more authority. I was sitting in the corner seats that night, about ten rows up, when Lloyd called an interference penalty and flashed a very emphatic signal. He was in the corner nearest me when the penalty occurred and before skating over to the timekeeper's bench, he looked back at me and said, "How's that Hoody, you think Scotty would be impressed?" The rink was still surrounded by wire mesh in those days, so I heard him clearly. We were both laughing as he skated away.

The weather was so nice in L.A. that I constantly found myself changing flight arrangements to spend as much time as I could in that beautiful, warm weather before heading back east or up north. The temperatures on these trips could change as much as eighty degrees, as for instance when going from L.A. to Minnesota. My flights were often scheduled to leave around noon, but often I would squeeze a little more time out by taking a flight late in the evening.

When the Roadrunners entered the league I found another place with great weather was Phoenix. I remember lying outside in the sun, sipping on a tall gin and tonic, reading the afternoon paper and thinking to myself, "Boy, this is the life."

I wasn't thinking that way one night in Phoenix when one of the wildest rhubarbs I had ever encountered broke out.

The Roadrunners were hosting the Portland Buckaroos at the Memorial Coliseum. We used to call their coach, Hal Laycoe, "the professor," because he thought he was an expert on everything there was to know, including officiating. Regardless of the subject, Hal was right and you were wrong. As a result, he was a fairly tough customer for referees. He was one of those coaches who would never admit that a referee did a good job, and he'd be the first guy to jump all over us for the slightest mistake.

That night there were two disputed goals, both against the Buckaroos. On the first one Portland thought they had scored off a wild scramble in front of the net, but I didn't see the puck cross the line. Even though the red light was on, I disallowed the goal. Naturally Hal wasn't too thrilled with my decision.

Later in the game a Phoenix forward took a hard slapshot that beat the Portland netminder along the ice, hit the iron middle plate of the net and bounced back into play. It happened so fast that the goal judge failed to turn on the light, but I saw it go in and stopped the action to award Phoenix a goal. Hal went bonkers. He tried to get my attention. When that failed, he began walking around the front row of seats towards the goal judge. I was getting ready to drop the puck when I heard a ruckus taking place down to my left. When I looked over that way, I couldn't believe what was happening.

Before Hal could even reach the goal judge, several fans began jostling him. Mel Pearson, seeing this, started climbing the screen to go into the crowd and rescue Laycoe. The entire Portland team swarmed onto the ice to follow Pearson and several players were hanging off the top of the screen and swinging their sticks at the crowd. Finally, the screen buckled under the weight and folded back onto the ice, taking seven or eight players crashing down with it.

I tried yelling at the players to settle down, but it was no use. There weren't too many punches exchanged, just a lot of pushing and shoving. As things began to quiet down, I looked halfway up towards the middle walkway and saw two exit doors suddenly swing open. Someone must have reported the incident because a dozen Arizona state troopers in riot gear burst into the arena and stomped towards the crowd of fans and players.

By then the commotion had pretty well subsided, but the screen was bent all to hell so I had to send both teams to the dressing room and summon the maintenance crew. I wasn't sure if any charges were going to be laid against the fans and I didn't much care. All I wanted to do was finish the damned game and get out of there.

Vancouver was another beautiful place that I always looked forward to visiting during my WHL days. Often I made a hotel in Vancouver my base while working games in Victoria, Seattle or Portland. I would catch the late bus, or the ferry if I was coming from Victoria, and go back to Vancouver after the game for a good night's sleep. It was much less of a hassle than checking in and out of different hotels and lugging suitcases back and forth between cities.

The Canucks played their home games at the old Vancouver Forum in the days before the Pacific Coliseum was built. The Forum was located on the grounds of the Pacific National Exhibition, as the Coliseum is now, and it had the highest boards in all of pro hockey. Trying to climb those boards, to avoid a flying puck or a player, was an exercise in futility. There was just no place to hide — it was like playing hockey in a bathtub.

The Pacific Northwest was always one of my favorite places to work. Vancouver, Victoria and Seattle were three of the most beautiful cities I'd ever seen, even though it was often quite rainy during the hockey months. Seattle had a decent arena but the officials' dressing quarters weren't conveniently located. We had to suit up in an adjacent building and then walk through a long corridor to reach the ice. After a tiring period of hockey, it was like walking three blocks back to our room; by the time we got there, we'd have to turn around and come out again. It took several years of bitching and moaning, but the Seattle people finally built us a mobile dressing unit right near the ice, which was a heck of a lot more convenient.

The head office of the WHL was in Seattle, so president Al Leader would often attend the Totems' games. Al had a reputation as being overly concerned about penalties called against the Seattle club, but I can honestly say that I personally never saw that side of him. Other officials told stories of how Al would visit their dressing quarters between periods and reprimand them for something they had called against the Totems.

I've often said I would like to retire in Victoria some day. On the times I decided not to set up base in Vancouver, I would stay at the Empress Hotel there. The Empress, like the city itself, was old and maintained many traditions of the Victorian age, such as serving afternoon tea in the lobby each day. It was an elegant and enchanting place, providing me with a pleasant change of pace.

Rudy Pilous was the Victoria Maple Leafs' coach and he had two rugged and willing players in the Hucul brothers, Fred and Sandy. The first Western League championship I worked was the 1965 series between the Maple Leafs and Hal Laycoe's battling Buckaroos. I alternated in three games with Lloyd Gilmour and Willie Papp — one of us refereeing and the other two working the lines. There were 4,077 disgruntled Leaf fans in the Memorial Arena after the fifth and final game as Portland's goalie, Don Head, earned a 3-0 shutout to clinch the Patrick Cup title for the Buckaroos in five games.

We got dressed and Lloyd, Willie, Murray Costello — the series supervisor — and I decided to cap the season off with a few ales. We were in my third floor hotel room having a couple when the four of us got into a little wrestling match. The window was open and on a dare from the other guys, I ended up throwing Murray's shoe out into the parking lot down below. Murray couldn't believe it and wanted to toss me out the window after it. I went down on my own and brought it back upstairs. Whenever I see Murray nowadays, we always laugh about that incident.

Despite his high-ranking position in the Western League, Murray had a laid-back sense of humor and his easy-going demeanor made our jobs more enjoyable. Before one period of a game in Portland in that '65 final, Lloyd, Willie and I skated around the ice and had a couple of laughs while waiting for the teams to come out. When we got into our dressing room after the period, Portland coach Hal Laycoe poked his head into the room and said, "You fellas should get serious out there."

Willie, who was tying his skate at the time, looked up and said, "Okay coach, I'll get him, what's his number?" The three of us broke up laughing again and Murray just rolled his eyes and walked out. He knew it was no use.

CARL VOSS RETIRED after the 1964-65 season and sent me a nice note just three days after I finished the WHL final. It was dated April 27, 1965, and said:

> Dear Bruce:
> Just a note to confirm my telephone conversation of today during which I was advised the NHL had awarded you a bonus in the amount of $500, less tax. This will be included in your final paycheck.
> Inasmuch as I may not have a chance to see you again, I would like to take this opportunity to express my thanks for the fine cooperation you have given me throughout the period of our association in the NHL.
> With kindest personal regards and best wishes for your continued success in the officiating business, I am
>
> Sincerely yours,
>
> Carl Voss

Underneath that letter, in my scrapbook, I wrote: Carl Voss . . . a good man who understood people." I'll always be indebted to him for having the confidence in me to bring me aboard the NHL staff. If I could start my own hall of fame for people I admire, he'd be the first to be inducted.

The NHL wasn't involved in supplying officials to the Western League the following year, 1965-66. The WHL hired its own people but I received another flattering note, this time from Murray Costello, just before the start of the season. In his letter of September 10, Murray wrote:

> Dear Bruce:
> Well, that's it! No chance we'll be seeing you this winter as we've hired our own staff. The NHL couldn't let any of the Big 5 come out this year and all of the direc-

tors felt that, of all the remaining referees, you're the only one who'd receive unanimous approval in this league (I was at the meeting when this was brought out).

If it should happen that we run into difficulties and have to request help from Scotty, you'll be the one we ask for. So, stay sharp!

I'll give the boys your regards.

Have a good season; will be looking for you on TV in the second half.

Murray

I received a $500 raise in base salary for the 1965-66 season, upping the total to $5,500. That was based on ninety dollars a game in the American Hockey League and sixty dollars a game in the Central League. It was my third season of officiating in professional hockey and I had a great deal of confidence in my ability. Voss had been responsible for much of that and Scotty Morrison, the new referee-in-chief, seemed like a good man as well.

I was in Cleveland to work an AHL game in mid-January when Scotty unexpectedly showed up at the hotel and told me some fantastic news. He said he wanted me to get my feet wet in the NHL and that I'd be working the Toronto-New York Rangers game on February 9 (1966) at Maple Leaf Gardens. I was having an excellent year in the minors so I had felt if somebody was called up I would have a chance, but still, the news came as a surprise.

MY FIRST NHL GAME

While I stood at center ice for the Canadian national anthem I tried to stop my legs from shaking.

O N JANUARY 25, 1965, I received a Canadian Pacific telegram from the National Hockey League at my house in Milton. It read:

NHL ASSIGNMENTS: GAMES ONE HUNDRED THIRTY EIGHT AND ONE HUNDRED FORTY SEVEN

The games referred to were New York at Toronto on Wednesday, February 9, and New York at Chicago on Sunday, February 13.

After being informed that I would be refereeing my first game in the NHL, my thoughts went back to the day seven years earlier when I decided to give full-time refereeing a shot. Even though there were no guarantees I would make it as a professional, I had told my board in Milton that I was quitting as manager of the arena. Finally to be able to say, after all the ups and downs, that I had made the correct decision was unbelievably gratifying.

Scotty Morrison, the referee-in-chief, could have summoned a number of minor-league prospects, but I was the one he selected. That made me feel pretty good, and the fact that my first game would be so close to home, in Toronto, only added to my enthusiasm.

I later found out that I was being pressed into service for veteran NHL referee Art Skov, who was ill and had to take some time off. Although I felt badly for Art, it was still a dream come true for me.

The local paper in Milton soon picked up on the story, creating a lot of hype. I was the first of the new young breed of officials to crack the big time.

This, of course, was during the six-team era before expansion, when there were only five referees in the NHL — Frank Udvari, Vern Buffey, Art Skov, John Ashley and Bill Friday — familiar names to most hockey fans. A new referee in the league was much more conspicuous under those circumstances than he is now, when there are twenty-one teams and fourteen or fifteen referees.

I believed the NHL selected me in part because of my firm standard of officiating and obvious success in the minor pro leagues. The league expected strong, authoritative direction from its referees. New, young referees had to be developed by the league because the current staff was getting on in years and expansion was looming.

The day before my NHL debut I began to grow fidgety. I kept busy with chores around my home and tried to stay calm, but it wasn't easy. I had decided not to take a lot of family and friends with me to Toronto because I felt it was important just to treat this game as another officiating assignment. Obviously, it was a special occasion for me, but I only wanted to do well, be accepted and keep things as routine as possible.

By the time I left Milton the next afternoon for the forty-five minute drive to Toronto, those calm, logical thoughts had been forced from mind, replaced by a nervous tension that grew even more intense when I walked into Maple Leaf Gardens. I was really wound up by the time I reached the dressing room.

John D'Amico and Brian Sopp, the two linesmen that night, both offered encouragement to help relax me before the game, but it didn't help much.

When I skated onto the ice I felt a mixture of amazement and fright. The sensation was similar to what I had felt before my first NHL exhibition game, in St. Catharines, four years

earlier. Then I had been very much in awe of my sur-
roundings, but now I was also the center of attention, when I
had no desire to be. I began skating around in figure eights to
calm my nerves and it felt like all 14,802 pairs of eyes were
staring right at me.

While I stood at center ice for the Canadian national anthem I tried to stop my legs from shaking. The anthem
seemed to go on forever. Fortunately they didn't play the
American anthem, too, as they do now.

Once it was all over and I got skating again I felt a lot better, especially after I dropped that first puck.

Thank God the game was a piece of cake! I didn't call my first
penalty until 2:05 of the second period, when I sent a Ranger
defenseman, Jim Neilson, off for hooking. Over the whole game
I only gave out five minor penalties. There was no fighting and I
don't even remember any pushing and shoving. It was one of
the easiest games I had ever worked, or, for that matter, ever
would work. Bob Pulford, Dave Keon and Ron Ellis scored for
Toronto and Terry Sawchuk earned a shutout as the Leafs won,
3-0.

After the game I felt like a million bucks. Scotty came
down to the room and offered his congratulations, which
made me feel even better.

The next day, in the *Toronto Star* game story, I was mentioned a couple of times. In the final paragraph Red Burnett
wrote:

> Rookie referee Bruce Hood made an excellent impres-
> sion in his NHL debut. It wasn't a tough game to handle,
> but Bruce was both competent and inconspicuous.

I didn't know it at the time, of course, but that would be one
of the last complimentary things ever said about me by Red
or the other Toronto papers.

The *Toronto Telegram* had a little piece about my debut as
well. It read:

REF HOOD HAD IT EASY

There's a ritual in the NHL to be followed when the
referee for that night's game is announced.

The fans boo. In Chicago, organist Al Melgard swings into "Three Blind Mice." In Toronto — the acknowledged seat of culture in the league — fans politely, but firmly, signify their displeasure with rumbling noises.

But, last night, when Bruce Hood came through the gate and stepped onto the ice for his NHL debut, there wasn't a sound.

"Here are the officials for tonight's game," the announcer said. "The referee — Bruce Hood; the linesmen, Brian Sopp and John D'Amico." There wasn't a murmur. The fans had never heard the name Bruce Hood before. It was his first NHL game.

Hood, who looks a little like Frank Udvari and a lot like Vern Buffey, skated figure eights while trying to calm the butterflies. "Sure I was nervous," he said. "Who wouldn't be?"

Hood, who refereed three years in the American League, was pressed into service because Art Skov has been sick the past several weeks with dizzy spells.

"I was happy that it wasn't a tough one," he said, when it was over. "I guess my turn will come soon enough."

How right I was.

WHISTLE WHILE
YOU WORK

So many fights are needless, needless, needless! Many times players don't even want to fight but do because they have to keep up the image of being a rough, tough hockey player.

WHAT'S A GAME in the life of a referee like?

On game day, officials are expected to be at the arena an hour and a half before starting time. It doesn't take that long to get dressed and ready, so there's time to lay the equipment out in the dressing room and then relax with a coffee or a soft drink.

In the dressing room before the game, officials go through a complete stretching program. This was started in the last five or six years of my career and there's no doubt that it enabled me to work a few years longer. I found it of great benefit because of my lower back problems. Stretching helps reduce injuries to officials and also increases the oxygen flowing to the brain, which is important when it comes to making those split-second decisions during the game.

When the officials go on the ice they are always led by the referee, and when they come off the ice, the referee is the first one to leave. There's no particular reason for that except tradition. It's much the same as goaltenders leading their teams out of the dressing room.

Once on the ice the officials skate around to loosen up. The linesmen check the nets, and the referee makes sure the off-ice officials are in place. By then the teams are supposed to be on the ice and ready to go. Getting the teams out used to be more of a problem than it is now. It's difficult to comprehend that in a big-league operation like the NHL, games used to be held up by coaches playing little mind games with their opponents. They may have felt they were gaining a psychological advantage by making the other team wait, or, as was often the case, they were just getting even for having had to wait when they were in the other team's building. The officials association proposed a rule change many years ago to put a stop to this. Finally it got so ridiculous that the present rule was instituted calling for a minor penalty to be assessed to any team not on the ice for the start of a period. It only took a few calls of that infraction before the teams started being more careful, and now that phase of the game is like clockwork.

During the game the referee is expected to follow ten or fifteen feet behind the play and a few feet out from the boards, so that he's out of the way but always in a position to see everything in front of him. As the play enters the zone, the referee passes the play and goes to the goal line eight or ten feet from the net. From that position he can move forward to see a close play around the net, or backward if there's a shot coming from the point that may deflect or be wide. He must be alert and flexible, not just with his body but also with his eyes. He must keep an eye on the shot, on the play at the point if someone goes out to check the shooter and on the contact in front of the net. In other words he must be aware of anything and everything that is going on.

Hockey is a contact sport, and hitting helps make the game the exciting sport it is. The referee has to have a feel for the play so that he can control the game without ruining it. If there is a lot of hitting going on, even if it's borderline legal, he should let it go unless the stick or an elbow is used. Any illegal use of the stick should be called, and is now, more than ever. The league has also cracked down on restraining fouls like hooking, holding and interference, which prevent the good players from showing their abilities and thereby hurt the game for the fans.

As most fans know, when the referee calls a penalty he raises his arm with his non-whistle hand and waits for the team that has committed the infraction to gain control of the puck. When it does he blows his whistle and then points at the player who committed the infraction and signals what the infraction was. He then skates to the penalty box and displays the signal to the timekeeper. In some instances — for example when two players have been roughing it up — the referee will probably skate backwards to the penalty box, so that he can keep an eye on what's going on, should they decide to mix it up again.

Problems arise when a second infraction takes place during a delayed penalty call. For example, say the referee has called a hooking penalty and during the delay a tripping infraction takes place. Then two players get into a fight and another player enters the altercation. The referee has to remember everything from the beginning and assess the penalties properly. He has to be sure he gets the right players and that additional players are sent to the box if a minor penalty is being tacked on to a five-minute major. It can get very complicated.

The linesmen are a great help in sorting things out. The referee can't possibly see everything all the time so a couple of extra pairs of eyes come in handy. Linesmen are not allowed to call minor penalties where judgment is involved, like hooking and holding, but are permitted to call delay-of-game penalties, unsportsmanlike penalties and infractions for too many men on the ice. They can also blow the whistle when objects are thrown onto the ice. Linesmen take a lot of abuse in the face-off circles and many just let it flow off their backs. The occasional unsportsmanlike call by them is great to see because it reminds the players that these fellows are in charge of the game, too, and trying to do a good job for everyone. The players have to respect that fact, whether they're happy with his work or not.

Linesmen are also permitted to call major penalties or match penalties. They couldn't call a minor for slashing, but they could call a major, the idea being that when an infraction that serious occurs and the referee doesn't see it, it will still be called. There's still one decision-maker for the judgment situations — the ones that might or might not be penalties —

while the major fouls are almost certain to be seen by one of the three officials.

Sometimes a player will get a quick breakout pass and before you know it he's heading in alone on the other team's goalie. The referee is at a disadvantage in that situation because he is still coming out of the other zone, which makes it difficult to get into position to see if the puck enters the net. The front linesman, however, is closer, and will skate into the zone with the play and point to the net if the puck goes in.

Linesmen are now also permitted to blow the whistle if the puck is batted ahead by hand to a teammate. It used to drive the players nuts when linesmen couldn't do that because sometimes they were in the best position to see it.

The key to the linesmen's efficiency is teamwork. The back linesman is in position to see if a pass comes from inside the blue line for a two-line offside, or from the player's own side of the red line for an icing. If that occurs, he will show it by pointing for an offside or raising his arm. The other linesman will acknowledge this and be in position to whistle the play if it is touched by a player from the team who shot it offside, or, if the defending team touches the puck first on an icing, he raises his arm to signal the back linesman to blow the whistle.

Breaks for television commercials are a necessity nowadays, and it's the linesmen who are told when they are going to occur. This is done through the use of a beeper, a light and compact unit about two inches by three inches and about an inch thick, taped to their sweatshirts or attached to their suspenders or waist area. When the linesman hears a series of beeps, he knows that a break will occur during that stoppage in play and that he is not to drop the puck until he hears another beep. Some units emit a vibration rather than a beep, which is beneficial when the crowd noise gets too loud.

Six half-minute commercial breaks are allowed per period but may not be used during a penalty, as that could give the team on the power play an advantage because it would allow them to rest their number one unit.

Line changes can sometimes be a problem. Coaches often want to match a particular line against another and the result is needless delays. The league instituted a rule a few years ago to eliminate the line juggling. After a certain length of time following a stoppage in play the referee raises his hand to indicate no further changes. Then the home team is allowed to make the final change.

The teams at first had quite a time adjusting to the new rule. I was standing there one night with my arm raised and the visiting players were skating right past me to the face-off spot like I didn't exist. I had to give them a penalty. They looked at me like I was nuts and I said, "Look, the rule's been in effect all season."

My personal philosophy — although the brass didn't agree with it — was to start raising my arm only if there were problems. Otherwise I didn't see the need.

When there is a dispute on a goal, the referee stops play immediately, unless he is certain that the puck did not enter the net. He shows this by emphatically waving the goal off. If there is some doubt, he stops the game and confers with the linesmen or the goal judge. At one time linesmen used to voice their opinions only if asked to do so by the referee. Nowadays if a linesman has seen something that the referee hasn't he is required to get to the referee and tell him, even if play is still going on. The reason for the change stems from the fact that there are more and better-trained full-time linesmen now. They used to be part-time and often lived in the city they were officiating in, so they couldn't be expected to be as reliable and competent as they are now.

When a fight breaks out during the game, the linesmen are expected to stand back, initially. The first thing they do is call out sweater colors to tell each other which player they will be taking when it comes time to break it up. They wait until the players go into a clinch, or fall to the ice, then jump in and take the player whose sweater they called. There's no point in their going in at the start of the fight because the combatants are too angry and aggressive. It's difficult enough, on skates, trying to control a player, and entering the fray at that point would usually mean the linesmen take some of the punches. Besides, the players are usually much bigger and wear more equipment. Once they use up some of their energy, it's much easier to take charge.

Incidentally, there is nothing in the linesmen's section of the rule book that tells them what to do to break up fights, which is strange, considering that it is a big part of their role and is taught to them by their superiors.

In regular-season games, if the referee gets injured and has to leave the ice, the senior linesman, or the one with the most refereeing experience, takes his place. The linesmen then work as a two-man team. The linesman appointed as referee is solely responsible for calling the "judgment penalties" described earlier and takes all the face-offs at the end face-off spot.

During the Stanley Cup play-offs the format changes. There is a standby referee for all games and a standby linesman for all deciding and final-series games. During the finals there is always a large contingent of officiating staff in attendance — the actual game officials, the standbys, the directors of officiating and the supervisors. It's good to have so many people around because there is as much pressure on the officials in the play-offs as there is on the players. A lot of kibitzing takes place during that time among the officiating staff, which helps to ease the tension and keep everyone loose. That's important because an official who is uptight won't perform at his highest level, which is true in any occupation.

THE TOUGHEST CALL in hockey is interference. It's a contact game and many times it's difficult to tell, especially in front of the net, who's pushing whom. It's a judgment penalty with a fine line between legal and illegal. So much of it goes on that it is often necessary to make a call to set the standard. If it's then called consistently, the teams will know what they can and cannot do, and play accordingly.

Consistency is important in all areas of penalty calling. For example, if something is let go in the first period and called in the second, or vice versa, then teams get really upset because they don't know what the referee is going to do and have no idea what limits they are expected to play within.

There's no question that it's a lot tougher to make some calls later in the game that were made more easily in the first period. Often the maturity of the official and his amount of experience will govern whether or not the call is made. Referees are human, the same as the players. Players don't want to take a penalty in a tight situation in the third period any more than a referee wants to give one.

But, when do you decide when an important part of the game occurs? Early in my career Fred Glover, then coach of the Oakland Seals, came up to me after a game the Seals had lost 8-3 and told me that a penalty call I had made against his team in the first period, which resulted in a power play goal being scored, affected the outcome of the game. If it was that important at that stage then shouldn't every part of the game be considered equally? Still, a referee does not want to call a borderline penalty in a close game. By the time the third period comes, players generally know the limits they have to play within. If those limits are overstepped, the referee has no choice but to call a penalty.

Billy Reay, the former Blackhawk coach, used to yell at me, "Don't referee by the score, Bruce." The problem with that is that players play according to the score. If a team is down by three or four goals late in the game a player might run around making trouble that he wouldn't have made if the game was close. So referees often have to officiate according to the score. Things have to be kept in perspective.

People forget that any referee has thoughts and feelings about the game. He's less likely to call a restraining foul against a team that's down and playing poorly than he is against a team that's up by five goals. It's only human nature and there's no reason to suggest that referees are not human.

There used to be larger disparities between officials as far as what they considered a penalty. In the past some referees used to let just about everything go and were loved by the teams that were hurt most by stricter officiating. It's not a knock on those officials; just that for the total picture, you have to have a standard of discipline, because wide variances can cause a lot of problems. The guy who lets things go may be liked more by some players, but if all the referees did that there would be sheer mayhem on the ice. The closer officials come to a consistent standard, the more respect there is for all officials.

One rule change that could eliminate about twelve pages in the rule book concerns, of course, fighting. There are lots of rules that cover everything around it — third-man-in, aggressor, leaving the bench and so on, but still not *the* rule. So many fights are needless, needless, needless! Many times players don't even want to fight but do because they have to keep up the image of being rough, tough hockey players. It's the mentality the players have grown up with, the same as when there is a stoppage in play and the players crowd around; pretty soon everybody is squared off — pushing, talking and staring at each other — to prove who's the toughest. The whole thing is ridiculous. In my mind, there is no place for fighting in hockey. There's no question about it, it should be banned. If players knew they would be ejected from the game for fighting, ninety percent of fights would not take place. Sometimes a player will get a burr under his saddle and fight regardless of the rules, as in Europe, where, even though combatants are always thrown out of the game, the odd fight still takes place.

In the NHL, the situation is one where everybody blames everybody else. They see that one team has an enforcer or two and they decide, well if they have those types, we need some, too. And that's just the way it is and will be, until fighting is removed from the game.

Most of the time, when a penalty is called a comment is made by the player. It doesn't necessarily mean a major confrontation. The player may say something like, "I hardly touched him," or "Didn't you see the play at the other end?" There are, of course, more emotional players, who swear and call the referee names. Usually, I didn't acknowledge that I heard them. The only time I called an unsportsmanlike conduct penalty or a misconduct, was when a player belittled me in front of the crowd or other players, or if the name-calling and cursing got too serious.

I didn't always just stand there and take their abuse quietly. There was often a little verbal battle, that worked as sort of a release for both of us, and afterwards we both felt better. With some players I earned respect that way and sometimes I developed more respect for the player, it he was able to take a little while he was giving it to you. Many times, though, a player couldn't wait to go and squeal to management if you swore at him, even though he had thrown a whole barrage of curses at you. Then the league would give you hell for swearing, because officials aren't supposed to do that sort of thing. It created a no-win situation.

In the dressing room after the game, the officials take a few minutes and relax with a soft drink or a beer. The talk is usually about the game — a dispute over a call, the spectacular play of an individual, the exciting finish. Then it's time to take off our sweaty equipment and hit the showers. Sometimes notes are prepared by the individual officials if an incident requires a report to the league. After that, the gear is packed up and they either rush off to the airport for a flight, or if not, then it's back to the hotel where the equipment is laid out to dry.

If the game has gone well, the referee and linesmen can feel a certain satisfaction. But even if the game hasn't gone well, all must quickly be forgotten because soon it will be time for another city, another game and another challenge.

INSIDE THE
OFFICIATING SYSTEM

Don't think for a moment that hockey games between officials would be the cleanest you'd ever see.

DURING MY EARLY YEARS with the NHL staff there were no special preparations for officials before the season started. We were provided with a poor-quality sweater and a single pull-on red armband. We were given a couple of exhibition games to work and a short rules briefing from the referee-in-chief. Then we were sent out to officiate the highest-caliber hockey in the world.

That changed dramatically when Scotty Morrison became referee-in-chief. He introduced a full-scale training camp that lasted up to a week. Complete medicals — including eye examinations, of course — along with fitness evaluations and conditioning programs all became part of the routine officials now go through every year.

Training camp for officials begins in the fall, shortly after the teams open their own. Centennial Park in Etobicoke, in the western part of Metropolitan Toronto, has been the site for many years. Previously it had been held in Kitchener or Brantford, both also in Ontario.

Training camp is held for more than to give officials the chance to get into shape for the coming season. Sessions are held to discuss rule applications and interpretations; the systems to be used for report filing and travel are clarified; and the general standards every official is expected to apply when carrying out his job are reinforced. It is the one time of year when everyone is together to discuss these matters, and the hope is that a higher measure of consistency will result.

The league has taken other steps in recent years to ensure consistency during the regular season. It now provides telephone hookups so that officials as a group can discuss various concerns with the league office. That proved beneficial this past season when it came to cracking down on restraining fouls and some of the more violent aspects of the game.

Physical conditioning was stressed first and foremost at the camps I attended. We were usually exhausted after our workouts, whether they took place on the ice, the sports field or the track. Every year new ideas were brought to the process of physical conditioning, with new programs instituted. By the end of every training camp we would be ready physically and armed with all the technical knowledge we would need for the season ahead. But one main ingredient was always missing.

Very little was ever done to prepare us mentally. An official can be in excellent shape and know all the rule applications, yet still not function at his top level if he isn't equipped to handle the mental strain that occurs during the long season. Many quality officials have left the business — either by their own choice or because the league dismissed them after it affected their work — because of the pressure. Many of them might have handled the stress — the pressure and the abuse from fans, players and management — much better if the problem had been addressed more often in training camp. Mental conditioning is that important. Many athletes receive psychological help to handle stress and enhance performances, and it certainly wouldn't hurt for officials to be exposed to that area as well.

The activity we enjoyed most at training camp — it was also part of our physical training regimen — was playing hockey. The games were always played between teams of officials. Sometimes teams were chosen so that the referees played against the linesmen, and sometimes it was officials from the east against officials from the west. Whatever the matchup, those contests were always competitive, as were those on the football field or baseball diamond. And don't think for a moment that hockey games between officials would be the cleanest you'd ever see. In fact at one point we got so aggressive that the games had to be stopped for a while until we agreed to tone them down a little.

When training camp was completed we would be assigned our exhibition game schedules. The nice part about those games was that many of them were played in smaller towns, or in minor-league cities that we never got to during the regular season. One year John D'Amico, Ron Finn and I officiated two games in Anchorage, Alaska, between the Winnipeg Jets and the Vancouver Canucks.

One of the functions of the exhibition season is to test new rules on a trial-run basis. One memorable experiment involved the "free face-off" rule, designed so that when the defending team caused a delay in play in their own end, for example by freezing the puck against the boards, the opposing team was awarded the puck at the corner face-off spot — without any competition. Everyone lined up as they would in a normal face-off except the defending center, who had to be outside the circle. The attacking center was then allowed to do anything he wanted with the puck except take a shot directly on goal. What usually happened was that he would draw it back to a big shooter at the top of the circle, who would blast it at the net. Goalkeepers in particular weren't too excited about that proposed rule, and after several tries the idea was discarded.

Rule changes tried out in the exhibition schedule rarely get a fair shake. Usually there's a lot of opposition to change from the teams, which is why it takes so long in the NHL to get anything done. Most changes are still the result of seeing new rules work in the Junior leagues or American League and following suit.

There have, however, been a number of excellent rule changes in recent years, rules that have picked up the pace of the game and made things easier for the officials. Many of the improvements have evolved by trial and error. The face-off system, for example, has changed tremendously over the years. There used to be all kinds of problems with players jockeying for position. Now the linesman simply waits until the players put their sticks down — visiting team first — and then drops the puck. Players who don't comply immediately with the linesman are thrown out of the face-off and can even receive a minor penalty if they make a fuss and delay the game longer.

Another rule change put in last year was directed at the delayed offside rule. If the puck enters the defending team's zone and an attacking player is caught inside the blue line, that player can now put himself back onside by making contact with the blue line. That has cut out unnecessary stoppages and helped keep the game moving.

THE NHL STAFF of officials is composed of eighteen referees and thirty-two linesmen. Twelve of the referees work a full slate of NHL games, while the other six work in the American and International leagues. One or two with the minor leagues also get some games in the NHL as they climb the ladder.

To develop officials, the NHL keeps twelve minor-league referees under contract. Close tabs are kept on them and only the best are selected to work NHL games. Files are also kept on many other officials around North America, with the idea of adding the top ones to the NHL staff.

Many officials never make it past the minor leagues because their evaluations indicate they don't have the tools to move up. Some who do make it encounter problems with the added pressure and the closer scrutiny their work is given, similar to what a player faces when rising from the minors.

Changes in staff may come about because of age, retirement or the release of an official. The Officials Association has a three-year agreement that states that an official cannot be released unless he finishes in the bottom third of the ratings for two years in a row. Retirement age is forty-five, based on contractual agreement; once past that age each official works under a series of one-year contracts and his rehiring is based on his ability to continue to do the job, and whether or not a replacement is ready to move up and take his place. The official's rapport with league brass is also a consideration.

The length of an official's career is generally longer than that of most players, but even so, it's limited, so they need to get as many of those top earning years in as possible before retiring.

The senior referees on the staff in the 1987-88 season were Dave Newell (43) and Bob Myers (47), both of whom joined the league in 1967, the year of expansion, when several new officials were brought into the NHL. These are the only two officials left who were founding members of the Officials Association in 1969. Newell has been its president for the last few years.

The Officiating Department of the NHL, which at one time was always headed by a referee-in-chief (first Carl Voss then Scotty Morrison), has changed its structure in recent years. During the 1987-88 season Jim Gregory was the vice president in charge of hockey operations, of which officiating is part; John McCauley was the director of officiating; and Bryan Lewis was the coordinator of development and a supervisor of officials. John Ashley, Matt Pavelich and Wally Harris were full-time, and Lou Maschio and Sam Sisco part-time, supervisors. John D'Amico, who retired from active duty during the 1987-88 season, was given the role of "coach."

The supervisor's job is to observe the game and the work of the officials and deal with team management concerning rule standards. He must file a report to the league giving his view of the official's work in areas such as rule application, effort, and rapport with the players on the ice. That analysis is crucial to the future of every referee or linesman.

Approximately 700 games a season over the various leagues are supervised, including between fifty and sixty percent of the NHL games.

All games in the American League are handled by the NHL staff of referees, as well as about fifty percent of those in the International League, fifty games each year in the Canadian Major Junior Leagues (QMJHL, WHL, OHL) and twenty-five games in the Central Collegiate Hockey Association (CCHA) at the American college level.

Referee assignments are usually given out a month in advance and average about three games a week. The referee usually travels by himself, unless he is going to the same city as the linesmen, which is rare because linesmen work more games—about ten more per season—and travel more. For games west of the Mississippi River, referees living in the east must travel the night prior to the game. We called that the "Vern Buffey rule" because it was instituted after Vern missed a game in Minnesota, after trying to fly on the day of the game and getting stopped by a snowstorm. The policy is a good one anyway because it allows the official to get a good night's rest before working, without having to worry about traveling.

For games in the east, the referee is allowed to fly out the day of the game but must leave by nine-thirty in the morning. Once I didn't make it in time and got caught red-handed by Scotty. The officials were known to stretch the travel rules on occasion. The odd thing about this particular time was that I didn't break the rule deliberately and it was the only time I was ever fined during my career.

I was scheduled to work Cleveland's home opener the year they entered the NHL, Wednesday, October 6, 1976. I had a reservation for a flight to Cleveland scheduled to leave at eight-fifteen a.m., and it was one of the few times I ever slept in when I was supposed to catch a flight. When I woke up I realized that there was no way I was going to make it to the airport on time.

I called the airline and found out there was another flight at ten-fifty so I booked myself on that one. It only takes about a half hour to fly across Lake Erie from Toronto to Cleveland and anytime the weather was bad and flights had to be cancelled, I could still drive there in five hours, so there was little danger of missing the game.

As I was walking down the corridor at the airport, who should happen to be there waiting for the same flight but Scotty Morrison. He saw me walking towards him and started shaking his head. I thought, "Oh, boy, this is it."

I walked up to him and told him that I had slept in and missed my earlier flight. The way he looked at me it was obvious he didn't believe me and thought I had done it on purpose.

We got on the plane and sat across the aisle from each other. I met a friend and the three of us had an amiable conversation during the flight. Scotty and I then took a cab to the hotel and were together after the game.

About five days later I got a letter in the mail that read "Strictly confidential" on the front. Inside, it said, "Due to your tardy clock you are hereby fined $50.00 for not being on the first flight in the morning."

I laughed when I read it. Of the many things that I had done intentionally that I probably should have or could have been fined for, I go and get fined for something accidental.

I got caught on another occasion trying to stretch the guidelines, this time by Frank Udvari, the supervisor of officials. And for doing something he taught me!

The expense reports from officials were okayed each Monday by Scotty Morrison, or by Frank when Scotty was out of town, as was the case this particular time. He went over my expense report and docked me for a claim I had made for mileage from Buffalo to Milton. He had attended the same game I was claiming for and knew that I had gotten a ride home from another official who was also putting in for the same trip.

Oddly enough, he had taught me tricks like that during his officiating days and was probably better than anyone at doing them. I guess that was how he knew what to look for on my expense sheet.

Every game is a road trip except for the occasional one close to home, and the assignments are arranged geographically to cut down on some of the travel. For example, some weeks I would fly to New York for a Wednesday-night game in Madison Square Garden, then take the train to Philadelphia for a game on Thursday, and go on to Pittsburgh for a game on Saturday night. Sunday morning I would fly home. The week before I might have gone to St. Louis for a Tuesday game, then on to Chicago for a Wednesday-night game, and back to Detroit for Friday night.

IF AN INCIDENT out of the ordinary takes place during a game, the officials are required to report it immediately after the game is over. This is done by a phone call to what is called the "Hot Line." Each official is expected to prepare his written report without consulting the other officials. The reports are then read into the tape machine by phone. If the league needs to act quickly on a matter, they have the transcribed report by the next morning. The written copy is sent along later for verification of the exact wording.

If a hearing is required, the main participants are called to a meeting, generally at the Montreal office, but sometimes in another location closest to where most of the participants are at the time. If it involves a player, then he is often accompanied by the general manager or the team lawyer, or both. The officials involved in the incident are also present, along with an officiating management representative, quite possibly a supervisor who was at the game and has submitted his own report.

At the hearing, a video is shown of the incident, if one is available, and reports from the officials are distributed. Then the player is asked if he agrees that the reports are factual, and if not, what his version is. Very seldom will the player dispute the officials' account, but frequently the person speaking on his behalf will question some aspect, which of course is his job. He doesn't want to see a player suspended, or if a suspension is imminent, doesn't want it to be for too long. Interestingly, whatever had taken place on the ice, the player almost always comes to the meeting very humble and seems truly sorry that the incident ever happened.

Generally, the teams are very respectful during these hearings. But there are some teams and individuals who, the same as they do away from the meeting room, will try to make the official feel like a low-class citizen. They become instant Perry Masons, cross-examining by means of innuendo. Their tone of voice and line of questioning is meant to cast doubt on the credibility of the officials' report.

The Hot Line reports from the officials do not necessarily have to concern a situation that resulted in a penalty. All game misconducts must be reported, but other problems, such as improper conditions or equipment, should be filed by telephone. For example, there might have been a problem with the glass, or improper markings on the ice or problems with the dressing room. Those types of things don't require a hearing, but are still reported on the Hot Line so that the league can get them corrected quickly.

When the regular schedule ends, all the officials are required to call the league office the next day at ten a.m. to find out their play-off assignments. Nobody knows where or with whom they are going to be working before that time.

There is a whole different set of procedures used in the play-offs, and the league does everything possible to ensure that those games are officiated to the highest standards.

Each of the play-off series has a series supervisor who has a number of responsibilities. For example, he deals with the off-ice officials who come in from other cities and looks after tickets on behalf of the league. But most important of all, of course, he is responsible for the on-ice officiating.

The day of the first game a noon meeting, with all the officiating staff present, is held to discuss the standards of officiating for the series. There is a noon meeting before each subsequent game of the series, in which the supervisor, the linesmen and the incoming referee discuss what happened in the previous game. The supervisor will reaffirm the standards and familiarize the new referee with the series to date, so he can use the same standards as the previous one and act accordingly when certain situations occur. The supervisor will inform him of any animosities that are building up and will tell him about any nonsense that has already taken place. It's best for the officials to be prepared as much as possible and it's important to attempt to keep a consistent standard throughout the series.

Referees are assigned to play-off games according to their ratings and experience. Linesmen are assigned in pairs and remain together throughout the play-offs, generally working two games in one city and then two games in another. In each series the best and most experienced referee available works the seventh game, if the series gets that far.

Officials are continually evaluated (See Appendix). Not only are the supervisory staff viewing their work and sitting in judgment, but so are the team general managers who must submit their ratings and comments on the staff. This latter procedure was viewed as something of a joke when the idea was introduced a number of years ago. The GMs always used to include some spicy comments in their reports, and no doubt still do, but I am sure their replies are more helpful now. Obviously, there will still be the usual bias, for and against, but that's only natural when one man is judging another.

If that isn't enough, all linesmen evaluate the referees, and vice versa. Again, this too can turn into a popularity contest.

As the play-offs go on, fewer officials are needed and more are dropped off according to their ratings. It takes ten referees and eighteen linesmen to cover the division semifinals. For the division finals it's eight and ten, then six and eight for the conference finals. For the Stanley Cup final, the top three referees and the top four linesmen are used.

Those who have the highest ratings go farthest in the play-offs and make the most money, and obviously that helps spur each official to do his very best.

Officiating in the National Hockey League is big business — more than half of the league's operating budget is spent on it. It may seem fairly simple from a fan's point of view, but obviously it's a lot more complicated than just pulling on a striped shirt and heading out onto the ice.

THE OFF-ICE TEAM

If the team was upset with the referee, the trainer would delay giving him a puck or throw it on the ice to the opposite end of the rink.

URING EACH GAME nine off-ice officials go about their jobs thanklessly, tirelessly and usually without pay. They're there because they love the game and want to be part of it. There are two goal judges, two penalty box attendants, one penalty timekeeper, one game timekeeper, an official scorer, a statistician and a stoppage-in-play recorder. Three alternates are also available, in case one of the regulars isn't able to make the game.

The official scorer, statistician and stoppage-in-play recorder all sit up in the press box. The job of the official scorer is to award the goals and assists. The referee only has to indicate who scored the goal, and even that is just a formality because the official scorer usually has the benefit of a television monitor. To keep track of the assists while the game is going on he continuously writes down the number of the last player who touched the puck. When the puck changes hands, he makes a slash on that line to indicate change of possession and starts over again. For example, he may record 5-7 / 9-7-19-9. If number 9 scores, the assists will be awarded to 19 and 7.

The stoppage-in-play recorder keeps track of that aspect of the game on a form listing each possible way that play can be halted. On the same form he records the actual time it takes to play each period and the entire game, and the number of face-offs in the end and neutral zones. This form was first used for research purposes but now is part of the regular stats sent to the league offices.

The official scorer is responsible for keeping data, and accumulating those sheets he doesn't do himself. These include the Official Report of Match, Score Sheet, Penalty Record and Official Statistics of Game forms. Often he will have somebody helping him compile some of the statistics — for example, by recording which players are on the ice when an even-strength goal is scored, so that the plus-minus statistic can be calculated later.

Right after the game the information is transferred by computer to the league office in Montreal. The actual forms are sent by courier afterward, as confirmation.

The penalty box attendants control the box doors and tell a penalized player when his penalty has expired. Straightening out a penalty situation can be confusing at times if several are called at once, but the off-ice officials have usually been involved in hockey most of their lives and are very knowledgeable, so there are few problems.

The odd time I may have had the penalties straight in my head but then told the penalty timekeeper the wrong players or infractions. And other times he may have written them down incorrectly. When the public address announcer didn't say the penalties correctly, I would have to go back and get it straightened out. In one building I had problems with this often — even the simplest things would get screwed up. This one guy, one of the few I ever had problems with, often ended up lecturing me, saying he hadn't got it wrong but that I had told it to him incorrectly. That was all I needed in the middle of a tough game — a lecture from the penalty timekeeper. The man has since retired.

The goal judges, to some degree, are window dressing — they're there to let the fans at the game and in the television audience know that a goal has been scored. Ninety-nine percent of the time the referee sees the play and knows whether the puck went into the net or not. Most of the time I never even noticed when the red light went on. There are now telephone hookups that allow the referee to go to the official's table and speak directly to the goal judge and hear his ac-count of what he saw — much easier than speaking through the solid glass behind the net.

The last thing a referee wants is to rely on the goal judge's version alone. He hopes that when there is a dispute, the goal judge and perhaps the linesmen will be able to confirm what he thought happened. However, when no one except the goal judge has witnessed the actual play, he has no alternative but to abide by his ruling.

Sometimes the goal judge will press the light button by mistake, when it looks for sure like the puck is about to enter the net but the goalie makes a miraculous save. It's easy to anticipate a goal in that situation. There's an old saying that goal judges should "sit on their hands" so that by the time they move them to press the button, they are sure the puck actually crossed the goal line.

Before the new Megnet system was instituted around the league, the puck would sometimes enter the net and then bounce right back out again. Once in Minnesota I saw clearly that the puck had entered the net and then come out faster than it had gone in. But the goal judge saw it differently and didn't put the light on. He was still shaking his head even af-ter I had been to the timer's bench to award the goal and was dropping the puck at center ice.

Goal judges sometimes have a hard time telling if the puck was entirely across the goal line, especially when the area be-hind the net is jammed with players. Since Wayne Gretzky started the practice of setting up behind the other team's net, it's become even harder with bodies bobbing back and forth and blocking the goal judge's field of view.

The off-ice officials also have miscellaneous duties. For example, they take care of the pucks used in the game. The pucks are kept frozen by the home team to keep them from bouncing too much. During the game they are put in a bucket with ice. It used to be the home team's respon-sibility to hand out the pucks, which meant if the team was upset with the referee, the trainer would delay giving him a puck or throw it on the ice to the opposite end of the rink. Lefty Wilson, in Detroit, used to be the best at pulling capers with the pucks. Thankfully, the league changed the rules so that they are now kept at the timer's bench.

Another duty of the off-ice officials is to give the players, linesmen and referee a five-minute and a two-minute warning, to make sure they come onto the ice at the proper time.

For all their responsibilities, there is little reward for these officials beyond being a part of the exciting world of hockey. Very few of them are actually paid; instead they get season tickets and then a chance to travel during the Stanley Cup play-offs — as neutral off-ice officials — during which time their costs are paid.

Off-ice officials are a special breed — some have worked since the old six-team era. There are fathers and sons involved. Some drive many miles to get to the rink for the games. They schedule vacation time and marriages around game dates, and some have sacrificed better positions with their regular employers in order to continue as off-ice officials. A dedicated group, they take as much pride in their work as the on-ice crew.

Off-ice officials at one time were referred to as the "minor officials," a somewhat degrading term, but that was changed and rightfully so. While they don't seem as important to the fans as the officials on the ice, without them there could be no hockey game.

AROUND THE LEAGUE

I was sure I was going throw up, right there at center ice in front of more than 17,000 people.

MY FAVORITE NHL city had to be New York. Not only was it a great place to visit but Madison Square Garden was one of the rinks I most enjoyed working in.

The people there often were wild and abrasive — and sometimes downright weird — but they were alive. When they started hooting and hollering they really added something to the game, and some nights they could be even more entertaining.

Every time there was a stoppage in play in one corner, this one guy, down close to the ice, would stand up and start pounding on the glass, shaking his fist and hollering at me. I don't think it mattered who the referee was, he did his little act just to entertain the people in his section.

One night I was just watching a game and happened to be down near his section between periods. He came up to me and introduced himself. "It's not anything personal," he explained. "I just like to have a lot of fun." We chatted for a while and it turned out that he was a pretty good guy.

The next time I refereed a game there the play came to a stop in his corner and he stood up at the glass holding out some candy in his hand. That got a few chuckles. But at the next stoppage he was right back to screaming at me and banging on the glass.

A lot of the Ranger fans' antics were amusing and I couldn't help but laugh sometimes. But one play-off game there against the Islanders, I wasn't laughing, and in fact came pretty close to getting sick.

Before the game had even started, the Ranger fans were voicing their dislike for the Islanders and getting on their favorite targets, Denis Potvin and Billy Smith. Just as the national anthem began, somebody threw some big dead fish out onto the ice. The rink attendants couldn't come out to clean them up until the anthem was finished, and the rotten flesh sent up a stench that was unbelievable! I had a touch of the flu that day and I was sure I was going to throw up, right there at center ice in front of more than 17,000 people. Somehow I made it through the anthem and rushed over to the side boards, where I gagged a few times before getting my stomach under control.

The rink attendants came out and cleaned up the fish, but all through the period the odor lingered in the area where they had landed, and every time the play went near there, the smell just took over. After the ice was flooded for the second period, it wasn't as bad, but still, just the thought of those fish turned my stomach for the rest of the game.

If the Rangers made the play-offs, they would work the hockey games around the circus, which comes to the Garden for a few weeks every April. It may be the only arena where you can see a three-ring circus in the afternoon and then come back in the evening for a hockey game. The circus brought with it another aroma — and I don't mean peanuts and popcorn. The pungent odor of the excrement of elephants and other animals would filter through the halls from the storage rooms and into our dressing room, and though it wasn't as bad as rotten fish, it still made the air repulsive.

There was always something going on at the Garden, and often I'd go there on off-nights to see what event was taking place. Whether it was a basketball game, a concert or the circus, it was always a good time-waster.

The officials stayed at a hotel right across the street, which was nice because of the convenience. In fact, the hotels in most cities were usually within ten minutes of the arena. But the hotel in Washington was at least a half-hour drive from the Capital Center, which caused problems one night when I forgot my referee sweater in the room closet. In any other city I would have had time to go back to the hotel, but not there. Fortunately, one of the off-ice officials happened to have his referee's equipment in his car, or I don't know what I would have done. After that it became something of a running joke every time I came to Washington. "By the way, did you remember your sweater?"

There's a lot of free time between and after games, and in each city the officials have a favorite hangout where they get together and unwind.

In New York the officials used to frequent a sports bar — it even had pictures of officials on the walls — across the street from the hotel. It was called the Blarney Rock. For me it was a great place to relax, listen to some stories, have a bite to eat and sip on a beer. I got to know the owners, the bartenders and the regulars, and spent hours just sitting around chatting. A place like that, where I knew a lot of people and they knew me, made being on the road a lot less of a strain.

Late at night, or in the early morning as was often the case, I would wander over to Pennsylvania Station, which is in the building right below Madison Square Garden, get a fresh bagel with cream cheese — they had just about the best you could get anywhere — pick up the early edition of the morning paper, head back to the hotel, and sleep in the next morning.

The next stop after New York usually was Philadelphia. Getting there meant another short walk to Penn Station and a leisurely train ride. Philadelphia may be known as the city of Brotherly Love, but they didn't love me too much. I could rarely work a game there without feeling front and center, and without being criticized in the press the following day.

Whether or not I agreed with the goon tactics the Flyers used in the seventies, there is no disputing that team's success over the years and little doubt that they are one of the best franchises in all of sport. They have done a remarkable job marketing the game and have a super organization, and should be commended.

The Philadelphia fans are another rambunctious bunch, a lot like the New York fans. One time we came up to the back entrance of the Spectrum and saw a burned-out car — it had been torched by rowdy fans coming out of a football game played that afternoon next door at Veterans Stadium.

The Spectrum has plenty of its own traditions, from Kate Smith's rendition of the national anthem, to the sign-holder, who gained his fame during the Flyers' Stanley Cup years. His slogans were very entertaining for the fans and the television viewers, but less so for the people he flashed them at — usually the referee or visiting goaltender.

The hangout for officials in Philadelphia was a little bar near the hotel. The bartender, a guy named Harvey, was a good friend to many of the officials. One night we took that friendship a little further than we should have and almost got ourselves in a lot of trouble.

Leon Stickle and I were sitting in there along with some of the regulars after the bar had closed, chatting with Harvey and finishing off our beers. All of a sudden about ten policemen burst into the place, surrounding all of us and guarding the exit doors. They hustled everybody out and took Harvey off to jail for serving beer after hours as part of a big crackdown for that sort of thing at the time in the city.

Leon and I followed the paddywagon with the idea of bailing Harvey out of jail. When we saw him at the police station, he didn't quite share our enthusiasm. "Just go home, fellas," he told us. "They'll make out a report and I'll probably go home in the morning. The boss will look after me."

We demanded to speak to somebody in charge. The sergeant who came to see to us looked at us like we were crazy. But we waited around and made a lot of noise, attracting a lot of attention. Finally Harvey came out again and said, "Hey guys, they're getting so upset, they're going to put you in here with me." We wanted no part of that, so we left. Later we found out the bar owner had been fined, but allowed to continue operating.

Each city around the league provided me with memories — some good and some not so good — and each city had something special about it. Sometimes it was as simple as the good ice I always looked forward to in Minnesota, or walking through the old Detroit Olympia, where I could soak up all that great hockey atmosphere.

ST. LOUIS WAS probably the city I worked in most often. I first started refereeing there in 1962, when it had a minor-league team that was playing out the remainder of Syracuse's schedule in the old Eastern Pro League. That league folded and the following year the Central Hockey League was formed. The St. Louis Braves became a farm team for the Chicago Blackhawks, playing in the old dilapidated arena with wooden seats and old boards, and chicken wire around the ice surface.

The arena was refurbished after the Salomon family — Sidney Salomon Jr. and Sidney Salomon III — became majority owners of the St. Louis expansion team. The franchise entered the league in 1967 along with Los Angeles, Minnesota, Pittsburgh, Philadelphia and Oakland.

St. Louis was the site of the first two games I refereed involving expansion teams. It was a treat to be there for the Blues' inaugural games in October 1967. Celebrities such as Arthur Godfrey, Anna Maria Albergetti and Guy Lombardo were on hand to help get the team off to a good start.

The Blues developed a solid core of fans very quickly. The fans would get up and start clapping and singing and have a great time. They really got behind their team and their enthusiasm carried over to the players, helping St. Louis to become one of the earliest expansion success stories.

The organist was a major contributor to the fans' enthusiasm, one of the first to jazz up the music. In fact he used to go overboard at times and play the organ even while the game was in progress, which proved to be distracting. The league drew up regulations to curtail that practice.

Some of the fans also went overboard at times. One guy used to sit behind the penalty box and get on the visiting players' cases. It got to the point where he was causing such a stir and generating so many complaints that they had to move him out of the section.

Every arena seemed to have one or two people like that. One time in Minnesota one of the vendors in the stands was down by the penalty box during a fractious game between the Flyers and the North Stars. He was upset with one of the Philadelphia players who had been penalized and tried to give him a kick. The Flyers came off the players' bench and flew across the ice to get the culprit, who wisely took off up into the stands. I got a good look at him, though, and later suggested to the Minnesota management that they tell him to contain himself. As it turned out, I actually got to know the young man and for years after, every time I came into the building to work, we would chat and reminisce about the time he introduced himself to the Philadelphia Flyers.

One of the pranks that fans, especially in Pittsburgh, used to get a kick out of involved throwing something on the ice, like a rubber chicken or a puck, with a string attached to it. When the linesman went over to pick it up, the fan would pull the string and gather it back in. Very entertaining for the fans, but, after a while, an annoyance to the officials. I used to enjoy it when a player used his stick to trap the item and break the string. Then it would be thrown in the garbage and the officials would have the last laugh.

The players were known to pull a prank or two themselves, like the night in Los Angeles when the national anthem couldn't be sung. The singer came out to the middle of the ice, everyone stood up and the organist started in with the first few bars of "The Star Spangled Banner." The singer began to join in, but she couldn't be heard because the microphone wasn't working. It had been tested before the game and had worked fine, so nobody could understand what had happened. That is, nobody except the Boston Bruins, who were the visiting team that night. The microphone cord stretched across the ice and through the door of the visiting team's bench to the outlet, and while all this was going on, there was a lot of suspicious snickering and guarded chuckling from the Boston players. I found out later that one of them had cut the cord with his skate.

Los Angeles is a city every official likes to go to, and not just for the great weather. The Forum itself is an interesting place to work a game, usually including a Hollywood celebrity or two in the crowd. Larry Mann, whom I got to know at Wayne Gretzky's tennis tournament, is a great hockey fan and would often come down to the dressing room to say hello. He is a very personable man who always provides a few laughs and keeps things light.

During the Kings' early years, the Forum staff weren't as proficient in manufacturing ice as they are now, so the playing conditions were horrendous at times. Part of the problem was that the ice constantly had to be put in and taken out for the many events taking place at the Forum.

One time conditions were so bad that the ice was breaking away all over the rink. When I found a foot-square piece of ice missing just inside one of the blue lines, I finally had to stop the game. Wren Blair of the visiting Minnesota team said he wasn't going to let his team play on that ice, and I didn't blame him — there was no question that it was dangerous. But I had no guidelines to follow in that situation, so I called Clarence Campbell in Montreal to find out what we should do.

Jack Kent Cooke, who owned the team at the time, stood by while I began explaining the situation to Mr. Campbell. Then he took the phone from me and started talking. "Now Clarence," he said, "you know we have a small problem here with the ice, but you have a fine young man here who I'm sure can handle the situation so that we will be able to go on with this hockey game."

Then he handed the phone back to me.

"There's no way we're stopping the game because of the ice conditions," Mr. Campbell told me, "so do what you need to do."

There I was, standing in this little room completely taken aback, first by the manner in which Cooke talked to the league president — I'd never heard him called by his first name or spoken to in such a patronizing tone — and second by the way Mr. Campbell seemed to jump to Cooke's wishes. The two bigwigs having decided on the course of action, I felt like whatever objections I had wouldn't matter anyway.

The Minnesota team ranted and raved about the decision to continue, and Blair kept saying he wanted to play the game under protest, which of course is not allowed in the NHL. The Los Angeles players weren't too excited about continuing either, but we were able to patch the ice up and finish the game.

CHICAGO STADIUM is a great place to watch a game, and the fans there are probably the loudest in the league. The first time I went there was in 1962, while I was refereeing in the IHL. I stopped in Chicago on my way to Minnesota, paid my two bucks and sat way up at the top. That was back when the Stadium used to squeeze in about 23,000 fans, before fire regulations cut it back to its present capacity of just over 17,000. I was in awe of the building and the boisterous fans. They were drinking, eating and playing cards long before the game started. It was quite a sight for a young man from a small town in Canada.

One of the most impressive things about Chicago Stadium is the gigantic pipe organ, said to be as loud as twenty-five brass bands. Whenever the officials came out onto the ice the organist would play "Three Blind Mice." The fans got a kick out of it. When the league clamped down on that type of thing, the organist played only the first three notes and then went on to something else. Often I'd look up and give the organist a wave.

As enthusiastic as the fans are in Chicago, a few times they went too far, or almost too far. One night I saw a fight going on in the upper deck. One guy had pinned the other right over the railing, and his victim could easily have fallen. That same game, the fans bombarded the ice with cherry bombs.

The officials' dressing room at Chicago is at one end of the rink behind the goal nets, close to the Blackhawk dressing room. That arrangement was less than ideal, and got very intimidating at times. Often after a tough period, we'd wait for the players to clear the ice and then head in and down the stairs, only to find a welcoming committee. If the coaches or players were upset over a particular call, they had themselves a captive audience. There was nowhere else for us to go, and little we could do about it. Billy Reay, when he was the Chicago coach, was especially notorious for that type of thing. Often he was accompanied by two or three players who wanted to bitch alongside him. Bill White got so upset once I thought he was going to kick our dressing room door down.

As many problems as I had in Boston with Harry Sinden

and the Boston press, things weren't all bad. Going back there during the 1987-88 playoffs while working with the Buffalo Sabre broadcasting crew, brought back a flood of memories. I ran into many old friends I hadn't seen for a few years. I reminisced with the fellows at the coffee stand where I used to go before each game and saw longtime friend Marge Prodanas. She has been a Bruin fan for thirty-three years and calls the officials "her boys." She would often bring us gifts, such as oranges and muffins, and is a very special lady in the eyes of the officials. She even attended Ray Scapinello's wedding in Guelph, Ontario.

Walking through the Garden, it was interesting to see the fans' reactions to seeing me there. Some people asked for my autograph and others told me how much they admired the job I used to do. One fan said, "Why did you ever retire? You and Andy van Hellemond were the best in the business. We need you."

I heard another fan say something that was probably more indicative of the way I was regarded by the Boston fans. "There goes Bruce Hood," he said. "He's as popular in Boston as Bucky Dent."

No arena compares with the Montreal Forum for class or tradition. It was always an honor to work there, and I never had any problem getting up for the games. Maple Leaf Gardens was similar in that respect, and holds many fond memories for me. I refereed my first NHL game there, and my thousandth.

At the same time, Toronto often was a tough place for me. I love the Gardens, and the city, but there is so much publicity wrapped around the Maple Leafs that nothing about them goes unnoticed. Because the Leafs had such poor teams almost every season I worked in the league (since then, they've gotten worse) and because there were so many Leaf fans around my hometown, I always got blamed and kept getting asked the same question: "How come you hate the Leafs so much?" Life would have been a lot easier for me and my family if they'd been a better team!

The truth, as far as the Leafs and I were concerned, is they always used a clutch-and-grab system of play that made refereeing their games even tougher. I always disliked that style, because it takes away from the game and doesn't allow the good players to stand out. Consequently I called a lot of infractions on them.

THERE WERE SOME cities we officials were never thrilled to go to. Nothing personal against the fans in Winnipeg, but when it was added to the NHL, it meant another cold, cold city. We were hoping for San Diego or Phoenix. We used to have a saying: "I spent a month in Winnipeg last night."

The Battle of Alberta was won by Edmonton in the 1987-88 play-offs — on the ice — but off the ice there are few cities anywhere that compare with Calgary for the warmth and friendliness of its people. They proved it to me when I was there for the Special Olympics in 1987, and they proved it to the world with the 1988 Winter Olympics.

Up the road in Edmonton they've perhaps got a little spoiled by having the Great One perform there along with his talented teammates. On a lot of nights, the fans just sit there, as if taking it all for granted.

The Auditorium in Buffalo is one of the oldest buildings in the league, and has many years' worth of great hockey memories dating from the Buffalo Bisons AHL team. There was a lot of excitement in Buffalo when that city was admitted to the NHL. They raised the roof — literally. The Auditorium needed to be expanded to provide enough seating for NHL standards, and that was the only way they could do it. It took weeks and weeks to get all the jacks in place and then up it went, all in one day.

Those early days of Sabre hockey with the French Connection — Gil Perreault, René Robert, Richard Martin — along with Jim Schoenfeld on the blue line and Roger Crozier in the nets, provided a lot of exciting games for Sabre fans. So did the skater who came out at the start of those early games with her famous sword skate dance, which she always finished off by letting go of the sword and sliding it from center ice into the net.

The Sabres bottomed out for a few years but are on their way back to being the exciting club they were for many years under the late Punch Imlach.

I always enjoyed visiting Vancouver, though I didn't always enjoy refereeing there. The Canucks usually had a rough time of it on the ice. Consequently the fans were miserable, and the atmosphere not very positive.

The city, with all its greenery and mountains, made up for it. It was a favorite of mine even before my refereeing days, and stayed that way when my career was starting, refereeing the old Canucks of the Western Hockey League, right through to the end of my career. I was there more recently to referee an old-timers game along with Lloyd Gilmour and Malcolm Ashford, both of whom are from B.C., and this time I was able to go to Whistler and ski — something I was never able to do during my refereeing career.

One of the things I miss about officiating is being able to see and explore different cities. Businessmen are usually in and out of a city in a flash, and vacationers see the sights and are gone. But officials go back again and again and have some spare time while they're there. I was able to build a relationship with each city — its streets, its people, its arenas — and for that, I feel very lucky.

WEIRD, WONDERFUL
AND WACKY GAMES

Finally I said to Mr. Campbell, "I've got a job to do here and I have to go." With that I hung up the phone.

Sunday, April 17, 1977
Philadelphia at Toronto

In the play-offs in 1977 the Leafs had gone into Philadelphia and won the first two games of the quarterfinal series. They lost the third one at home in overtime and were leading the fourth in the third period, 5-2. The Flyers came back to tie the game and then Reggie Leach scored for the Flyers at 19:10 of the first overtime. Philadelphia won the next two games to take the series.

The fourth game of the series was a wild affair. I had to eject Moose Dupont in the second period for beating up on Mike Pelyk. In the third there was more trouble. Gary Dornhoefer, who was famous for standing in front of the other team's goalie and creating havoc, knocked Toronto goalie Mike Palmateer down, so I gave him a minor penalty. With all the antics that followed, I ended up throwing him out of the game, along with Ross Lonsberry, who wouldn't shut up.

It's unusual for three players from one team to be thrown out of the game, as opposed to none for the other team, and the Flyers weren't happy about it. "Hockey Night in Canada" had a camera behind the Flyer bench with an open mike so when Bobby Clarke yelled out "Hood, you fucking queer!" the whole country was listening in.

Ten years later people still tell me about the time they heard him shout that on national television.

Sunday, September 21, 1975
Montreal at Philadelphia (Exhibition)

The two teams had played the night before in Montreal. Apparently Scotty Bowman was upset that the Flyers had pushed his team around so much. He wanted the Canadiens to play it tougher and it wasn't long after the opening face-off that he got his wish and the fights began. In the first period I called nineteen penalties. Over the whole game I handed out a total of 334 penalty minutes.

At 18:15 of the third period Bobby Clarke and Doug Risebrough got into a fight, which touched off a bench-clearing brawl that just kept going on and on. Fights were taking place on both sides of the rink, and since nobody seemed to care about the game anymore, I called it and sent both teams to their dressing rooms. To my knowledge it's the only time an NHL game was ever halted before its completion.

People asked me afterward if I would have stopped the game had it taken place during the regular season. My answer was that I didn't think the players would have gone crazy like that if it was going to mean two points in the standings and likely suspensions.

Saturday, January 22, 1983
Chicago at Toronto

Chicago was leading by a score of 3-2 with fifty-six seconds left in the game. Jim Korn of Toronto was in front of the Chicago net creating a screen and caused a disturbance when he pushed Keith Brown, the Chicago defenseman, back into the crease. That blocked the goaltender, Murray Bannerman, who couldn't move across the goalmouth to stop a shot from Dan Daoust. The puck went in the net. I immediately ruled no goal and called a penalty on Korn.

That call was not at all popular in Toronto and made headlines in all the newspapers. Everybody had something to say about it. The only person who was quoted as agreeing with me was the Chicago coach, Orval Tessier, and even that was twisted.

"That was the only right call he made all night" is what Tessier said.

I took a lot of heat after that game. A few weeks later, coincidentally or not, I received a letter from Scotty Morrison telling me I was not going to be rehired the following year. That decision was later rescinded. It bothered me that all this fuss had taken place that probably wouldn't have, had it happened in any other city. A linesman in the game said after that it was, "the right call, against the wrong team, in the wrong city."

I've never once doubted that the call I made in that game was the right one.

Sunday, February 14, 1971
Pittsburgh at Minnesota

Jude Drouin had been acting up the whole night — a real pain in the neck — and had something to say every time I made a call. I had already warned him once and had no intention of putting up with more. We had a saying that carried over from the days when misconducts cost twenty-five dollars, that a player who is bothersome throughout a game uses up portions of it. Drouin had already spent $24.95.

Later in the game Pittsburgh scored on a power play. I was getting ready to drop the puck at center ice when he skated up to me and made some remark about how I and other officials were all the same. I asked him to repeat it, which he did. The remark in itself wasn't serious, but he had just spent his last nickel, and I gave him a misconduct.

Drouin went crazy! He came charging at me with his fists clenched like he was going to hit me. His teammates intervened so I don't know if he would have or not. He had spent the whole amount for a game misconduct and Drouin was gone. I went over to the penalty timekeeper to report it.

Then Drouin came charging at me again, this time with his stick. The linesman stepped in his way, but he still managed to get in a pretty good blow that hit me on the shoulder. The other linesman also tried to restrain him, and finally his teammates dragged him away and off the ice.

At the hearing Drouin agreed with the facts as I had reported them but said he hadn't been trying to hit me with the stick, just the glass close to me, and that the stick had slid down and struck me on the shoulder.

He ended up with a fine and a three-game suspension, which was pretty hefty in those days.

Sunday, January 21, 1966
Chicago at Boston

This was the night I was unofficially selected the first star of the game by the writers.

Ted Green and Doug Mohns had met along the boards. After a little jousting with their sticks Mohns took a poke at Green with his stick. Green then brought his stick up and chopped down right on top of Mohns's head. Fortunately for Mohns, he was one of the few players at the time who wore a helmet. The two then started swinging at each other. The two linesmen, Ed Butler and Claude Bechard, tried to break them up and both got hit by sticks.

At the time there hadn't been a match penalty in the league for years, but I went right to the penalty box and called one on both of them. Though my resolve was firm, my knees were shaking as I made the call.

The writers praised the call, and even made me the first star of the game. In Boston, yet!

Sunday, October 13, 1968
Los Angeles at Oakland

Carol Vadnais of Oakland and Dale Rolfe of L.A. got involved in an altercation in the third period and after it had broken up, Rolfe gave Vadnais a hard slash. I assessed an additional major to Rolfe and that was the end of it . . . or so I thought.

I was coming off the ice after the game when suddenly my path was blocked by a man who deliberately bumped into me. I stepped back, surprised, and said, "Who are you?"

"You know fucking well who I am," he screamed. I didn't know then, but it was Larry Regan, the Kings' general manager.

He drew back his fist and punched me right in the mouth, cutting my lower lip. Then he grabbed my shirt and tried to hit me again. The linesmen and a policeman finally broke it up, but it wasn't easy — we got into a quite a tussle. When he grabbed my shirt, he got his hand wrapped up in it and couldn't let go. We ended up with my arm around his neck and the linesmen draped between us trying to pull us apart.

That incident really shook me. It was one thing to be verbally abused, but I had never actually been punched before. Even worse was the aftermath.

The league was in no hurry to investigate. Two weeks later I was in Toronto to referee a game on a Saturday night. As I was preparing for the game I received a call from Clarence Campbell. This was about half an hour before game time and I had to leave the dressing room and go across the hall to the telephone.

He was sitting with Jack Kent Cooke in Los Angeles getting Regan's side of the story, and was going over my report of the game. He began to question me, and by his manner I could tell he was intent on challenging my accuracy and finding a loophole in my report.

I was bothered with both the line of questioning and the timing. It didn't seem to matter to him that I was getting ready to go on the ice. There was no doubt in my mind as to what had happened, and that it had been deliberate. The man had come up to me and punched me in the mouth. Both linesmen had filed their reports to the league saying the same thing.

Finally I said to Mr. Campbell, "I've got a job to do here and I have to go." With that I hung up the phone.

Regan was fined $1,000 by the league and suspended for three weeks. During that time the Kings sent him on a scouting trip to Europe. When he got back Regan said it was the best vacation he ever had. He also said that ticket sales hadn't been very good and that something had been needed to stir fan interest. I suppose he thought himself some kind of hero.

In my mind, the way the whole thing was handled was ridiculous. It was not a serious matter to Regan, and Mr. Campbell didn't seem overly concerned, either. But it was no joke to me.

That incident is what sparked my personal desire to form the Officials Association the following summer. If the league wasn't going to protect its officials, then we would do it ourselves.

Regan went on to head up the Canadian Oldtimers' Hockey Association and has done a fine job with that. He was also responsible for the series known as "Relive the Dream," which reunited the participants of the first Canada-Russia series.

Thursday, March 7, 1968
Boston and Philadelphia at Toronto

This was considered a home game for the Flyers — they'd been forced out of the Spectrum after its roof had blown off. The game included the most vicious stick-swinging battle I have ever seen. Eddie Shack of the Bruins and Larry Zeidel of the Flyers were the culprits. They went at it, hitting each other in the head. Blood was pouring out of both of them.

This incident was the climax of a feud between the two. Shack's comment after was that he had to keep his stick up when around players like Zeidel. He added that he was there to score goals, not fight the village idiot.

I issued match penalties to both players. Later Shack was suspended for three games, and Zeidel for four.

Wednesday, March 28, 1973
Philadelphia at Buffalo

Larry Hillman of Buffalo and Dave Schultz of Philadelphia got their sticks up with just a little over a minute gone in the first period. While those two were being ushered to the penalty box, Tracy Pratt came over and had words with Dave Schultz. Then the two of them started to fight. Jim Lorentz of Buffalo jumped in as the third man, and as if that wasn't enough, the Flyers' Don Saleski grabbed Gerry Meehan and those two went at it.

I had to throw all of them out of the game, but Schultz and Saleski refused to go. The complete disregard for the officiating I saw in that game was typical of the goon-era Flyers. So was what happened in the game's last minute: Buffalo's Don Luce had a breakaway on an empty net. The Flyers' Barry Ashbee threw his stick to break it up and a goal stick came flying out on the ice from the Philadelphia bench.

That game was not televised in Buffalo, but it was back to Philadelphia, and since I was going there that same week, the league asked me to pick up the tape of the game so they could review it, for possible further discipline.

I took the tape to Montreal. We put it in the video recorder and sat down to watch the incidents that had taken place early in the game. To our surprise, the picture on the tape was blank at the start and came on after the incident was over. We could hear the commentators, but that was all.

Maybe the tape had been altered. Only the Flyers know that for sure.

Sunday, May 10, 1970
St. Louis at Boston

This was my first Stanley Cup final play-off game. It was incredibly hot that afternoon in the Boston Garden.

It was to be the final game of the championship. After regulation time the score was still tied. In the first overtime period, with less than a minute gone, Bobby Orr took the puck into the St. Louis zone and passed it to Derek Sanderson in the corner. Sanderson passed it back and Orr put the puck between Glenn Hall's legs. That goal was the source of a well-known photograph that shows Orr flying through the air with his stick raised in victory after a check by Noel Picard.

It had happened so fast, only forty seconds into the overtime, that it came as a shock to me, my first Stanley Cup final game ending so quickly. It was only a few seconds after the puck went in that I realized that was it, the culmination of a long and memorable season.

I waited for the teams to shake hands and leave the ice and then went into our dressing room. Only then did I realize I hadn't gone over to the timekeeper to give him the goal scorer's number. It seemed so inconsequential after what had taken place.

Sunday, February 5, 1967
Toronto at New York Rangers

This was my second game in the NHL and it was not as easy as the first. I was called in on an emergency basis to cover for Vern Buffey, who had been injured. I remember other officials telling me that when the shit hits the fan, it's usually while you're filling in for someone. They were right.

I made a mistake during that game. I wasn't mentally prepared and when the time came for me to react, I choked.

Peter Stemkowski of Toronto took a shot on net that I was sure had gone in and bounced right back out. The goal light didn't go on, but I didn't do anything. Play carried on, and by the time I realized I should have stopped the play and checked with the goal judge and linesmen, it was too late.

Also during the game there was a brawl involving Shack and Bob Baun of the Leafs and Vic Hadfield and Orland Kurtenbach of the Rangers. I gave Baun two five-minute majors, Kurtenbach a major, Hadfield a minor and a major, and I gave Eddie Shack two minors. Imlach and Shack didn't feel Shack deserved anything and said so in the newspapers. Shack's quote was, "Aw, that Hood had to take care of his buddy, Hadfield. He (Hadfield) lets him play free on his golf course in the summer."

After the game Matt Pavelich and I rushed to catch a flight back to Toronto. It turned out the Leafs were on the same plane. Matt was talking to some reporters on the flight and came back to me and said, "Don't read the papers tomorrow. Punch has really been ranting and raving."

We arrived in Toronto and I picked my car up at the airport. On the way home I got a speeding ticket, which made my day complete. The policeman who gave me the ticket knew who I was and had been listening to the game on the radio. Even he commented on how poor a job I had done that night.

The next morning I read the papers, despite the warning, and sure enough, Punch had gone to town. One quote said: "That was the worse refereed game I've seen, and you can quote me. We *not* only get beat in penalties, but we get robbed in goals also." That was the start of many more such quotes from him.

Thursday, December 27, 1979
St. Louis at Detroit

For the first-ever hockey game in the Joe Louis Sports Arena I stood at center ice, dropped the puck and then promptly fell flat on the ice when the puck came into my feet. A roar went up from the crowd, so you could say I was the recipient of the first official cheer ever heard at a hockey game at Joe Louis arena.

11

THE GOON ERA

*"Hoody, we've got to sell this game to the people here in
Tennessee. They've never seen anything like it, so let 'em
go at it, will you?"*

IF YOU DEFINE a goon as a player whose hockey skills are
limited and whose main role on a team is to fight and intimidate
opponents, you could say the goon era started when intimidation
and fighting became a key part of some teams' game plans.

If you're looking for the specific time when that strategy
began, look no further than the 1967-68 season, the time of
the first expansion, when the NHL grew from six to twelve
teams. There's no doubt that the demand for twice as many
players diluted the on-ice product, with players who never
would have made one of the original six teams suddenly
wearing an expansion team sweater.

It follows reason that the quality of playmaking had to suffer when less adept players entered the league. It also follows
that those players would look for ways to stop the better
players. Put together that had to mean a higher incidence of
restraining fouls like hooking, holding and interference. That
of course led to frustration on everyone's part, which in turn
led to more slashing and stickwork and finally to brawling.
As the saying goes, if you can't beat them on the ice, beat
them in the alley.

Intimidation had played a major role in the league before
expansion, but in a different sense. When the Canadiens, Red

Wings and Maple Leafs were winning Stanley Cups in the years before expansion, the talent possessed by those teams was the intimidating factor. It's only in the past twenty years that on-ice intimidation has come to mean the use of brute force as well as — or rather than — skill.

I think the league thought it necessary to allow that type of hockey in order to bring fans into the arenas of the many new expansion cities.

That attitude was typified by something the late Eddie Bush told me on the night of the first home game for Memphis after it joined the Central Hockey League. At the end of the first period, he came down to me and said, "Hoody, we've got to sell this game to the people here in Tennessee. They've never seen anything like it, so let 'em go at it, will you?"

He was right about their not having seen ice hockey before. After the game many of the fans came down to ice level to touch the ice and look at the sharp blades on the players' skates. They couldn't believe it!

I think the league got caught up in the type of thinking ex-emplified by Bush and didn't hold the reins as tight as they should have. The fact that we officials began barking at the NHL's heels after the summer of 1969 (the year the officials' association was formed) is one indicator that we disagreed from the start with what was taking place. But we weren't running the league. As loud as we protested, it all fell on deaf ears, and goon hockey was allowed to develop.

The Boston Bruins, or the Big Bad Bruins as they were called, set the early standard for goon hockey in the late sixties and early seventies. But, interestingly, the Bruins didn't have any goons as such. They had Ted Green, John McKenzie and Wayne Cashman in the lineup, but they also had Bobby Orr, Phil Esposito and Gerry Cheevers. All of those players could play the game, which gave the Bruins the right combination of toughness and skill — the best form of intimidation a team can have.

When the World Hockey Association came along in 1972, twelve more professional teams needed players. At the same time, the NHL added the Islanders and the Atlanta Flames as expansion franchises, bringing the number of NHL teams to eighteen. This only diluted the product more.

The NHL was heavily involved with starting franchises, shifting franchises, fighting lawsuits and trying to prevent many of the top stars from defecting to the new league. (Bobby Hull, Derek Sanderson, Bernie Parent, Ted Green and J.C. Tremblay were some of those who eventually did switch leagues.) It seems the league lost sight of the most important thing of all — the game.

But these developments mirrored larger social developments. There was a rebellion against authority and responsibility by the young people of the time and it seemed to carry over to hockey, with rules there to be challenged rather than followed. "The Love Generation" wanted to do their "own thing," which basically meant the opposite of what society so long had dictated was proper. Hockey players lost respect for officials and proper moral standards.

Philadelphia's Broad Street Bullies came out of the changed professional hockey picture and the game hasn't been the same since. Coach Fred Shero's system was to create as much havoc as possible. He knew his team would be penalized for many but not all infractions. They had good goaltending and good penalty killing so they did almost anything they wanted. And they used their intimidating tactics before and especially after the whistle.

They'd glove an opponent in the face after play had been halted, or lean against an opponent after the whistle, or use their sticks on the back of an opposing player's legs. And on top of all that, they'd mouth off constantly. These were just some of the tactics they perfected. The result? Opposing players were looking over their shoulders for the Flyers rather than for the puck.

Dave Schultz was the notorious leader of the Broad Street Bullies, ably assisted by Don Saleski, Moose Dupont, Ed Van Impe, Gary Dornhoefer, Tom Bladon and Mad Dog Kelly. Once one Flyer got involved in an altercation, the others weren't far behind to lend a hand.

But the fault ultimately lies not with the Bruins or the Flyers or expansion, or with the formation of the WHA but with the league. They allowed it to happen. I'm not sure you can point to any one person as the guilty party. Certainly the enforcers weren't to blame. They were only doing their job and trying to make a living.

Whatever the cause, the result has been a damaged sport. Perhaps the most unsettling thing of all is that every team now carries at least one designated fighter. Check one of the better players a little too hard and you know on the next shift the enforcer is going to come out to settle the score. So of course the other team brings its designated tough guy out, and away they go.

It has gotten so ridiculous that many fights now start before the puck is dropped, while the players are setting up for the face-off. Everybody knows why the goons are out there, so why waste time playing hockey?

Where does it end? The truth is most teams would rather not carry goons. But they have to, if only because the other teams do, and every coach and and general manager knows it. Many GMs, coaches and players have been quoted in past years in support of banning fighting from the game. What is it going to take to get everybody on-side?

THE OFFICIALS
SPEAK UP

"I hope those fellas have other jobs to go to."

IN THE MID-SIXTIES Scotty Morrison, the NHL's referee-in-chief, worked directly under the supervision of Clarence Campbell, who was then president of the league. Mr. Campbell was directly involved in all major decisions concerning refereeing. Because of that, I don't believe that Scotty was ever as strong in that capacity as he could have been. The referee-in-chief has to stand up and be counted. When the coaches, owners or general managers spouted off about the officiating, Scotty should have had the clout to put a stop to it, or at least explain the referee's side and stick up for his officials when necessary.

Unfortunately, while Mr. Campbell still reigned, general managers and coaches seemed to be able to say anything they wanted about the officiating and get away with it. Seldom was anything done or said on behalf of the officials. This put the officials in a compromising position. Though we were expected to maintain a high level of respect on the ice, doing that was all but impossible when it was open season on officials in the press.

Whether or not it was Mr. Campbell's desire not to ruffle the feathers of team owners and management, it was clear that bitching about the officiating went on far too much and that the officials themselves had to bear the brunt of it. Mr. Campbell once commented that he worked for the owners and had to abide by their wishes. That may be okay in the business world, where a board of directors perhaps will tell their chief executive officer what policies to abide by. But the NHL operated in a far more emotional climate and the owners' decisions were often based on personal gain and so were not necessarily rational. A strong leader was needed to balance things. Mr. Campbell was just that in most areas, but not in his dealings with the officials.

Other problems for officials added up and made it difficult for us to do our jobs properly. Things just got worse. Finally we had to do something about it on our own.

I had heard that Joe Kane, a lawyer who at the time was also the president of the Central League, was sympathetic to our cause and supportive of the officials' movement to establish representation. I met him for lunch in Kansas City near the end of the 1968-69 season, when there for a game. We talked extensively about the problems, especially the abuse. Joe knew of my run-in with Larry Regan, the Los Angeles Kings' general manager, in the fall of 1968. And we talked about how how the teams used the media far too much to get back at officials, with little or no retaliation from their targets.

After the season ended I talked to Joe several more times and then arranged a meeting with him at my house for July 2, 1969. Bob Sloan and Ron Wicks also attended.

That night marked the unofficial start of the National Hockey League Referees and Linesmen Association. We summarized all of the complaints that we knew about, laid some groundwork for the future and drew up lists of staff names for Sloan, Wicks and myself to contact concerning a meeting, which we scheduled at the Cambridge Hotel in Toronto for July 14, 1969.

I spent that summer building a porch on the back of my house and helping coordinate the building of the Association. Hardly a day went by that I wasn't on the phone with Joe or an official, as we worked on putting the pieces together. I used to put the phone out through the window of my den to save having to go in the house. I must have climbed up and down my stepladder a hundred times to talk on the phone.

At that first meeting the officials agreed to proceed with the Association and retain Joe Kane as our representative. Bill Friday was elected president and Vern Buffey, vice president. I was selected as the secretary-treasurer. Other members were Lloyd Gilmour, Ron Wicks, Bob Sloan, Wally Harris, John D'Amico, Tom Smith, Dave Newell, Brent Casselman, Bryan Lewis, John McCauley, Ron Ego, Pat Shetler, Will Norris, George Ashley, Ed Butler, Bob Myers and Malcolm Ashford. All the officials except for John Ashley, Art Skov, Matt Pavelich, Claude Bechard and Neil Armstrong agreed to be in the Association.

We made up a list of items to discuss with the league. But we felt recognition of our Association had to be the first concern.

It wasn't that easy. Several phone calls to the league office in Montreal, and to Scotty Morrison, yielded no results. Scotty took the month of July off in those days to go to his cottage in Haliburton where there was no phone. We had to call the store at the marina nearby so they could give him the message when he came in. He was pretty surprised when he got the message to call Joe, and wasn't too pleased about what was taking place.

On Thursday, August 22, the Board of Governors of the NHL informed the Association that it would neither recognize nor meet with us. Clarence Campbell relayed the reasons in a press release:

1. The governors erred in recognizing the NHL Players' Association because it had caused the NHL expense, inconvenience and embarrassment.
2. The Governors were satisfied that the officials have no grievances.
3. If any grievances did exist, they could be resolved without an Association.

According to his response, problems with the NHL concerning salaries, pensions, medical plans, training camp, equipment and lack of support for the officials were figments of our imagination. Besides that, our right by law to bargain together for common interests was being ignored.

If the NHL governors thought that we would be satisfied by their decision, they were dead wrong.

Joe Kane made a last-ditch effort to avoid the matter going public by telephoning each of the governors. As a result, Bill Jennings, the chairman of the Board of Governors, asked Joe on September 1, 1969, to withhold the Association's demand for recognition pending the decision of the National Labor Relations Board in Washington on the application of the baseball umpires to form an association. He said that the NHL supported the American and National baseball leagues in the hearings and that the NHL would embarrass those leagues if it granted recognition to our Association now.

He also said that the league was agreeable to giving each member of the Association a noncontributory pension and medical plan similar to the one the players had and would remove the holdback percentage on our salaries.

The latter offer addressed another one of our main grievances. At the time, every official was required to sign a uniform contract with the NHL guaranteeing only seventy-five percent of his previous year's income. The remaining twenty-five percent was withheld pending satisfactory performance of duties. The official had no way of knowing if he had received an increase or a decrease in salary. Suffice it to say, this type of contract was no longer acceptable to us.

Part of the reason there was no set salary was that officials under NHL contracts were paid according to the number of games they worked, and where they worked those games. They were paid less for minor-league games, of course, and had no say where or how often they would work. Furthermore, if at any time the NHL decided it no longer wanted an official, whatever the reason, he was gone and that was that.

The agreement between Kane and Jennings was acceptable, pending ratification by our Association, but with the understanding that as soon as the decision in Washington was made, the Association would demand recognition. Jennings suggested that in the meantime the officials should meet with Scotty Morrison to outline their grievances.

On September 8 the NHL announced to the officials in the Association that it would not proceed with the agreement made between Jennings and Kane. They offered no explanation.

In a story by George Gross in the Toronto *Telegram*, Clarence Campbell was quoted as saying he might resign because of it. He also stated, "I hope those fellas have other jobs to go to."

Scotty Morrison indicated he also was close to resigning, and was quoted in the article as saying, "You would like to do something, but then you realize you have seven kids and a wife to look after."

In the same article Kane said that he intended to have the matter brought before the House of Commons in Ottawa. "It's no longer just a sports-page story. Everybody should know there's an employer in Canada who thinks he's beyond the law."

We went to training camp while all this was going on, but decided at a meeting that we would leave camp until such time as the Association was recognized. That decision was given to Scotty at approximately midnight on Sunday. The NHL had until six p.m. Monday to act on it. On Monday afternoon the Association was informed that the NHL governors had decided not to recognize the Association. At six that evening we walked out.

That night we all met at Bill Friday's house in Hamilton just down the road from the training camp in Brantford. I think we were all in shock that we had actually left camp. Five of the officials had declined to be part of the walkout. There were others who hesitated — especially after being taunted by Frank Udvari about losing their jobs — but they believed in the Association and came anyway. Joe Kane was there to tell us what to do, and it was his guidance that kept us together.

The next day we set up our own training camp at Lambton Arena in Toronto and arranged a press conference so we could tell the public what was going on. The officials from out of town boarded with the members who lived in the area, and we went about getting ourselves ready for the season of hockey we hoped was still ahead of us.

The strike lasted six days. We agreed to abandon our demand for immediate recognition. In return the NHL addressed seven of our eight grievances. The most important of those was the salary holdback issue, but we were also offered improved salaries, pensions, medical coverage and life insurance, and increased exhibition and play-off game fees. We would have gained little or none of that without the Association.

There's also little doubt we wouldn't have been able to accomplish as much as we did without the help of Joe Kane. He was never recognized by the NHL, who wanted no part of an outside agent. But he seemed to have the right answers, the enthusiasm and the ability to talk to the right people. Interestingly, he had been touted as a possible successor to Clarence Campbell and he might have been the logical choice. He was a lawyer and a sportsman. He also was dedicated and experienced and had a good head on his shoulders. Joe is now a judge in Toronto.

As the 1969-70 season progressed, word got around that the Association would probably be recognized, even though we had gone back to work and had settled some differences. The sentiment was that recognition would come more easily if we didn't have Joe Kane involved with us. The reasoning was that the league was already unhappy having to deal with the Players' Association through another lawyer, Al Eagleson. So it was decided we would dismiss his services and go it alone.

If the comments still being heard in the press are any indication the Association is still a long way from meeting its main objective, which is to put a gag on the people who have a tendency to mouth off. I'm sure that if Joe had stayed on, that would have come about a lot faster — he had a knack for getting to the right people and getting the important things done. It was probably my mistake, because I was instrumental in getting Joe dismissed. I was working to get the results that we needed and at the same time trying to stay in the good books of management so that three or four of the officials and three or four from the league and could sit down together and hammer out agreements.

It's interesting that the people we were dealing with — in the initial stages they were Brian O'Neill, Scotty Morrison and Frank Udvari — agreed with us about the major problem, which is abuse of officials, and agreed that it shouldn't take place, but they weren't able to do anything about it, either. I was looking for something that was beyond anyone's power to accomplish. I guess you can't sit on both sides of the table at once. We needed to take a firm stand and Joe Kane would have been the man to lead us. Once we lost

A favorite picture of mine — the NHL officiating staff in 1979, taken outside Milton Memorial Arena, site of our training camp while on strike, or lockout as the League called it. FRONT: Ray Scapinello, Ron Wicks, Will Norris, Randy Mitton, Matt Pavelich, John McCauley, Gerard Gauthier, Ron Finn, Claude Bechard, John D'Amico, Ryan Bozak. BACK: me, Bob Hodges, Bryan Lewis, Don Koharski, Kevin Collins, Andy van Hellemond, Leon Stickle, Gord Groseker, Jim Christison, Bob Kileger, Swede Knox, Bob Luther, Wally Harris, Greg Madill, Dave Newell, Bob Myers.

Up and coming NHLers? This group attended our 1986-87 referee school at the University of Guelph. Held in August each year, more than 2,000 students have attended over the years. Staff in front are Neal Dagle, audio-video expert; Kevin Hook, sports/pro shop; Father Jim Armstrong, assistant camp director; Mark Pare; me; Don Koharski; John D'Amico; Dan McCourt — all were NHL staff members and school instructors. The two lovely ladies are Marilyn, my daughter and our camp administrator, and Linda Stewart, aerobics instructor.

Bruce and the boys get together for a little tennis! Ron Ellis, Frank Mahovlich, Ralph Mellanby, TV producer, Simon McGrail, IIHF doctor, me, Fred Walker, CBC Radio, Don Goodwin, CBC TV. (Pam Gollish)

Game number 1,000 — the first referee ever to do it. Scotty Morrison was on hand at Maple Leaf Gardens to make a presentation to Joanne and me.

Right on! (Pam Gollish)

Joanne and I enjoy the good life on a cruise after my retirement.

Back home in my travel office. Jamaica again? Sounds like a good idea.

Our children Randy, Marilyn and Kevin in 1980, along with Cleo (quite a dog). They gave us this photo, framed, for our twenty-fifth wedding anniversary.

It was the league's option whether or not they wanted to rehire him, and if they did, it was to be for one year at a time.

In the final year of the three-year contract, when I was forty-six, I received a registered letter from the league on Valentine's day telling me that my services would no longer be required after the end of the 1982-83 season. I called it the "Valentine's day massacre." To say I was shocked would be an understatement.

Scotty had not said a word about it so I had no indication whatsoever that it was going to happen. The letter said the decision was extremely difficult and too personal and important to deal with in a letter — even though that's what I was holding in my hand.

It appeared that Scotty was using the clause in the agreement as a way to get rid of me without having to take the responsibility for the decision. In the letter, he enclosed a copy of the section of the contract that dealt with the age part, almost as if to say, "Look, there it is, it's not my decision." I was in good condition, was at the top of my game and was having one of my best seasons, so it was difficult for me to think otherwise.

It was very difficult emotionally to hear that I was no longer considered capable of doing a job I had been at for more than twenty years. However, I couldn't let it affect me when I went out on the ice. We were heading into the toughest part of the schedule and I still had a job to do — at least for a little while longer.

As it turned out I had longer than I thought. I was told the following summer that because of my good year, they wanted me back for another one. I worked the season and things went well, although injuries finally took their toll. I retired at the end of the 1983-84 season. As I was in Scotty's office getting my settlement with the league in place, he mentioned that it was too bad there wasn't a supervisor's position open. I wasn't interested in one at the time anyway, and besides, I'm sure Scotty wouldn't have felt comfortable with me in that job.

The three-year agreement in 1979 extended to the end of the 1982-83 season. Subsequent three-year agreements have carried the Association through to the end of the 1987-88 season.

Before the start of the 1988-89 season a new agreement will be necessary. Meetings have been under way and the officials are expressing the same concerns that have existed since day one in 1969: the elimination of further abuse of officials, increased salaries, job security and better job conditions.

One thing the Association has now that it didn't at the start is solidarity. New officials coming on staff are now automatically a part of the Association. They have seen the benefits and are 100 percent behind it. This will help the Association remain strong, which will mean a better chance to accomplish its goals.

I was impressed with the fact that in the summer of 1987 the Association went to the league to complain that the game wasn't being officiated in the manner it should be and that there was far too much being let go. The play-offs that year had turned into a ridiculous affair, with far too much clutching and grabbing, interference and other nonsense happening after the whistle. It was great to see them stand up and be counted that way. I'm sure the fact that they came front and center helped to make a better product in the 1987-88 season, and laid a solid foundation for the future.

I hope the Association continues its efforts, because it is working in the best interests of the game, to ensure that hockey becomes as good a sport as it can be.

DEALING WITH MANAGEMENT

"That's the trouble with you Hood. You're finding fault with so many things all the time. Why don't you just do your job?"

W HEN I FIRST BECAME part of the NHL officiating staff I was on cloud nine. I was happy to be there and wanted to do the best job I could to please my bosses.

After my first few years, working in the minor leagues, I felt good about the way things had gone. If I hadn't been rehired after any of those seasons, I probably would have gone into the business world, disappointed but happy for the memory of having been there at all.

With expansion there was a need for more officials at the NHL level. I had developed pretty well and it was looking more and more like officiating was going to be a career for me — for a few years, anyway.

While officiating in the minors I often wondered about all the abuse from players, managers and sportswriters that was heaped on the likes of NHL referees Red Storey, Eddie Powers and Frank Udvari. But I didn't worry too much about it because it seemed a long way away from me.

As I grew in experience and knowledge I formed opinions about where changes could and should be made for better working conditions for officials.

I suppose I could have just sat back, collected my paychecks and enjoyed life, but problems that were not being dealt with properly by management nagged at me. By hurting our ability to officiate well, they also hurt the game. If these conditions didn't need to exist, then why should they?

Because of this Bruce Hood was often looked upon by management as a complainer or troublemaker or, in less polite words, a shit disturber. Clarence Campbell once told Scotty Morrison, the referee-in-chief, "You'd better straighten that young man out."

Carl Voss, my first referee-in-chief, I considered a class act in every respect. When he retired, Scotty Morrison took over and would be the referee-in-chief over the remainder of my career, and longer. He has since been named the NHL's Vice President for Project Development and is currently involved in relocating the Hockey Hall of Fame from the Canadian National Exhibition grounds to downtown Toronto.

Scotty is a devoted family man and is a lot of fun to be around. He likes to tell jokes and seems just generally to enjoy life. It would be difficult for anyone not to like him. It was unfortunate that as the years progressed our working relationship started to deteriorate. My involvement in the Officials Association, along with my ongoing concern over the lack of support for the officials, made it look like I was always finding fault.

I owe a lot to Scotty. A lot of other officials came and went during my span in the league. Some of them retired on their own, but many others were tried and tested and didn't make it. Scotty was the one who gave me the chance to progress up the ladder in the NHL, and he stuck with me.

The amount of abuse a referee has to endure can be incredible, and maybe I wasn't thick-skinned enough to let it slide by. As much as I enjoyed officiating, there were times when it could be extremely difficult. Some support from the league would have gone a long way in helping me through those times, but I didn't often get it.

It's common for players to lose their confidence. A coach or general manager will do what he can to help a player because he knows that player will be of more use to the team with his confidence intact. Officials can lose their confidence, too. If somebody from the brass had given me some support during the rough times, my frame of mind would have been better and I would have been better able to handle the problems. It wouldn't have even taken that much, just something like, "Bruce, we know it's tough right now and things aren't going well, but just hang in there and things will get better. You've proven you can do the job, so just go out there and do it the way you can and remember that we're with you all the way."

Instead, every time you picked up a newspaper you'd read how a coach, a player or a general manager was questioning the competence and integrity of a referee or linesman. Blaming a loss on the officials was done with alarming regularity. Punch Imlach used to do it all the time in Toronto, right under the noses of the officiating brass, but nothing was done to support the officials.

Without any kind of backup or support, it's easy to begin doubting yourself. I went through one period where I had gotten a lot of flak over some games and was really down on myself, to the point where I thought my career was over. I talked to Scotty about it and he said to me, "How am I going to explain to the general managers that you've lost your confidence?"

I worked out my problems by myself that time, knowing I wasn't going to get any help from management.

Another time I had a grueling three-week road trip out west, for games in the Western Hockey League as well as the NHL. In one stretch I had to work five straight Portland Buckaroos road games and then go back into their home arena for a sixth.

Before the end of that stretch I'd had it up to my eyeballs with hockey and confrontations and couldn't take any more. I finally called Scotty on a Friday from Seattle, barely even able to talk, and told him that because of the shape I was in, I couldn't referee any more.

My schedule involved Western League games in Seattle on Friday and Portland on Sunday, followed by a flight to St. Louis for an NHL game. Scotty suggested that I work the Friday game because he didn't have time to get anyone else, but head home after that. I did the game, but I wasn't myself. I didn't even feel like I was the referee, but just there for the skate and to watch. It was a horrible feeling! I was dying inside. After the game was over I caught a flight home.

Joanne picked me up at the airport and on the way to Milton I broke down. After seeing her my emotions just took over. When I got home I called Scotty and we talked. He said to take a few days off and meet him on Tuesday for lunch.

At lunch he pointed out that I had a job to do, that I'd done it well in the past and that it would be just a matter of maintaining the same standard in the future.

If he had given me some support earlier, I probably wouldn't have been sitting there talking to him then. I had no desire to be babysat and patted on the head every time I did a good job. But at the same time, there could be so much pressure in the games that a little backup would help you know you weren't out there alone.

He rearranged my schedule and I was back on the job the following Saturday. My first game was in Montreal and it went well — I was up for it and gained confidence as I went along. After the game I went out for a few beers with the two linesmen, Ron Ego and Bob Myers. We talked things over and they were a great help in making me feel better about the whole situation. The next day, refreshed and armed with a better attitude, I took the train to Quebec to do an AHL game. What a difference a week makes! And what a difference there is between having no confidence and feeling good about yourself again!

Scotty had his own problems to worry about at the time. I was talking at the Toronto airport one day to Jack Button, who was the assistant general manager of the Pittsburgh Penguins at the time, and he told me he had heard through the grapevine that people were upset with the job Scotty was doing, and that seven out of the twelve teams wanted him removed from his position.

I called Scotty and told him what I had heard, as a favor to him so he would know what was going on behind his back. He didn't appreciate my good intentions and told me that I should mind my own business, and that the only reason I was telling him these things was that I wanted his job. His reaction shocked me!

One year at training camp everything was disorganized and it was clear that Scotty, perhaps due to expansion and the added responsibility, hadn't prepared properly for the camp.

The officials were upset. Frank Udvari, who had retired as a referee to become a supervisor of officials and work with Scotty, was particularly perturbed. He wanted the league brass to know what was going on but couldn't very well make the complaint himself, because it would look like he was undermining Scotty. So he talked to me about it — at that time we were friends and still on good terms — and suggested that a list of problems submitted to the league office in Montreal that appeared to come from a senior official would help rectify the situation. Since I could understand his position and was also concerned, I agreed. Frank indicated that he had already been in contact with Brian O'Neill over the issue, and that he agreed with the plan.

Scotty was very upset when Mr. Campbell confronted him with the list of complaints "submitted by a senior referee." He never knew Frank had initiated it and made it known he planned to find out who the senior referee was.

I don't know if Scotty ever found out for sure that it was me who was involved, but by narrowing down the field, he probably came up with a pretty good idea. And all I had done was agree with Frank and Brian O'Neill . . .

I also had a confrontation with Scotty over work permits. Each year every official from Canada receives a permit with an H1 classification, which allows him to work in the United States as a specialist. It's fairly routine. All the Canadian hockey players are required to do the same thing, with the teams submitting their player lists each year for approval. In the case of the officials, the league draws up the petition and submits it to the U.S. immigration authorities for approval.

After training camp this particular season one of my assignments was an exhibition game in Buffalo. When I got to the border at Fort Erie, directly across the Niagara River from Buffalo, I answered the official's questions at the booth by telling him I was from Milton, Ontario, and that I was going to referee a game in Buffalo. I said that I wanted to get my visa permit from them and get it stamped and approved for the season ahead.

I parked my car and went inside the immigration office while they looked up the petition. But there was nothing on file and they refused to let me into the country to work the game. I was five minutes away from Memorial Auditorium and there was nothing I could do.

There was no time to get someone else to work the game, and I had to be there, so I got back into my car, and crossed the border at Niagara Falls. When asked why I was entering the United States, I said I was going to see a hockey game, which was true. I was sent right through.

I made it to the game, although it had to be delayed for five minutes because of my late arrival.

The next morning I called Scotty from my home and told him about my problem at the border, including the fact that the petition wasn't there.

His response was immediate. "That's the trouble with you, Hood. You're finding fault with so many things all the time. Why don't you just do your job?"

I couldn't believe it! I was so upset I could hardly speak!

Scotty had got it into his head that I was after his job, and that could very well have been the reason for his reaction. It would be hard for anyone to be objective under those circumstances. He probably felt I was contesting his authority.

It wasn't true. We were all supposed to be part of the same team and my aim was to help him not hinder him, in his job.

Frank Udvari, the supervisor of officials at that time, was one of the most knowledgeable people I've ever met in the world of officiating, a man whose work as a referee I admired greatly. If you were on his good side he would do anything for you, but if you were on his bad side you hardly existed as far as he was concerned. I had a turn on both sides, so I know how much help and how much of a hindrance he could be to an official.

Frank always had to be front and center. When we were riding to the arena in a cab, of course he rode in front and the referee and the two linesmen in the back. If he was cracking jokes, everybody was loose and did the same — the officials were always careful to follow Frank's mood. More often, though, there would be icy silence on the way to and from the rink.

When I first started he was very supportive. He supervised many of my games in the minor leagues and was instrumental in getting me to believe in myself. He definitely helped me make it to the NHL. After an AHL game once, in Baltimore we went for a walk and he told me my future looked good in the NHL. He went on to say that my career would be finishing about the same time he retired as supervisor and that I'd be able to move into his job!

His opinion of me changed with time and circumstances, and I saw his other side, the one reserved for officials he didn't care for.

A few examples of his treatment of officials illustrate one of the problems I felt management was overlooking — lack of support for the job we were doing on the ice.

One time Frank attended a Saturday-night game on Long Island between the Islanders and Philadelphia. I was officiating, along with linesmen Ray Scapinello and Bob Luther. Bob was from St. Louis and one of the first American officials to come onto the staff. He always gave 100 percent, but he was not one of "Frank's boys." Before the game Frank came into the dressing room, nodded to Bob and me, and then completely ignored the fact that Bob and I were there and carried on a conversation exclusively with Ray.

Put yourself in the same position, whatever line of work you're in. If your boss came into a small room and ignored you, you'd feel awfully strange about it and it wouldn't exactly fill you with confidence in your work.

Meanwhile, down the hall, we could hear the Islanders and Flyers whooping it up and getting psyched for the game. This was also a time for the officials to get psyched. Usually the adrenaline would start pumping and we'd be anxious to get out on the ice.

I left the dressing room with my thoughts not completely on the task ahead. How much that was responsible for one of the poorest officiating jobs I ever did, I don't know, but I just didn't have it that night and I knew it. All kinds of things were going on and I was letting a lot of it go. I was second-guessing myself. My rhythm was off. An obvious infraction would occur and I'd find myself thinking, after it was too late, that I should have called a penalty. I didn't feel comfortable on the ice at all. I had an off night — and every official in any sport will admit to some of those.

When it was over Frank came into the dressing room and told me that it was one of the worst jobs of officiating that he'd ever seen. It wasn't that I didn't deserve the lecture, but I got the distinct impression that he enjoyed being able to dress me down.

At another game, this time in Boston, he was the same way in the dressing room before the game — completely cool to me. At the end of the first period he came in and started giving me hell because I hadn't called a penalty when Boston defenseman Dallas Smith knocked his team's net off the moorings. This had happened during a flurry during the first couple of minutes of play and I hadn't seen how it happened. If it had occurred later in the game, with Boston perhaps pressured in their own end for an extended time, then I could have anticipated it and watched for it. But at the time, if there had been two penalties called in twenty-five years for that infraction it would have been a surprise to me. Yet he chose to come in at the end of the period and chastise me for missing it.

That was indicative of where I stood with him, when he had something to say I just listened quietly. There was no chance for a rebuttal or explanation, because he was likely to go off the deep end when he thought someone was questioning him.

Support from Frank would have gone a long way, not only for me but also for other officials. Frank came through a tough era for officials and said many times that had it not been for the support he got from Clarence Campbell, he certainly wouldn't have lasted. While he was appreciative of the help he'd received himself, it didn't bother him at all that he was adversely affecting the confidence of the officials in his charge. He didn't hesitate to belittle them or make them question themselves or their abilities.

I DIDN'T ENDEAR myself to management with my involvement in the Officials Association. One time I not only upset them but many of my fellow officials as well.

At training camp in 1975 the Association issued a press release on the topic of public abuse, criticism and intimidation of officials. It cited a new rule that was meant to eliminate excessive on-ice "talking" and discussed the question of officials using the media to defend themselves when attacks were made on their competence or integrity. Finally, it mentioned the agreement between the league and the officials that officials would not reply publicly through the media as long as the league did its job to protect officials from abuse.

At camp the day after the release was issued Don Ramsay from the *Globe and Mail* showed up and spent a long time talking with Scotty about rule changes for the coming season and how the training camp operated. He had a few pictures taken and then left.

I happened to see him in the parking lot and asked him if he had seen our press release from the day before. I told him not to forget the Association and the support we were looking for. We chatted for a few minutes and I emphasized some of the things in the release. I had no expectation of being quoted — in fact the purpose of the release was to ensure that we wouldn't have to speak out individually.

When I came down for breakfast at the hotel the following morning, most of the officials were already there. As I entered the room I quickly got the uncomfortable feeling that everybody in the room was watching me.

It didn't take long to find out what was going on. Ron Wicks came up to me as I was preparing my plate at the buffet and said, "Have you seen the morning paper yet? It's possible you're not too popular at a couple of tables here this morning."

I got a look at the article and my appetite for breakfast suddenly left as my stomach did flip-flops. Ramsay's story focused not on the topics he had discussed with Scotty — those were included later in the story — but on what I had told him.

To quote myself, I had said, "I'm sick and tired of this one-sided situation. Players and coaches have been running off at the mouth and if the league doesn't do something to curb continuation of the situation, we'll have no recourse but to defend ourselves publicly."

I went on to give an example of one such attack. "This guy told the press we threw him out of a game for the game's betterment. He said we had a grudge against him. I think we're entitled to defend ourselves on such statements."

It wasn't my place at the time to speak out as an individual — that was the purpose of the Officials Association. As a group we were trying to instigate changes in the proper way and I regretted that my personal comments may have undermined our efforts.

Scotty and his staff were all glaring in my direction, as were a few of the officials who had jumped on the management bandwagon. Probably the right thing to do would have been to arrange a meeting with Scotty to clear the air, but I didn't feel very confident at the time about explaining my position, and I thought with the mood Scotty appeared to be in, it wouldn't do any good anyway, at least not until he cooled off.

That day at the arena Frank made all of us pay for my remarks by skating us like never before, until we were ready to drop.

The officials had enough problems dealing with fans, players and team management without having to go up against our own bosses. We needed someone on our side to support us and to offer constructive criticism. The officiating team at the time lacked that positive leadership and guidance that is so important when it comes to the successful operation of any team.

14

FELLOW OFFICIALS — JUST REGULAR GUYS

We'd shift all the furniture in an official's room out into the stairwell or laundry room. When the victim came back he would be greeted by nothing but bare walls.

IN THE EARLY sixties, at the year-end banquet for officials in the Ontario Hockey League, Bill Friday was holding court. A number of us were huddled around, listening attentively as Bill told us what a great life professional refereeing was. He had been signed to the NHL staff the previous year and had just finished working a season in the minors. Bill told about the travel, about seeing all the sights in the various cities, about being under the bright lights.

I was almost drooling, thinking what a wonderful and exciting life it must be. I never dreamed that I too would be there some day. A year later I was working in the International League and that dream was starting to take shape. A year after that I was signed by the NHL.

The NHL meetings in my first professional year, 1963-64, were held at the Royal York Hotel in Toronto. As I was crossing the street to reach the hotel, Bill Friday saw me and waited for me to join him at the entrance.

"What do you think of joining a company that replaces a third of its staff every year?" he asked.

It wasn't the greatest introduction to the NHL, but that's the way the system worked then. Staffing decisions were based on the previous year's performance, so officials had little security.

There were only six NHL teams when I joined the pool of officials. To begin with I was signed to work exclusively in the minor leagues, but even the veteran referees were required to work some games in the minors. As the old saying goes, familiarity breeds contempt; with a maximum of three games on any one night, referees would see the same NHL teams much too often.

Games in the American League were a good training ground for up-and-coming officials. They also allowed veteran officials to get away from the pressure once in a while. The hockey in the American League was of excellent quality then, and it was often said that the top teams in that league could beat the bottom teams in the NHL.

The numbers that officials wore on their sweaters were assigned according to seniority: when I joined, Frank Udvari was number 1; Vern Buffey, 2; John Ashley, 3; Art Skov, 4; and Bill Friday, 5. Then there was a gap for linesmen — Ron Wicks, 6; Matt Pavelich, 7; Neil Armstrong, 8; and George Hayes, 9. Then they started back at 10 with the minor-league referees: Art Casterton was 10; Tom Smith was 11; I was number 12; 13 was vacant; Bob Sloan wore 14; and Kenny McLeod, 15.

When somebody retired or was let go, everyone moved up a number. I got all the way to number 1 and was the last referee to wear it before the league eliminated the practice.

When expansion came along in 1967, there was a need for more officials at the NHL level and the number system became outdated. For example, Matt Pavelich and Neil Armstrong had worn their numbers for so long they didn't want to give them up, and John D'Amico was proudly wearing George Hayes's old number 9, which George had actually requested go to John. That meant linesmen were wearing lower numbers than referees. Besides all that, it was thought that people might think a referee with a high number might be an inferior official.

Back then when there were so few officials compared with now, everyone got to know the referees and linesmen better because they saw them more often. Certainly, most hockey fans who were following the game around the time I joined the staff in the sixties are familiar with many of the officials' names of that time, and with the names of some of the legends who came before them.

Red Storey is one of the best known and best liked of all officials. Anybody who has heard him speak on the banquet circuit knows what a great storyteller he is. He was a deserving winner of the 1987 Hockey News King Clancy Memorial Award for dedication to the sport. I didn't know Red until after he left the game. Even at his age he still referees seventy to eighty old-timers' games a year, to raise money for various charities. Though it seems like he's been around forever, he didn't have a particularly long career as an NHL referee. He was another official who left the game because of the lack of support from the league.

It's said Bill Chadwick was the first official ever to use signals on the ice so that people would know what was going on in the game. I never saw "The Big Whistle" officiate, but I heard some of his comments while he was working on Ranger broadcasts in New York. He gained a reputation in his early broadcasting years of being something of a hatchet man when it came to officials. As he went along, he mellowed a little and analyzed the game with more of an eye to the officials' side of things. Bill is said to have refereed all his years with only one eye, a remarkable achievement when you consider how difficult a job it is with two! In recent years he has done public-relations work for the Rangers.

Eddie Powers left the NHL staff before I joined. He also had problems with lack of league support. I admired his work, though I didn't get to see many of his games until the play-offs, the only time games were televised in those days. The summer I joined the league we were both working for Mohawk Raceway near my home, and I showed him the contract I had signed. He told me how pleased he was the league was finally getting the salaries closer to where they should be.

FRANK UDVARI, WHO later became my supervisor, and Vern Buffey were the two senior referees in 1963. Even at that time Buffey was very concerned about the abuse officials had to endure, and he didn't hesitate to speak up about it. When comments were made in the press about the work of John Ashley by Bill Jennings of the Rangers, Vern was quoted as saying that Ashley had forgotten more about hockey than Jennings would ever know. He was reprimanded, and on another occasion when he complained publicly about the quality of the ice at Maple Leaf Gardens, he was fined. Anyone could say anything about officials, but the moment an official spoke out, the league jumped all over him.

Vern went on to become the referee-in-chief of the World Hockey Association.

Art Skov was a conscientious, hard-working referee with a strong feel for the game. I commented to him once about how ignorant the fans in the buildings could be and how much they could annoy me at times.

He told me to go to a game one night when I wasn't refereeing. He said I would see that the same people who bothered me were doing the very same thing to whoever happened to be refereeing that night. It wasn't personal, he said, just aimed at the striped shirt and what it represents. I quickly learned how right he was.

As good a referee as Art was, he used to have quite a time in training camp when we were given rules exams. He knew the rules fine, but had a hard time putting answers down on paper. He'd say, "If you put the players on the ice and have the situation happen, then I could call it, but on a piece of paper it's tough."

He wasn't the only official with that problem — the exams could get complicated. A question might start off with Team A getting a penalty, then Team B getting a penalty a minute later, followed by a goal by Team A, followed by another penalty to Team B, and so on. Pretty soon the numbers and letters would start to run together.

Bill Friday, the senior referee in 1969, became the first president of the Officials Association. It was a surprise to me that he even wanted the position, but he worked hard and did a good job. In 1972 Vern Buffey invited Bill to join him in the WHA, a major decision that worked out well for Bill, who retired at the age of fifty-three, with no need to find another job. How many people can do that?

In Seattle many years ago in the WHL, Bill got tagged with the nickname "Crisco," compliments of a woman who used to sit along the boards. When he asked her why she called him that, she said it was because he had such a fat posterior — i.e., lard ass.

A lot of credit goes to Bill for the work he put in to get officials recognized by the government as athletes, so that we, like the players, could defer income. It was a long process. Bill's lawyer drafted a twelve-page letter stating all the reasons why officials should be under the same tax classification as players. I supported the issue with seven additional pages through the advice of John Zoppas, my Manufacturers' Life rep and financial adviser, who also advised many other officials and the Officials Association.

We got the okay from the government and were able to purchase annuities that deferred part of our salaries till after we were finished refereeing. That's why Bill was able to retire at the age of fifty-three. The Canadian government recently changed the laws regarding deferrals, but for many of us Bill's efforts were a great help for the future. Salary deferrals allowed me to go into business for myself when I retired from officiating.

When John McCauley joined the NHL staff he dropped in at my house and I explained to him what he could expect as an NHL employee. We had been friends before that, through our lacrosse ties with the pro league and the Ontario Lacrosse Association. Both of us had worked together with officials to improve the rules.

John was known as one of the best wheeler-dealers on the staff. We could always depend on him to tell us where all the good shopping deals were in the various cities around the league.

John had his share of disagreements with the NHL brass, and his share of complaints about the operation. He was active in the Officials Association, working his way up the ladder to become its president, the position he was in when the first three-year contract for officials was instituted.

During the 1979 all-star series against the Soviet Union, played in New York, John got into an argument with a fan over the officiating — he was in the Blarney Rock bar near Madison Square Garden — and got punched. He hit his head on the counter and hurt his eye so badly he needed a series of operations and long rehabilitation before he could go back to officiating.

Shortly after that the NHL offered him the position of director of officiating, which he now holds. Fans who followed the infamous "doughnut incident" in the 1987-88 play-offs will remember John. He ended up sitting at the timekeeper's bench where he could advise the amateur officials who'd been brought in to work the game. The referees and linesmen had walked out of the game following New Jersey Devils coach John Schoenfield's verbal abuse of referee Kohalski.

John used to talk a lot about being a general manager in the league. He's a strong judge of players and their abilities, and it seems to me that he would do an excellent job. It will be interesting to see if it ever comes about.

Bryan Lewis was also active in the Association. Through his creative newsletters he kept us up to date on the facts and the news, and entertained us with gossip and plenty of humor. Bryan also ran the officials ball team, which revealed his excellent organizing skills. He also worked for a time at my referee school, as did John McCauley and many other officials. Bryan is now a supervisor of officials in the NHL. He is also involved in developing up-and-coming officials, which is why it's especially funny to remember what he used to call supervisors when he was an on-ice official — he'd note their presence by stating, "The spies are in town again."

The officials ball team was established the same year as the Association, in 1969. We went around Ontario playing different organizations to raise money for charity. It was for a good cause and we had a lot of fun doing it. Before the games even started, we would present our opponents with a trophy bearing an inscription that thanked them for participating, plus our regrets that they had lost the game. Next, we'd give the umpire a *Playboy* magazine to use as a rule book, then we'd hand him a home plate that was three times the normal size so our pitcher would have an easier time.

We did all the things on the ball field that we couldn't do on the ice — we cheated a lot. Sometimes we'd go to third rather than first if we got a hit, or if we were down by a few runs, and someone hit a homer, the whole team would round the bases and we'd count all the runs.

Lloyd Gilmour was one of the more colorful referees in the league. One of the most colorful things about him was his language, which made it difficult for him to work as a television analyst, though he was one with the Vancouver Canucks after retiring as a referee.

Once when refereeing a game in Atlanta between the Flames and Philadelphia a bench-clearing brawl erupted and went on for about twenty-five minutes. When it was finally over so many infractions had taken place that Lloyd just figured to hell with it — he called a couple of majors on the original combatants and went on with the game. Many nights I'd thought of doing the same, because it's often impossible to get it all straightened out properly anyway. The league didn't think too much of what he'd done, however, and told Lloyd in no uncertain terms. They also passed the message along to the rest of us not to get the same idea in our heads.

Lloyd was the referee for the fog bowl in Buffalo in 1975, that famous play-off game between the Sabres and Philadelphia. It was summer weather outside, which made for so much fog on the ice that they had to recruit the rink attendants to skate around with sheets to try to get rid of it. He was there again for that famous game in Philadelphia in 1976 when the Soviet players were so upset at all the rough stuff that they left the ice after Ed Van Impe cross-checked one of them, refusing to play any more.

Lloyd was a fun guy to be around. He always liked to have a good time and was usually at the center of any party. Some of my happiest days of officiating occurred while working the Western Hockey League finals one year with Lloyd and Willie Papp.

Lloyd now has a bar and restaurant in Nanaimo, B.C. which he named the NHL — Nanaimo Harbour Lights. It's filled with mementos from Lloyd's career in the NHL and WHL.

At twenty years of age, Ron Wicks was the youngest official ever hired for the NHL staff. He worked as a linesman for three years before becoming a referee. Our nickname for Ron was "Professor," or "Lawyer." In training camp discussion sessions, Ron used to get right down to the nitty-gritty of a rule, analyzing it every which way. It used to tee the guys off at times, and we used to tease him about it, but it was probably something *we* should have done more often. He probably did the most work on the staff in personal pension, medical and dental coverage. He was continually digging up facts on these subjects and bringing them to everyone's attention, including the league's.

Ron officiated in more than 1,000 games, but he almost quit during his early years as a referee. He disallowed a Los Angeles goal late in a game near the end of the season that could have meant first place for the Kings. Instead the game ended in a tie and Philadelphia took the division. Jack Kent Cooke was incensed and said that his team had been bilked out of first place by a greenhorn official. Ron was almost ready to pack it in right then. Three weeks later Clarence Campbell issued a press release saying that he had made the right call. Ron was finally able to enjoy his first real meal after three weeks of agony.

Ron is the only official to have worked the Stanley Cup finals and the All-Star game as both a referee and linesman. He holds the record of twenty-six years as an official in the NHL!

I SAW THE LINESMEN more often than other referees. We worked together as a team, and most of us got along very well off the ice as well — we'd go places together after and between games. As happens in most careers, the common bond of our work kept us on the same wavelength. The odd time there might be an official not everyone got along with, but that didn't affect the on-ice product. We all had our jobs to do.

Linesmen vary in how much they like to get involved when there's an incident on the ice. Some of them, like John D'Amico, were very thorough and were right there when there was a job to be done. On occasion John almost took it to the extreme. When there was a skirmish at the far end of the rink, he'd sometimes leave his position at the blue line and go rushing in to prevent a fight. But sometimes the players would go their separate ways and John would have to rush to get back in the play because the referee hadn't blown the whistle. But getting involved was the way he worked.

It was also the way he taught at my refereeing school. He'd tell his students that they should work with the referee, support him, make themselves available to him and stay aware at all times of what was going on during the game.

John has been involved with my school every year since it started. He's an exceptional instructor and has great rapport with the students. He's always well prepared and is usually the first one on the ice. He really enjoys teaching other officials and it shows in the tremendous job he does.

John is very particular about his equipment and we enjoyed having a little fun with him sometimes. He had shin pads marked "L" for the left one and "R" for the right. Since both pads looked exactly the same to us, we added an L to the one he had marked for right and an R to the one he had marked for left, so that each pad said "LR." He just shook his head when he saw it and I don't know if he ever figured out which was which.

When there were only six teams in the league, there were also only a few full-time linesmen. The ones they brought in on nights when there was a full slate of games were known as "weekend commandos." Bobby Frampton was from Montreal, Walt Atanas lived in Feeding Hills, Massachusetts, Bill Clements was from the Detroit area, and Bill Morrison lived in Bowmanville, Ontario. They all did a great job and were highly qualified. I worked with all of them except Bill Morrison, who had retired by the time I reached the NHL. Frampton went on to be in charge of referees for the WHA, Atanas became a scout for the Philadelphia Flyers and Clements took charge of the minor officials for the Detroit Red Wings.

My first year on the league staff turned out to be George Hayes's last and I only worked one game with him. But it didn't matter — George was my idol. I respected him for the authority he could exert over the players and for his forthrightness — he called a spade a spade. When I stepped out onto the ice with him for that one game, I was on the ice with a legend, and it meant a lot to me.

During that game, an exhibition match in London, Ontario, he called an offside. He was standing at the face-off spot waiting for the other linesman to bring him the puck, when Bob Pulford of the Leafs skated up to question the call. George gave a quick, jerking motion with his thumb and said, "Get the fuck out of here." I looked over at him as Pulford scurried away and he gave me a wink and a little grin.

We talked about it after the game and George suggested I shouldn't let the guys start to run me or they'd do it all the time. He also told me I had the tools to do the job and a good feel for the game, and that if I worked hard I would be a success. I was just a raw rookie, and hearing that from George Hayes was a tremendous boost to my confidence. I never forgot his advice.

He and I have something in common: he was the first linesman to officiate in 1,000 league games, and I was the first to referee in 1,000. He ended up doing more than 1,700 games, and worked eleven all-star games.

George had some run-ins over the years with Clarence Campbell and Carl Voss. The most contentious issue, and the one that eventually led to his "retirement" from the league, involved his refusal to take an eye test as ordered by Mr. Campbell. It got to the point that whenever he came to Montreal to officiate a game, he wouldn't answer the phone in his hotel room — he knew it was probably the league calling him again, to tell him about an appointment they had set up for his eye test.

He always said he knew his eyes were okay because he could still read the labels on liquor bottles. He never did give in, and as a result the league dismissed him. It's ironic, in that nowadays many NHL officials have less-than-perfect vision, wearing glasses off the ice and contact lenses during the games.

When I got a letter from the league at the start of my second season that started off by saying, "Gentlemen: This season all officials will be given eye examinations . . ." my thoughts were with George.

In 1988, twenty-three years after departing from the league and the year after his death, George was finally admitted to the Hockey Hall of Fame. Others have made it into the Hall with fewer years of service, and having contributed less. George Hayes should have been there at least twenty years earlier, when he was first eligible.

Neil Armstrong was another full-time linesman working in the NHL at the time. His nickname was "Skinny," or "Tanglefoot." Neil was his own man and did things his own way. He didn't participate in the Association in the beginning and didn't join until it became compulsory. Even then he didn't get involved in it to any degree. But that was Neil. He was a golf pro originally and operated a golf course during the off-season, in his hometown of Sarnia. After his officiating career ended he became a scout for the Montreal Canadiens.

Many officials will always remember him as the best gin rummy player on the staff. The amount of money he won from the other guys over the course of the season almost amounted to a second salary.

Gin rummy was the favorite game of the officials on game day, and while Neil was the best, John Ashley was close to his league. When Will Norris was learning to play, he used to get beaten so severely by Neil that one time he threw the cards out the hotel window in frustration, from seventeen floors up.

Will Norris was the officials' in-house tour guide. In Los Angeles, San Francisco or Atlanta, he wouldn't waste a day off sitting around the hotel. He always had activities planned and was always taking other officials around on one of his famous city tours.

Will was also one of the best pranksters on the officiating staff. Many afternoons, during my pregame rest, I would hear a knock at the door. It would be someone from room service with a hamburger, or the hotel bellman with orders to pick up my luggage, or a maid with a roll of toilet paper or box of Kleenex. Of course I'd ordered none of it, and rarely had to look past Will to find the culprit. He even used to do this from other cities, by long distance. His shenanigans were always funny, never malicious, and indicative of the camaraderie among officials.

Will worked at my referee school over the years and was an excellent instructor. He now works for the Ontario Hockey Association as its director of officiating — a natural position for him given the interest he has in the profession.

I didn't mind pulling a few pranks myself when the chance arose. One time I saw Ryan Bozak checking into the Holiday Inn, where we used to stay on Long Island. While he was filling out the registration form, I snuck up from behind and took his luggage. I went around the corner and up the stairs and hid it in my room, then went down the back stairs and in the back way to the bar off the lobby. A few minutes later I wandered out into the lobby and said, "Hi, Boze, when did you get in?"

He was standing around looking bewildered, and explained that somebody had stolen his luggage. He also told me that the security people in the hotel had phoned the police and that there had been a witness to the theft.

Well, I thought, this is really developing. I suggested we have a beer and wait for the police. While we were doing that he told me that, according to the witness, the thief had been a blond guy. Very interesting, considering my hair was jet black.

After watching him squirm for a while, I decided I had to tell him what had really happened. We had a good laugh over it and then remembered the police were on their way. When they arrived we went and explained to them that the luggage had turned up, that it hadn't been stolen after all. They looked at us as if we were nuts, suspicion of an inside job written all over their faces.

At the old Madison Hotel in Boston, which no longer exists, we used to pull a lot of weird antics. We'd shift all the furniture in an official's room out onto the stairwell or laundry room. When the victim came back he would be greeted by nothing but bare walls.

One night we planned to pull the prank again, but the official we had in mind was wary of us and extremely cautious. We pulled it off anyway. A group of eight or nine of us were next door at the bar, talking and having a drink with some local fans. One of the guys and I said we were going for a bite to eat but would be back. The victim didn't catch on, and away we went to do the job on his room. When we returned to the hotel later on it was quite a scene. We walked down the hall nonchalantly and waited for him to open the door to his room. When he did, and saw what had happened, he threw a fit. We quickly rushed into our own rooms and locked our doors, leaving him with an empty room.

Matt Pavelich worked as a carny before joining the staff. He might have gone on to become a top referee except for some unfortunate timing. Carl Voss came to see him referee an AHL game in Rochester one year, and there happened to be a stick fight in the third period. Carl had left at the end of the second period and after hearing of the incident didn't give Matt many more opportunities to prove himself as a referee. Matt had the ability, as do many linesmen who have moved on to become referees, and he should have been given more of a chance.

One day in Detroit, Matt and I were discussing an incident that had taken place the previous night between Art Skov and Carl, during which Art had tossed a skate in frustration. I asked Matt what he thought of Carl and he answered by asking what I thought of him. I said I thought he was a pretty good guy. Matt told me then that's the way I should take him, and that I shouldn't judge Carl or anyone else in the business by what somebody else said. I applied that advice through the rest of my career. It's easy to be influenced by another person's opinions, which are often fueled by jealousy, resentment or personal dislike. I couldn't let myself get into a situation where I made judgments based on somebody else's feelings.

Matt now works as a supervisor of officials. He was one of the people who refused to join the Association at the start. But later he did. At one time he was even its vice president.

DURING THE EARLY years of officiating it was a struggle to find ways to save money, and Matt was one of the best. Every nickel was important. We used to kid him about it by running ahead of him to check phone booths. If there was a coin on the sidewalk, Matt would have his foot on it before we could bend down to pick it up, prompting more good-natured kidding.

Jim Christison was working the lines in Pittsburgh one night when I was refereeing. He took a face-off to the right of the Pittsburgh net. The Pittsburgh center pulled the puck back to Tim Horton, who at the time had one of the hardest shots in the league. Horton tried to clear the puck out of his own end and hit Jim on the leg with it. He went down to the ice immediately, on his hands and knees with the puck directly in front of him. Though the puck was still in play, Jim just reached out with his hand and grabbed it, all the while writhing in pain. The players were all around him attempting to play the puck, and wondering what was going on. Then Jim realized he shouldn't have the puck and slid it along the ice away from him. I blew the whistle when I realized he was injured and went over to see how he was. He was still on his hands and knees kind of crawling along to ease the pain. Then he let loose with a string of cuss words and finished it off with, " . . . that hurt!"

I started to laugh at his predicament, and then so did he. Soon we were both down on the ice laughing, oblivious to the players, the fans and the game. In the end, Jim skated off the injury and we went on with the game.

Jim is a diabetic, and his need to maintain a proper diet puts heavy demands on him. Traveling all over North America is a tough task for him, and the league has arranged his schedule so that he doesn't have to work several nights in a row. That gives him a chance to "build up" between assignments.

I once had an experience similar to Jim's, in which I instinctively handled the puck. It also happened in Pittsburgh. I was along the side boards when a defenseman at the point shot the puck around. I was perched on the boards, with my hands on top for support, when the puck deflected up and hit me just above the wrist. It hurt like hell and I dropped to the ice, rubbing my wrist. I looked around for the puck and there it was, still sitting on top of the boards. I hadn't blown the whistle yet to stop play, and I was upset at getting hit, so I just took a swat at the puck to knock it back onto the ice. As soon as the players got over their surprise, play continued right on.

A few weeks later I was again working in Pittsburgh, and a couple of fans called me over to the boards and told me it was the funniest thing they'd ever seen during a game. I kind of chuckled to myself when I heard that because I thought the way the Penguins played some nights back then was pretty funny too.

Leon Stickle is from my hometown of Milton. Watching him officiate local games, I knew he had the attributes to become a good NHL official. He came to my referee's school and as a result got invited to the NHL's training camp, and he has worked as a linesman in the league ever since. As a player he was a hard-nosed defenseman on the local junior team who was always ready to scrap. Leon has excellent rapport with the players in the league. I always enjoyed working with him because he kept things loose with his good sense of humor.

Leon and I were both present in 1979 when one of the officials made the much-publicized statement that American officials weren't as good as Canadian officials and the NHL was just catering to them to keep them on staff and ensure American content. Jim Kernaghan reported the comment in the *Toronto Star* but refused to reveal his source. The brass went nuts. We got letters from Scotty challenging the official who said it to come forward. The American officials all received letters of apology. I'm pretty sure the brass thought I made the comment, but only those who were there that evening know who it really was. And we're not telling!

Don Koharski has the right attitude and deportment for an NHL official. He started out as a linesman in the NHL, then went back to the minors to become a referee before rising back to the NHL. He really had to work his way up the ladder.

Don has established himself in the top ranks of NHL officials and was the first referee to officiate in the Canada Cup finals in a game with a Canadian team involved.

Don is from Nova Scotia and has that easygoing down-east attitude. When he was working in the NHL as a linesman, before going down to referee in the minors, he told us, "Look, when I come back to the NHL and I'm working the games up here, don't you old retired guys be bugging me for tickets to the games!" When a friend of mine called me after I retired to see if I could get him some tickets for a game in Montreal, the first person I thought of calling was Don. Remembering his joking remark, I was delighted to ask for tickets. And he came through with them, too.

Don's nature was typified when, about a week after the "doughnut incident" in the 1988 play-offs, he reportedly forgave New Jersey coach Jim Schoenfeld for their disagreement and assured him that yes, he was still invited to his golf tournament that summer.

Andy van Hellemond is considered by many to be the best referee in the game today and he's certainly one of my favorites. He always jokes about how he got his break when I was injured and he was called up as a replacement. As for the officials, he has done as much for them as anyone. He doesn't hesitate to stand up and be counted.

Kerry Fraser is another one who's very articulate when it comes to explaining the officials' side of things. He's been through some tough times himself and knows the effects of having to put up with the abuse that goes with being an official.

OVER THE YEARS I tried to help other officials when they ran into problems. If I knew about a problem, I'd call the official up to tell him that he wasn't alone, and that every other official, including myself, had gone through similar trials. I'd explain that it was just part of the game and urge him not to let it affect him. Other officials did the same thing for me once I joined the staff, so I was always happy to offer the same type of help. I appreciated it when I received it, and know the people I tried to help felt the same way. I used to get letters from up-and-coming officials, some who are in the league now, thanking me for helping them through a rough spot. When I retired I received many letters thanking me for my support and advice, and for helping form the Association way back in the early days.

When I think about what I miss most about the business, the first thing that comes to mind is the camaraderie between the officials, and the times we shared traveling, sightseeing or just sitting around talking. Just as players have withdrawal symptoms after leaving the game, so do officials.

THE PLAYERS — UP
CLOSE AND PERSONAL

"Hoody, will you please tell the linesmen to drop the puck as quickly as possible when I'm on the ice? That way the fans won't notice I'm out here and won't get on my ass. They hate my guts in this place!"

Bobby Hull

Bobby Hull's booming slapshot is a legend now, and was a terror to every goaltender he faced. But imagine standing directly in front of him just as he was winding up to let that big shot go — without the protective equipment of a goaltender, or even of a defenseman.

It happened to me.

During a game in 1968 at the Montreal Forum, the Canadiens were bringing the puck out of their own zone against the Blackhawks. Before they got to the blue line, Hull intercepted a pass and turned around to blast it at the net.

I had been following the play out of the Montreal end and was in the path between him and the net, about eight feet away. I remember thinking right then, "If he shoots that puck, it's all over for me."

But he actually *waited* for me to scramble out of the way, his stick cocked in the air, and only then let the shot go!

I saw him after the game and said, "Thanks." He gave me a wink and a grin. Nothing else was said — he knew what I was talking about.

Bobby Hull was a class act all the way. Only once in all the games I officiated did he say anything even slightly derogatory. Bryan Watson, the pesky Detroit checker, was shadowing him one night and giving him a rough time. Midway through the game, Hull looked at me with a frown and said, "Gonna let that guy do that all night?"

Hull was amazingly strong. In fact his strength may have cost the Blackhawks a few power plays over the years. He could have two or three guys draped all over him and still keep going. Anybody else would have stopped or fallen to the ice. But not him. It was difficult to call a restraining foul against someone who wasn't being restrained. So I gave him a few breaks in other situations. First of all, any time he did go down from a check, a penalty was almost automatic. Second, I would let him get away with the odd hook or hold because of the many transgressions against him that I couldn't call.

That may sound like an odd thing for a referee to admit, but I did what I thought was fair. Hull was in a category all by himself, even in the minds of the officials.

Bryan Watson

"Bugsy" was probably one of the best shadowers I ever saw in the NHL. He wasn't tremendously talented, but he was hard-nosed and determined. When he had a job to check a player, he'd practically get into his opponent's hip pocket and live with him. While I admired the job he did, still I had to make sure it was legal, which it usually was. Later, towards the end of his NHL career, he started to cheat a little and took some bad penalties.

John Ferguson

Plain and simple, John Ferguson scared the wits out of me. He was one of the most renowned tough guys in the history of the NHL, and the ferocity and intensity he brought to the game was intimidating, even to the officials.

Every time "Fergie" stepped on the ice, it was like a do-or-die situation for him. He looked and acted like he was always one step away from exploding, and that's what scared me. I always figured if he ever snapped, he'd go right through the end boards and take someone with him.

Most people remember Ferguson as a great fighter, and he was, but he didn't go out of his way to look for scraps. One look into his eyes was usually enough to warn opposing players not to mess with him.

Ferguson used another form of intimidation just as well: he had a habit of cutting through the opposing team's goal crease on his way back up the ice and dumping the goaltender. By the time he did this, everyone's attention, including my own, was usually focused up the ice where the play was headed.

One night I looked back and saw Gerry Cheevers skating towards me waving his arms and stick. He was pretty upset. Apparently Ferguson had cut through the crease and dumped him. After that I made a point of keeping an eye on him until he got out of the other team's end.

Ferguson wasn't as hard for officials to handle as you would think. If he made a fuss after I gave him a penalty, I knew that it was mostly out of frustration and a result of his tremendous intensity. He didn't do it on purpose to show up the officials, like some players did. It was genuine, and I usually just looked the other way.

His intensity as the general manager of the Winnipeg Jets is just as high, and he can get very upset when a penalty call goes against his team, or if he feels one of his players isn't putting out.

Bob Pulford

I always thought that someone should have taken Bob Pulford aside and tried to convince him that the world wasn't such a bad place. He had to be one of the most miserable and most negative players on the ice that I ever came across.

It always looked to me that the last place he wanted to be was at the hockey rink. He always had a frown on his face and was always mumbling something. I used to routinely tell him to shut up, and it got so I almost expected him to complain even when the other team got a penalty.

Pulford is actually a likable guy, but I would never have known it if I hadn't met him in a bar one night during the latter stages of his career. I had never seen him smile before then, but that night we had some laughs and talked over old times.

The next time I saw him on the ice, he was back to being his miserable self.

Stan Mikita

Mikita was a tremendous hockey player throughout his long career with the Chicago Blackhawks. He was also a tremendous pain in the neck throughout my long career as a referee. He always had something sarcastic to say and wouldn't think twice about belittling an official on or off the ice. He had a mean streak that didn't show through during his Lady-Byng-winning seasons of 1966-67 and 1967-68.

After some calls he would stand there on the ice and shake his head or roll his eyes, just to make sure everybody in the building knew who he thought was the biggest moron on earth that night. After a Chicago penalty he might yell at me, "What the hell's going on out here, ya trying to ruin the fucking game? They didn't come here to see you."

One night when the Balckhawks visited Atlanta, before the Flames moved to Calgary, things weren't going right for him. Without any provocation that I could see, he came up to me and said, "What are you doing here? You don't know anything about the game."

But Mikita was also one of the few players who'd maintain his sarcasm away from the rink. After the game that night, I happened to be at the airport at the same time as the Blackhawks. He said something like, "Hey boys, it's the blind man," and eighteen professional hockey players had a laugh at my expense in a crowded airport.

As little respect as I had for Mikita the man, no one could question his hockey-playing ability — it carried him to the Hall of Fame. He was phenomenal at face-offs, and linesmen had an easier time with him than I ever did. They even used him as an example to other players jockeying for position in the face-off circle. The linesmen would say that if they would set down their sticks like Mikita did, they'd probably win a lot more face-offs.

Reggie Fleming

I once called Reggie a name I had no business calling him, and regretted it instantly. It was on a Saturday night in the Montreal Forum. Reggie was playing with the Rangers, and the Canadiens had just scored a goal. He came at me whining about a hook or something he thought I had missed. I said, "Okay, C.H., that's enough."

He whirled around and yelled, "What did you say!"

I knew instantly that I had made a mistake. C.H. was short for Cement Head, a name I had heard him called by some of his friends, and understandably I wasn't one of the privileged few who could call him that and get away with it.

He came up to me, nose to nose, and laid into me with that high-pitched, raspy voice of his. "Who do you think you are? You can't talk to me like that!" He went up one side of me and down the other and there was nothing I could do.

I said, "Hey, all right, let's get the game going." After that he was always Reggie.

Carl Brewer

Carl used to be known as "The Professor." No detail escaped his attention. If there was a little piece of thread on the ice, he would be the one to see it and pick it up.

Carl was a very talented player, cool under pressure and very adept at moving out of his own zone. He was also very articulate and extremely smart.

He used to cut the palms out of his gloves so that he could hold onto another player without the referee knowing. The officials eventually caught on, but it worked for a while. The league even put a rule in the book to stop that sort of thing.

Carl acted very aloof on the ice. When he got a penalty, it was almost as if arguing with the referee about it was beneath him.

Brewer's ill-fated comeback in 1979–80 was a source of amusement for many hockey observers, and certainly did nothing for his dignity. He was forty-one years old, much heavier than he'd been in his prime, and was bald as an eagle.

One night in Detroit he got involved in a scuffle with a Red Wing player who seemed more intent on removing Brewer's helmet, as if showing off that bald head would be a thrill for the fans, than on landing a punch. It reminded me of a wrestling match in which one of the grapplers is trying to remove his opponent's mask.

Jean Beliveau

One word describes Jean Beliveau — class. He had it in every sense of the word. He had dignity and poise and was all business when it came to dealing with officials. If he had a question to ask, he asked it in an intelligent way, and always appeared to accept the answer.

Jean did, however, let it slip one night. Bob Sloan had given another Montreal player a penalty during a game in Toronto and Jean took his glove off and went over to shake Sloan's hand — to show him up and make him look silly. Sloan, rightfully, gave him a misconduct.

The next night I was the referee and Jean came up to me on the ice and said, "When you see Bob Sloan, apologize for me. That was not me. It was out of character and I felt badly afterward."

That was a typical move from a class man. Jean Beliveau was and is my idol.

Gordie Howe

I was always awed by Howe when he came on the ice. He was a legend, and acted like it. When he got a penalty he would go to the box without a word, as if it was just another part of his job.

Howe is a great public-relations man for hockey, much the same as Wayne Gretzky. I could sit for hours just listening to his hockey stories, and once had the opportunity to do just that. We were both at a fantasy hockey camp in Lake Placid, and as he told story after story, the people who had paid their money to attend, sat there in awe. I have to admit; I was a little in awe myself.

I think the elbows thing with him was a little overrated. He was taller than most players, and when he went in along the boards his elbows would naturally be at their ear level. But there was no doubt he could use them on purpose if he wanted to, and he sometimes did.

At that fantasy camp, one of the players was checking a little too aggressively as Howe carried the puck up the ice. The guy was hooking him and whacking at his ankles. Howe glanced back over his shoulder and I knew right then the guy had gone too far. As soon as the player caught up, Howe's elbow went out like a flash, and he no longer had a pest on his tail. I guess if the fellow wanted to experience the realism of playing hockey against Gordie Howe, he got what he paid for.

Bobby Clarke

I was not too popular around the Philadelphia Flyer organization during the goon years of the mid-seventies. But I don't think any player disliked me as much as Bobby Clarke did.

Clarke would skate in little circles about fifteen feet away from me, scowling and making remarks about the "goddamned refereeing." Never once, in all my years of officiating, did he confront me face-to-face, but he never stopped yapping away with biting, sarcastic comments, either.

Clarke also had a way of getting on the nerves of the linesmen. He'd stand around the face-off circle looking around, then position his teammates, then tug at his right elbow pad, then his left. The linesman finally would have to say, "Okay, Clarkie, get your stick in here."

Clarke would retort with something like, "Shut up, the people didn't come here to see you."

Clarke was also one of the worst stick men I ever saw. His most notorious tactic was to jab an opponent in back of the leg with the point of his stick. I called a lot of penalties on him and became very unpopular with the fans and the Philadelphia organization. Perhaps he thought it was okay for him to do that because of who he was, but I didn't care; a penalty was a penalty. In any case, it was the Flyers' philosophy to take everything to the limit, to see what they could get away with, and Clarke's stick work certainly was part of the strategy.

Still, I had a great deal of respect for Clarke's endless drive and determination. Even on nights when his team wasn't going well, he'd hop over the boards and give his utmost effort. His dedication to the game could never be questioned.

While in Buffalo to work on a Sabre telecast just after retiring, I saw Clarke, who is now the Flyers' general manager, in the lobby of the local Hilton. He nodded hello, came up to shake hands and said jokingly, "Jeezus, are you back to get us again?"

Bob Gainey

The first time I met Bob Gainey was on Grand Bahama Island in the summer of 1973. I was down there to relax and play golf with friends. He was there doing the same thing with some of his Junior teammates from Peterborough.

We were sitting on the patio outside my room when Bob and his chums came along and joined us. We started chatting about hockey and Bob mentioned that he had been drafted by the Canadiens, the defending Stanley Cup champions that year.

My first reaction was that he had almost no chance of making that team, so I said to him, "How do you think you'll like playing in Halifax next year?" It wasn't a smart-aleck remark; Halifax was the Montreal farm club at the time, and just about everybody played there first after they were drafted.

As it turned out, Bob was one of the only Montreal draft picks who never spent a day in the minors. We have both been involved in charity work with the Special Olympics program, and when we get together we often joke about my comment.

On the ice Bob was another NHL Jekyll and Hyde. He'd always come up with some kind of taunting, sarcastic remark, no matter what the situation was.

One time he had something to say about an incident that had occurred. I said to him, "Hey, you just play the game and keep quiet," and then skated back to my spot beside the net for the face-off. Bob went over to his position on left wing. When I looked back, he made a gesture toward me by grabbing his crotch. I skated right over to him and said, "You know, that was a pretty low-class thing you just did."

He looked back at me with a "Who me?" expression on his face, and seemed surprised that I had confronted him.

In my books, it was serious enough that I could have given him a misconduct, but I rarely took an isolated incident to that extreme. If he had made a spectacle of himself in front of all 17,000 fans, he would have been gone in a second. As it was, the gesture was meant strictly for me and I doubted if anybody else had even seen it. So I overlooked it, at least as far as calling a penalty.

After the game I went back to the hotel and checked for messages at the front desk. I was given one that said to call Bob Gainey. At first I thought it was one of the linesmen playing a joke on me, but I called the number on the message anyway.

Gainey answered the phone and when I said who it was, his voice sounded very humble. "Bruce," he said, "I wanted to call you and apologize for what I did on the ice tonight. I don't know what made me do it — the game wasn't going too well for me and I just got frustrated and carried away. I wanted to let you know that I'm very sorry. I'm not usually that type of person."

I thanked him for his call and said I could understand his situation, and hung up the phone with a whole new respect for him. It was a special moment: people tend to forget that players and officials are all human beings, and that we have feelings just like anybody else.

Ken Linseman

When he was playing for Philadelphia, Linseman earned his nickname, "The Rat," and it was definitely an apt title. He would circle around behind a scrum of players and cause all kinds of trouble. Players would be pushing and shoving and Linseman would be there poking players in the legs or pulling their feet out from under them.

When he absolutely has to pair off with somebody, he goes looking for the other team's Lady Byng candidate. A classic example is what happened a few years ago in Buffalo, after he'd been traded to the Bruins. Defenseman Mike Ramsey checked Linseman in front of the net and Linseman fell to the ice, face down. There was no movement from him whatsoever. A couple of his teammates came over to challenge Ramsey and when they arrived, Linseman quickly sprung to his feet and went around behind the pack. He had to pair off with somebody so he grabbed Bill Hajt, one of the least troublesome players in the league. It was so typical.

His tactics often put opposing players off their game, which of course was the whole point, and at the same time he causes the officials all kinds of grief. A very talented hockey player, and one of the best there is at face-offs, he can be a real asset to a club. And he sure as heck keeps the officials tuned to the game when he's playing.

Mike Pelyk

At times during his career Mike Pelyk fell into disfavor with
the Maple Leaf Gardens faithful. One night before a game, he
skated up to me and said, "Hoody, will you please tell the
linesmen to drop the puck as quickly as possible when I'm on
the ice? That way the fans won't notice I'm out here and
won't get on my ass. They hate my guts in this place!"

No problem, Mike.

I told the linesmen.

Wayne Gretzky

Wayne was labeled a complainer by the officials when he first
came into the league. He seemed to have something to say
about everything and was constantly moaning and groaning.
John D'Amico got so upset with him one time that he really
laid into him, telling him to just play the game and not try to
run everything on the ice.

Eventually Wayne came to realize that he isn't special as
far as the officials are concerned. He's learned that he doesn't
get any breaks for his team by constantly whining and has
made a turnaround.

I remember Clarence Campbell coming to a game in
Montreal one night when Gretzky first entered the league.
Campbell came into our dressing room before the game to
hang up his coat, and chatted for a few minutes as he often
did. He said he had wanted to come out and see for himself
just how good this young man Gretzky really was.

After the game he came back to the dressing room to get
his coat, and I asked him what he thought of Gretzky.

"Well, I really haven't seen him do too much yet," he
answered. Then he put his coat on and left.

The linesmen and I looked at each other and then checked
the scoring sheet, and sure enough, he had scored a goal and
earned two assists.

But that's the way Gretzky is. Mr. Campbell had been looking for somebody like Beliveau, who could control and
dominate a game. But with Gretzky, it's difficult to see just
how spectacular he really is until you study him on video in
slow motion — as I have done while analyzing Sabres games
— because he does so many amazing things in a routine way.

He controls the game as much with his mind as with his physical skills. He can read the play far in advance and seems to know what the other players are going to do before they know themselves. Actually, he does control and dominate a game like Beliveau did, but doesn't stand out. Is Gretzky the best player I ever saw? That's hard to say, because he isn't as spectacular as many of his predecessors. As far as having a feel for the game, there has been no one better. There have been better skaters, better shooters and better stickhandlers, but none of them have put it all together like Gretzky has. He does it all, both on and off the ice, and has been a great asset to the sport of hockey.

Dave Semenko

If it's possible for a referee to have such a thing as a favorite enforcer, then Dave Semenko was my man. Many of the goons around the league are a real pain to deal with, causing a lot of problems with their cheap stuff after the whistle, and just generally making nuisances of themselves.

Dave Semenko was different. He earned his reputation by bodyguarding Wayne Gretzky and he was always there in case somebody wanted to make trouble for his charge. But the only form of intimidation he ever used was just being present on the ice. And he never mouthed off at the officials — a respectable goon, if you will. If enforcers have to be in hockey, that's the type they should be.

Perhaps Semenko had been a "problem goon" at an earlier stage of his career, but he never was when I dealt with him. And I only take people the way I find them.

I always had a soft spot for "Big Sam." He stopped in at my house on the way back from Gretzky's tennis tournament one time and met my family. He is very respectable and very likable, and even — so some say — gave Gretzky a run for his money in Edmonton, when it came to popularity.

Paul MacLean

It was one of those nights when I had taken as much as I could. Paul MacLean had been yapping all through the game at just about everything, and he was getting on my nerves.

On one play he was going into the other team's end when he got a little hook, but not enough for me to issue a penalty. Play was still going on at this point and he started hollering at me. Well, I got mad, one of the few times I ever did, at least while play was still going on. I followed him out of the zone up the ice, yapping back at him, and stayed on his case all the way into his own zone, and even after play had stopped. I told him just to play the game, that I would be the referee, and that he didn't know what he was talking about. I even followed him to the players' bench. I completely forgot about the game and just let go on him, releasing all my frustrations.

It felt good at the time, but afterwards it bothered me. I knew well enough that some players were going to take their frustrations out on me, and should have remembered it wasn't fair for me to take my own out on a player.

I was going down east to play in Rick Vaive's golf tournament in Prince Edward Island the following summer and I knew Paul made his summer home in Nova Scotia. While down there I made it a point to talk to him about it. I apologized, explaining to him what I thought of my own actions and how unnecessary it had been for me to behave that way. We ended up having a laugh over it.

I got to know MacLean and his family on a personal level and struck up a friendship with them. I'm always pleased to see him do well, and watch for his name in the scoring summaries.

Phil Esposito

Phil Esposito held the record for most goals in a season, before Wayne Gretzky came along. In my book, he still holds the record for complaining and bitching.

When Phil was in Boston he was easily the biggest complainer in the league. He wasn't like other players, who would get upset about a penalty being called against them. He was much more worried about penalties that weren't called.

Phil would set himself up in the slot and wait for his rugged wingers, Ken Hodge and Wayne Cashman, to dig the puck out for him. He'd give it that quick release and bang, the puck was in the net.

The other teams knew what he was doing and weren't inclined to stand by and watch. That meant he got more than his share of attention and had to fight for position. Though he was a pretty big guy himself and could shove with the best of them, he often ended up flat on the ice. Sometimes it seemed to me that he spent more time lying down than he did standing up.

I wasn't inclined to call penalties that often in that situation because most of the time it looked to me like he was just as much at fault, if not more.

Whenever he did go down, he'd look up at me with his arms outstretched as if to say, "How the hell do you think I got here?"

Anybody could see what he meant. This went on constantly. He liked to bring the wrath of the "Gallery Gods" at the Garden down on me, and knew just how to do it. Phil would do anything to gain an edge for his team, and wasn't beyond using the fans to intimidate officials. There were plenty of other players on the Big Bad Bruins who could intimidate the opposition, so he rarely got into it with opposing players — his target was the referee.

Most of the time I tried to ignore him, but one night in Boston against the Rangers he went too far and I threw him out of the game. A few minutes later Vic Hadfield of New York locked skates with Carol Vadnais of the Bruins. As I was helping pull the skates apart, Hadfield's skate blade cut my hand badly enough that I had to leave the game for repairs.

While I was on my way to the first-aid room I had to walk by Phil, who was still pacing back and forth in the Boston dressing room. He made some comment to the effect that I was not on his list of favorite people. I told him that I didn't care whether he liked me or not as long as I had his respect. He passed our conversation on to reporters, and the next day it was in the Boston papers, word for word.

Later, after Phil was traded to the Rangers, he lost some of his enthusiasm for the game and didn't take himself quite as seriously. After all the years of grief he had caused me, he was now a pleasure to be around on the ice. We had fun chatting about this or that and he was a completely different person.

Still, it's hard to think of Phil without remembering that look on his face, as if somebody had just picked his wallet, right in front of a policeman.

Wayne Cashman

I had as much respect for Wayne Cashman the hockey player as I did for Chris Nilan—close to nil. They were the same type of player. But at least Nilan would drop his gloves and fight. Cashman would make sure his stick was in position to ward off any takers.

He was one of the Big Bad Bruins and nobody played the intimidation role better. He would give a guy a little shove in the face after the play was over and then sneer at him. He made sure everyone knew that if you messed with him, you messed with all the Bruins. He liked that power and took advantage of it. When a guy was down, Cashman always looked ready to kick him.

Wayne Cashman was a hell of a hockey player in his own right and could dig that puck out of the corner with the best of them, but I'm sure he was a lot more effective knowing that the opposing players were worrying as much about him and his teammates as they were about the puck.

His intimidation tactics worked so well on his opponents that he tried them out on referees as well. Or maybe he just did it because he enjoyed it. He'd stand about three feet away from me and hold the stick upside down, studying the blade. Then he'd say something like, "I'd like to gouge somebody's eyes out with this stick." Meaning my eyes, of course.

He knew I couldn't call a misconduct penalty for that.

One Saturday night in Boston the Bruins were leading the Islanders 2-1 late in the game. Cashman was leaving the ice as I was skating by the Boston bench.

"Get in the game, you fucking asshole!" he hollered at me.

There was no way I could allow him to get away with that, and I called a bench penalty. The Islanders tied the game up and I took a lot of heat.

I called him that time, but there were plenty of others when he got away with it. I even started giving it back to him. He'd say to me, "I'd like to meet you in an alley sometime," and I'd say, "You've never had any guts on the ice—what makes you think you'll have any in the alley?"

That way I didn't lose my self-esteem. But still, it got to the point where the first time he would say something I'd tell him, "Don't mess with me tonight." That seemed to work pretty well, because then he'd know that I wasn't in the mood to accept any of his bullshit, and that he'd get a misconduct penalty faster than he usually would.

John McKenzie

He was reckless, a guy who just didn't give a damn. That's the best way I can define him. Some nights he reminded me of a fox going into a chicken house. He'd fly into those corners at full speed, arms and elbows flying, and come out with the puck on his stick and a grin on his face. He loved it!

He was part of the Big Bad Bruins, who, by the way, were the first team I ever saw that didn't wear ties while traveling. When I saw them at the airport they were always loud and rambunctious. And always in the middle of the pack, having a good time as usual, was John McKenzie.

Bobby Orr

I knew about Bobby Orr long before he made it to the NHL with Boston in 1966. As a young hotshot defenseman, he was the talk of the town when his Parry Sound peewee team came to play in Milton. By the time he reached the Junior A level with Oshawa, at the age of fifteen, he was already a hockey legend in Ontario. And we all know what he did after that.

Orr revolutionized the sport like no other player before or since. Until his chronic knee problems forced him out of the game in 1979, he was a dazzlingly powerful skater who could summon incredible bursts of speed. He was the first defenseman to handle the puck with authority in the offensive zone, and thanks mainly to his lead, an entirely new game strategy was born. While some of his scoring records have since been surpassed, no NHL player has ever handled the puck as brilliantly and naturally at both ends of the ice as Bobby Orr did in his prime.

Having said all that, I must also say that Bobby Orr was one of the most difficult players I ever had to deal with. He had as foul a mouth as any player I ever came across. Some nights he'd stand ten feet away from me and call me a "fucking idiot," or unleash a torrent of abuse.

When he got a penalty, he rarely just accepted it. Instead he'd storm towards the box at full speed to show everyone he was disgusted with the call, then throw his stick down and slam the door for good measure.

In the early seventies, I got to know Bobby on a personal level at the sports camp he operated with Mike Walton in Orillia, Ontario. Once again I was reminded that the nastier a player is on the ice, the more pleasant he's likely to be off it. Bobby, as it turned out, was a classy, humble individual, and I grew to respect him a great deal more as a person.

Tiger Williams

Tiger marched to the beat of a different drummer, there is no doubt about that. He had a theory about everything. I would talk to him about a different rule or situation and most of the time his theories made sense. He told me that he had passed along many of those thoughts to people in the league at different times, but that they hadn't been very well received.

One of the points he made was that a player who wears a face mask and starts a fight should be penalized extra. Interestingly, the league is considering it for a rule change.

I was involved with him at the Special Olympics in Calgary in 1987 and was extremely impressed with the work he did. He was coaching a team in the floor hockey division and his enthusiasm rubbed off on the players. He had them bouncing all the time, and it was great to see.

While we were both in Los Angeles for the all-star game, we had quite a talk about how he felt the officials were getting on his case. I said to him that if he gave the officials less flak and just played the game, he probably wouldn't be as conspicuous as he believed he was. We have an old saying in refereeing that if a player got one penalty, he probably deserved two or three, and if he got three penalties, he probably deserved four or five. I think that saying applied to Tiger Williams.

Larry Robinson

I saw Larry as something of a General when he was out on the ice because he always seemed to be in control — moving the puck out of his zone, taking charge in front of the net or of anything else. He was one of the players whose styles I admired most. Part of the reason was that he played the game the way I always wanted to play when I was a defenseman.

He doesn't hesitate to say something when he thinks a play hasn't been called properly, but still shows a great deal of respect for the officials. Because of that, the officials respect him.

Ken Dryden

I first saw Ken Dryden while refereeing a game in New York that was one of his first in the NHL, and just prior to the Stanley Cup play-off year in which he performed so spectacularly. In just that one game there was something about him that made it evident he was a little special.

I was always impressed by the high level of intensity he showed on the ice. He wouldn't hesistate to chastise his teammates if they weren't playing well or moving the puck out of their own end properly. He'd slap his stick on the ice and holler at his defensemen to "get in the game."

Back when the rules weren't as strict about goaltenders freezing the puck, he used to do it whenever he thought his team needed a line change. He was almost like an assistant coach on the ice. I talked to him one night about freezing the puck too much and he replied, "Well, we're due for a change, therefore I had to stop the play." He said it in such a logical way — as he always did whenever he talked to me — that I couldn't very well argue with him.

The Plager Brothers

The Plager brothers were a big hit in St. Louis, back in the early days of expansion. Barclay, who has since passed on, played with as much intensity as any player I ever officiated with. When he got a penalty, he'd skate as fast as he could to the penalty box, plunk himself down and sit there shaking his head. I could never figure out whether he was upset with himself or upset with me.

Billy was the youngest of the three and didn't play as much.

Bob was probably one of the last of the hip-checkers in the league. He used to use it a lot on players that didn't have the puck, however, so he took the odd penalty for it. I was going off the ice in Madison Square Garden one night, back when the visiting team used the same exit, and he made some comment about a play that had happened just before the end of the period. I told him just to play the game, and he snapped back, "I pay more in income tax than you make."

He said it to get a rise out of me because I wasn't interested in listening to his complaints, but I thought about what he said, realized he was probably right and had to laugh. I replied, "I have to agree with you, but nevertheless, I have to be the boss."

We both ended up laughing over it.

Brian Spencer

"Spinner" Spencer was not enormously talented as a hockey player, but he did have a way of stirring the fans up into a frenzy, which no doubt helped him stay around for parts of ten seasons in the NHL.

I knew him from his early years in pro hockey through to his retirement and found him to be a very personable individual.

I saw him one night in the parking lot of Buffalo Memorial Auditorium after a game. He told me that he and his wife were separated and that he wasn't even allowed to get his tools to fix his van because the sheriff had made his home off-limits.

That was somewhat indicative of his up-and-down lifestyle which came to such a tragic end when he was murdered in Florida in 1988. Hockey made him a somebody, but after his playing career was over he wasn't able to find himself. It was a sorry end to someone who was so well-liked as a player.

THERE WERE many players I knew on a personal level. Officials have the chance to meet and get to know the players off the ice at various events in the off-season. Some of the players are very friendly, leaving the game on the ice. Others are not — maybe that's just their nature, or maybe they still hold a grudge against officials.

My personal philosophy was to be friendly with the players, but to be sure and keep my own space. I didn't feel it was right to get too close because I didn't want anybody to think that my being friends with a certain player affected my calls once the game started.

So I generally kept at arm's length. Still, I enjoyed talking to them, and they have my utmost admiration and respect.

16

BLOWING THE WHISTLE ON GMS AND COACHES

He said that if Bruce Hood was refereeing a Bruin game, the smart thing would be to bet on the other team.

I NEVER DID have much tolerance for people yelling at me, right from the first time I started refereeing.

Chirp Brenchly was the coach of the Port Huron Flags in the International League. It was one of my first games in the league and I hadn't learned yet that he was always in a foul mood. I was trying to concentrate on the game and make the right calls, and all the while Brenchley was screaming at me. I wasn't used to that, and I didn't appreciate it. I had to wonder if I was doing the right thing out there.

After a while I learned that it was just his nature, as it is for many coaches. My attitude was that if I had to put up with all that stuff from a coach, then there was no way a coach was going to get any breaks from me. If they thought they were gaining an edge for their team, they were wrong. The result was that the more vociferous coaches disliked me all the more. I was never in the best books of the people who tended to mouth off.

A referee is satisfied after a game if he feels he's done things right and made all the correct calls. But sometimes someone comes along and tries to make you feel like a complete incompetent, and there goes the good feeling.

This made it difficult for me to keep an open mind on the ice. Instead of calling the game as best I could, my concentration would be affected and I'd end up wondering whether I should have made the calls I did.

I should never have taken it so personally but sometimes it was impossible not to. My job was difficult enough without that kind of abuse. Although I had great respect for many general managers and coaches, I had none for those who were constantly on my case during a game or who constantly spouted off to the press or who carried the game outside the arena.

Scotty Bowman wasn't the toughest coach I ever had to deal with, but he was close. If I had been perfect I don't think he would have been satisfied. As a result we had many run-ins.

He was constantly badgering me from behind the bench. If nothing had happened during the game that he could yap about, he would start hollering about a dispute in an earlier game — even if he hadn't been involved in it. When he questioned me about something it was always in a sneering, sarcastic way, as if he was trying to convince me I was inferior.

I did receive some vindication after one incident with Bowman. It happened during a play-off game between Buffalo and Montreal when he was coaching the Canadiens. During the second period Sabre coach Joe Crozier challenged the size of Ken Dryden's goal pads.

I got a tape and made the measurement at the referee's crease by the timer's bench, with Bowman leaning over the boards looking on. The pads were too wide by about an inch. Maybe Bowman didn't trust my eyes, because he sent to the Canadiens's dressing room for their own measuring device in the shape of a U, cut to the maximum dimension for a goal pad — ten inches. I took the device from him and attempted to place it over one of the pads, but it wouldn't go.

I held the measuring device in place and looked up at Bowman. He didn't have anything to say. It was the first time I had ever dealt with him that he couldn't deny being wrong. The minor penalty I handed him was a pleasure to assess.

Chicago had two of the toughest coaches to deal with — first Billy Reay, and later on Orval Tessier — and a general manager, Tommy Ivan, who was just as bad. I'd pass Ivan in

the hallway and he'd give me a look that said I was somebody that shouldn't be treated with equal respect.

Tessier never had a good thing to say about an official in
his life, I'm sure. He treated them with disdain and didn't
seem to care what he said about them. Judging by some of
the things he allegedly said about his players, it was apparent
he treated them the same.

Reay didn't have much good to say either, and he always
seemed to be in a bad mood around the game. In Chicago
once I jumped up on the boards by the home bench to avoid
the play. There's no glass, of course, in front of players'
benches, and I jumped up on the Blackhawk bench door. As I
was perched on the ledge, I started to fall back. Reay was
right there and could have reached with his hand to support
me. Instead he moved back and let me fall all the way to the
floor. As I picked myself up to get back onto the ice, Reay
was right beside me, nattering in my ear and giving me heck
about something.

One time I actually gave a coach the opportunity to back
up his threats. Bobby Kromm, who later coached with
Detroit, was coaching a game in Kansas City in the Central
League at the time, while I was there doing some scouting
during one of my injuries. One night I saw him follow an
official up the stairs and all the way to his dressing room,
where he stood banging on the door. I went up to him and
asked what the problem was. He started cursing and swearing and calling down the official, saying among other things,
that he was yellow. I said, "I'll tell you what. If you really
want to prove how tough you are, I'll let you go in the room
with him and I'll send the two linesmen out. Then you can
decide who's yellow." He looked at me like I was nuts and
walked away.

Wren Blair, the coach of the Minnesota North Stars in their
early years, was another character behind the bench. One
night he started taking his frustrations out on one of the
linesmen, so I assessed a bench minor. There was no way
he'd have any of that. He refused to put a player in the box. I
told him that we weren't starting the game until he did. He
still refused, so I gave him a delay-of-game penalty. That did
the trick — then they were two men short.

Blair had a sense of humor though. One season I refereed four of their first six games, and then read in the local paper that he said he was going to check his roster to see if Bruce Hood was a member of his hockey team.

DISAGREEMENTS WITH coaches and general managers were part of the job. The old saying applies — if you can't stand the heat, stay out of the kitchen. Speaking as one who was in the kitchen a lot, I still disagree with the complete lack of respect shown by some coaches and general managers, who were prepared to sacrifice the official for the sake of personal gain.

That's not to say they were all like that. Most of them were fair and had respect for the job the referee had to do on the ice.

Emile Francis was one of those. Some nights he went off the deep end and got a little over-excited, but most of the time he treated the officials like human beings. You could discuss a rule of call with him and he would take the time to listen, and then discuss it in an intelligent way.

Glen Sather of Edmonton is like that, too — at least in his dealings with me. Of course you can afford to be in a better mood when Wayne Gretzky and company are the team you're coaching.

Lou Nanne was usually loose and easy to deal with. He didn't have any reservations about giving his viewpoint, but he would always listen to what you had to say.

I always enjoyed working games when Eddie Johnston was behind the bench. He is just a plain, ordinary, nice guy.

Cliff Fletcher in Calgary is a good example of one of the class people in the league. When I had occasion to come across him away from the ice, he was always very respectful. I, like any official, couldn't help but appreciate people like that.

Generally a GM or coach will have the same personality off the ice as he did on the ice. Gerry Meehan, Buffalo GM, is an excellent example of that. He was a gentleman hockey player — hard working and very dedicated. When he was the captain of the Sabres, I knew when he came to ask a question it would be an intelligent one. He wouldn't always agree with my call, but the conversation wouldn't degenerate into personal attacks on my character. He had great respect for the game of hockey when he was a player and is the same way as a general manager.

Al Arbour was a no-nonsense type as a player — and later as a coach. He never caused grief for the officials either way. Al is also right near the top of the list of class people in the league, as is Islander general manager Bill Torrey.

We used to be told by the league that if there was something that needed to be explained to the teams, we were to speak only to the captains. I always thought it made more sense to talk directly to the coach because by the time the captain relayed the information to him, it could be twisted around. Every time I did that, however, the league would tell me to use proper procedure. In Arbour's case, I liked speaking directly to him anyway, because he was easy to talk to.

Bryan Murray of Washington at first seemed to be a nice guy. I met him for the first time before the first Capitals game I officiated after he became coach. We shook hands and chatted for a while and I wished him good luck.

The game wasn't five minutes old when he started yelling and screaming at me. I kept looking at him, confused, because nothing had gone on yet. He saw me watching him with my puzzled look and screamed, "Just watch the game — don't look at me!"

Wow, I thought, we've got a beaut here. I never could figure him out. The things I thought he should bitch about, he didn't, and the things that were routine, he'd yap like crazy.

Toe Blake used to be intimidating, but in a different way, because I don't think he intended to be. But he was one coach who scared me. I had great respect for him and all his accomplishments as coach of the Montreal Canadiens, and used to work extra hard in those games to make sure I did an exceptional job. I used to just hope I did well enough to keep him off my case. Most of the time things worked out okay, but when he let out a roar . . .

Don Cherry does most of his roaring on television now, and is also known for his sense of humor. But I didn't laugh at much he had to say when he was coach of the Bruins. He caused me a lot of grief — he was always being quoted as saying how terrible the refereeing was, and many of his comments were directed at me. The most memorable one was when he said that if Bruce Hood was refereeing a Bruin game, the smart thing would be to bet on the other team.

I appeared on Don Cherry's television show after my career was over and we had a few laughs over the things he used to say, but they weren't too funny when he first said them.

Once, in another of his classic statements, he said he knew why the referees don't call many penalties when the Bruins and Flyers are playing — either they're hoping they kill each other, or they can't figure out which team they hate the most.

Don Cherry, with his flamboyant style, is a celebrity now as a commentator on "Hockey Night in Canada." I often completely disagree with his opinions, especially those regarding on-ice fighting and goon tactics. Whether or not his comments reflect what is best for the game, he's the type of person that people like to listen to.

I like Don personally, and we have been at many banquets together. I also know his wife Rose and his family. But whatever I think about him now, when he was a coach with Boston, he said a lot of things that made my job very tough. Now, of course, he can say whatever he likes without fear of retribution, and on many nights the referees are still his favorite target. Once a coach always a coach.

CHERRY AND HARRY Sinden were about equal when it came to verbal abuse of the officials. But it was Sinden who gave me the most trouble, during and even after my career.

I first ran across Sinden around 1956 when he was playing Senior hockey for the Whitby Dunlops and I was playing for the Milton Pontiacs. His team beat us on their way to winning the Allan Cup. I bumped into him next when I was refereeing in the International League. He was the playing coach of the Kingston team in the Eastern Pro League, which at the time played an interlocking schedule with the IHL.

I got to know more about him the following year, when the Eastern League folded and he moved to Minneapolis in the

Central League, again as a playing coach. He'd spout off over anything and everything that didn't go his way. He had absolutely no respect for referees. He still doesn't today.

Night after night I had to put up with his abusive language and actions. One time, Carl Voss, the referee-in-chief, came to see and supervise one of my games. I told the Minneapolis captain to tell Harry to keep it down and not talk so much, because Carl Voss was in the stands. I wanted to make a good impression and the last thing I wanted to do was deal with Sinden's antics the whole game.

The captain went and told him. While we were all skating around for the pre-game warmup, Sinden came up to me and said, "You do your fucking job out here and don't worry about me. Do your job right and I won't have to yap at you."

There was one time, however, early in both our NHL careers, when he actually congratulated me for a call I made. It was the night after I had given Ted Green and Doug Mohns match penalties — the first in many years in the NHL — for a stick-swinging duel. It must have been the call of my life, for Sinden to say anything complimentary to me.

There's no doubt that he was the most abusive player, coach or general manager I ever came across. During the Big Bad Bruin era, when it was open season on officials, it seemed like I couldn't pick up a newspaper without reading quotes from him that were critical of me. In fact it seemed at times that he and Don Cherry were holding some sort of contest to see who could bad mouth me the most.

A person would need a pretty strong character to go on the road away from home and family, and continually read quotes directed at his abilities, qualities and integrity — and then go out and referee a game without any animosity, hang-ups or bad feelings carrying over.

Even recently, years after my career ended, Sinden is still somewhat less than friendly. I ran into him, Cliff Fletcher and Tom Watt at the Olympics in Calgary. Fletcher and Watt were very receptive and very polite, but not Sinden. My son, Kevin, who was with me, later commented on how coolly Sinden had acted towards me.

During the 1987-88 play-offs, after my retirement, I had a confrontation with Sinden in Buffalo. The television studio, visitors' dressing room and officials' dressing room are all in the same area at the Auditorium. I was standing in the hall outside the studio when Sinden walked by. Staring straight ahead, he said to me, " I heard what you had to say about our hockey team the other night."

I said, "I beg your pardon?"

He continued, "I heard what you had to say about us. You bailed out on the Sabres the other night and now you dump on us. You were a horse-shit referee and you're a horse-shit television commentator."

I blew my stack and yelled back at him, first noting what I thought were the similarities between his hockey playing and management skills. Then I said, "You haven't got the guts to talk to your hockey team, you can't holler at the officials because they're in the dressing room, and now you're taking out your frustration on me. That shows how much class you've got."

He took a few steps towards me. I couldn't believe it. I didn't think he would be stupid enough to take a swing at me. He didn't.

There was another odd thing about it. After the game, I had been in the officials' room to check on referee Bill Mc-Creary, who had been hit with a puck. He was all right and I spent a few minutes talking with the guys. Before leaving the room, I said jokingly, "I'd better leave because Sinden might see me in here."

Fifteen minutes later our exchange took place.

The next night in the same hallway he went crazy again. This time he was upset at the refereeing job of Kerry Fraser. Coaches Terry O'Reilly and John Cunniff had to restrain him — they almost had to drag him to the floor. He was struggling and kicking. He even kicked at our studio door — Danny Gare opened it once and Sinden grabbed the rope handle and slammed it shut. He was like an animal. The guard outside the officials' room said Sinden kicked at him while trying to get into the room.

Afterwards, he spoke to the press about the integrity of the whole officiating staff.

What about him and the integrity of the game?

His attitude and actions are absurd and shouldn't be condoned in the game of hockey. Instead, the Boston media, many times, follows Sinden's cue. Sometimes their opinions are so slanted in Boston's favor, it's ridiculous. Their stories many times focus on the officials and accuse them of being anti-Bruin.

I never had a problem with an owner, although Ed Snider in Philadelphia was photographed down by the boards shaking his fist at me one night when I threw Bobby Clarke out of the game. I didn't see him but he was later fined for it when the photograph was sent to the league. Usually I had very little contact with owners, and that's the way I liked it. I've since got to know some and have enjoyed their company away from the game. Most teams are run like a business and each person has his job to do. The owners don't get involved that much, Harold Ballard being an exception, of course.

Most of the coaches and general managers were okay to deal with the majority of the time. But a few think their own interests are more important than the interests of the game, and that hurts hockey. They are in a position to affect the public perception with their actions and comments. That's a big responsibility—one that should be taken seriously.

THE INTERNATIONAL
CONNECTION

He told me that the Soviet Union people had said that I was to take it easy on them and not give them so many penalties.

INTERNATIONAL HOCKEY WAS something special, even way back in 1954 when a group of us huddled around a radio at the old Milton arena listening to Foster Hewitt, the voice of hockey in Canada, broadcast the world championships from Europe.

International hockey then was nothing compared with what it is today. From that famous Canada-Russia series in 1972, through the Americans' rise to gold at the Lake Placid Olympics, to any Canada Cup and, for that matter, any time it's country against country on ice — there's nothing that can beat it for intensity and excitement.

International hockey has come a long way since that day in 1954. The caliber of international officiating, unfortunately, has not kept pace. Although dramatic improvements have been made, European officiating still has a poor reputation. Many North American teams are warned by their coaches when they go overseas that the officiating will not be what they're used to. Getting upset over it, they're told, will only throw them off their game.

Part of that poor reputation stems from the inequities in the way referees are selected for tournaments. To start with, many countries have an alternating system for choosing the officials they send, so that the best from that country may not be sent in the first place. On top of that, the International Ice Hockey Federation rules state that officials for each game must be from neutral countries. Also, officials are carefully selected so that they seldom referee games that may affect the position of their own countries in the standings. The result is absolutely ludicrous, with the least qualified officials often refereeing the most crucial games. Many times these officials come from countries that are not major hockey powers with no exposure to top-level hockey.

The 1987 World Junior Championship final in Piestany, Czechoslovakia, provided a good example of that. In that game, Canada and the Soviet Union staged a wild brawl that ended with both teams being expelled from the tournament. The referee was a fellow from Norway by the name of Hans Ronning, and he very likely wouldn't have been officiating the game at all if not for the neutrality rule.

Actually I felt sorry for the Norwegian because I knew he was in over his head. If he'd been exposed to the elements of the North American or Soviet game, he probably would have been prepared to handle it. Without that exposure, he certainly wasn't. There's no question that they should have had a more qualified referee doing the game, but of course referees from Canada and the Soviet Union were ruled out, and due to the importance of the game to their own countries' chances, so were those from Sweden and Finland.

It's obvious that times are changing, however, and a more commonsense approach is developing as a result of changes in the International Ice Hockey Federation officiating committee. For example, at the Canada Cup tournament in 1987 NHL referee Don Koharski, who is Canadian, refereed some of Team Canada's games. The message is getting clearer that every referee has a lot of pride in his work and calls a game in the fairest way he can, without any bias towards his home country.

This is a vast improvement in attitude over those earlier years exemplified by Viktor Dombroski of the Soviet Union, whom many people will remember for his questionable calls in international games. There were many who felt he let his allegiance to his country come through in his work.

Steps had been taken to improve officiating as far back as the 1976 Canada Cup, when all of the countries involved in the tournament sent referees and linesmen over to Canada for a training camp. Included were Bill Friday, representing the WHA, and me, representing the NHL. The point of the training camp was to begin standardizing the system of officiating that would be used in the tournament, to get us into condition and to give us a chance to get to know one another.

Workouts included on-ice training at Upper Canada College in Toronto, as well as European-style dry-land training. Off the ice we played soccer, and the European officials could handle that ball as well as any pro hockey player could handle a puck. I would run up and down the field for half an hour, never get near the ball and still feel like I had a great workout. As impressive as the Europeans were on the soccer fields, when we hit the ice it was our turn to excel.

Off the ice and away from the playing fields we learned that the Soviet officials had one up on all of us in another area. One afternoon, after we had finished our workouts for the day, the Soviets invited us back to their hotel room for a drink. Pretty well all of the communication was in hand signals, and "drink" as you can imagine, was not too difficult to understand.

When these fellows hand-signal drink, they really mean it! About eight of us went along and when we got to the room one of the Russians took out some bottles of vodka, then got some hotel glasses and filled them all about three-quarters full — no mix, no ice, just Russian vodka!

Not willing to be ungracious guests we all tipped our glasses, knocked them back and thought that was that. Except that wasn't that, because the Russians pulled out more bottles and poured another round. This was about four-thirty in the afternoon and we had been planning to go out for dinner that night. Whether or not we made it, I'm not sure. In fact I don't remember much of the rest of that day at all. That Russian vodka really knocked me for a loop!

The first game I refereed in the tournament was between the Soviet Union and Czechoslovakia at the Montreal Forum. The two countries had had a stormy political relationship for many years, especially since 1968, when Russian tanks rolled through the streets of Prague. This was the first game played between these two teams in North America — excluding the Olympics and World Championships — and the political situation combined with the excitement of the tournament made for a highly emotional environment. The tensions off the ice carried over to the rink for both teams.

Aggie Kuklowitz, a former pro hockey player, is now the sports rep for Air Canada, and in that capacity has spent some time in the Soviet Union. He has become fairly well-known over the years as an interpreter for the Soviet hockey team. Aggie came to me before the game and told me to let him know if I had any questions or problems and he would be there at the boards to translate for me. I appreciated his presence because sometimes it's difficult explaining something to players who can speak English, let alone to those who can't.

The level of play in that game was unbelievable. The ice surfaces here are much smaller than those in Europe so there was more contact than either team was accustomed to. In the early going, bodies were flying all over the place. There was the usual number of penalties. With all that speed and contact it was one of the most exciting games I'd ever been involved in.

At the end of the first period Aggie came to our dressing room. He was very hyper, obviously caught up in all the excitement. He had just come from the Russian dressing room and he told me that the Soviet Union people said that I was to take it easy on them and not give them so many penalties. I wondered what the heck that was all about, but of course I paid no attention to their request and refereed the rest of the game in my normal fashion.

The Czechs went on to win that game 5-3 but lost to Canada in the finals. I couldn't referee any of those final games because of the neutral-country rule, but the whole tournament was a thrill for me. It was my first experience of the exciting world of international hockey and it set the stage for much more to come.

MY NEXT INVOLVEMENT with international hockey was also my first hockey experience overseas. In 1979 John

D'Amico and I were invited to Kiev, in the Soviet Union, for a week as part of a five-year agreement that would see exchanges of hockey officials and coaches.

We went to Toronto airport on Sunday, September 2. Our flight was scheduled for seven-twenty that evening but ended up not leaving until midnight. We arrived in Frankfurt fifteen minutes before our connecting flight to Moscow was scheduled to leave. We missed that and had to scramble for other arrangements, and just managed to get the last two seats on another flight.

The airport people in Frankfurt whisked us through the terminal on a golf cart to catch the other flight. As we turned one corner I almost fell off the cart in surprise. Standing in front of us, looking ready for action, was a guard with a machine gun across his chest. I had never seen anything like that before.

We got to Moscow in time for lunch and were met by Andrei Starovoitov, head of the Soviet Union Ice Hockey Federation officiating program, as well as the controversial head of the IIHF referees committee. He welcomed us to the Soviet Union and introduced us to a lady by the name of Valentina, who would be our escort and interpreter for the entire trip. Valentina was a big woman, almost six feet tall, and though pretty she left the impression she could pin you in a wrestling match.

After we left Mr. Starovoitov we proceeded to another airport in Moscow and spent the next twenty-four hours wondering if we would ever get to Kiev. I had heard about the inefficiency in the Soviet system, but I hadn't realized I was going to find out firsthand.

Our flight was scheduled to leave Moscow at nine-twenty that evening, but that turned out to be wishful thinking. The flight was delayed again and again, until finally we had to spend the entire night there.

The next day I made some phone calls to the Canadian embassy, which in turn got in touch with the Sports Federation in Moscow to find out what was going on. We were not in the best of moods at this point and were almost ready to go home. We got a flight, finally. But that didn't make us feel any better. At the time there was a lot of talk about the

Soviets spending so much money on their space program that they couldn't afford to look after their in-country planes. As we proceeded along the tarmac to board our flight we saw this for ourselves: we passed plane after plane that had been taken out of operation, all in various states of disrepair, including some with missing engines.

This didn't exactly inspire confidence in our plane. Inside it was loaded half with people and half with cargo. The cargo, mostly sacks of wheat, was piled at the back of the plane and wasn't even tied down. Any kind of a rough landing and everything would have spilled forward onto us.

Two days after leaving Toronto we finally made it to Kiev, exhausted from the host of problems with our flight plans. Years later, when I had my own travel agency, I learned the nightmares that can surface in flight arrangements, but I have never come across anything as ridiculous as that trip.

To top it all off, when we got there nobody came to meet us. We waited awhile and then finally got in a cab and went to the Sports Federation building ourselves. Although we still weren't in the best of spirits, all was pretty much forgiven when we met a chap who had waited at the Kiev airport until three a.m. the previous night.

We left there and after learning firsthand about Soviet driving attitudes — anything goes — we finally got to our hotel. It was beside the Dnieper River and offered a nice view of a beautiful city. The very narrow cobblestoned streets reminded me of Quebec City.

We met a representative from the Soviet Ice Hockey Federation and learned that we were supposed to officiate in a game that night. That wasn't a very good idea as far as we were concerned, because we hadn't been to bed in two days and our energy was sapped, so we ended up just watching.

It was my first chance to see, in person, a game played on the larger European ice surfaces. There was less body contact because of the size of the rink, but the speed of the game was faster.

While in Kiev we put on a clinic for the Russian officials and officiated games in the tournament that was taking place between teams from Russia, Poland and Czechoslovakia. We also did some sightseeing and took part in a phenomenon that is very popular over there — pin exchanging. We had brought about 200 little maple leaf pins. All kinds of people, even those not involved in hockey, were anxious to make some kind of trade or deal for those pins. Once one person found out we had Canada pins, it seemed others came out of the woodwork to try to get one for themselves.

I was used to having a cola between periods, but in Russia, at the time, neither Coke nor Pepsi was readily available. When the trainer of the local hockey team heard that I wanted one, he showed up with a couple of Pepsis. All he wanted, of course, were more pins.

I spent some time evaluating the style and system of the Russian officiating. They had a different system for linesmen that took us a while to understand. The main difference was that the linesman who got the puck after a stoppage in play went to the face-off location, even if it wasn't in his end, and stayed there to drop the puck. In the North American game, the linesman working a given half of the ice surface takes all the face-offs in his end only. The other linesman gets the puck and hands it to him.

I thought the referee did not get as involved in the play as he could have. A lot of calls were made — or not made — from a distance. I felt they should have tried to get closer to the play. Generally, though, the wider ice surface is better for the referee because there is extra room for him to skate, and less chance of injury.

The European referees were fortunate in that the teams over there were more disciplined and showed the officials more respect, which made the games easier to control. That, among other reasons, is why North American referees would probably be able to adjust to the European game easily, while Europeans would have a more difficult time adapting to the North American style.

I think this has been proven over the years. The more frequent body contact in the North American game requires more judgment. The European referees sometimes couldn't believe their eyes when they worked a game with a North American team. In recent years, however, European players have converted, to some degree, to the North American style, and the quality of European officiating has improved tremendously.

The Soviet people were friendly and the countryside beautiful. A touching moment for me came after the tournament when we were set to board the train to Moscow. The officials we had worked with showed up at the train station to say a final farewell and present us with gifts. I received a beautiful silver samovar.

We took the overnight train to Moscow and spent the next day touring the city with Valentina. We saw the Kremlin and Red Square, took a ride on the subway to admire the clean and astonishingly beautiful stations, and saw the site of the 1980 Summer Olympics. We capped the day off at the Canadian embassy, where we visited with one of the officials, Jim Wright—and where I enjoyed my first Canadian beer in a week.

We headed to the airport and said our farewells to Valentina, who had turned out to be a super friend and escort, and then climbed on our plane for the long flight home. When we landed in Toronto we were exhausted, but also satisfied and feeling lucky to have been able to make such a memorable trip. On our return we reported to the NHL training camp in Toronto and jumped right into another season — my sixteenth.

IN 1981 I HAD another opportunity to work a Canada Cup series. Another training camp was held for officials from all the countries, this time in Edmonton. It was a fun camp; we worked hard, but we also got a chance to play some hockey, and one thing we found out for certain was that North American officials are far better at hockey than European officials.

We had some fun off the ice as well. One night Andy van Hellemond, who was the other Canadian referee, organized an evening at the racetrack. A big fan of horse racing, he arranged to get us into the dining room for dinner and a night of picking the horses.

The Russian referee had never seen a harness race in his life and obviously couldn't read the program. But he'd study the horses very carefully and, when he had made up his mind, show us on his fingers the number of the horse he thought would win. I wasn't picking any winners myself, so after a while I thought what the heck, I'd go with his system. And I started winning! On the final race of the night he picked horse number 4, so I bet it as well. We had to return to the hotel before that race was run, but I checked the paper the next day and sure enough I had won another.

Right away I went looking for Aggie, our interpreter, and got him to ask the Russian referee how he did it. The guy had picked four winners in a row! The Russian explained that he had watched the horses in their warm-ups to see how the drivers handled them. He decided if the drivers had to restrain them, those were the horses who were ready to go and would most likely win. Any handicapper will tell you there's more to it than that, but for that night, at least, he had the right system.

The night before the tournament opened, the teams and pretty well everyone else — coaches, general managers and sponsors — gathered for a banquet. We officials were seated at the back, right beside the kitchen where the waiters and waitresses brought the food into the room.

After dinner came the introductions. Everyone, including the organ player, who was seated beside us, was introduced. Everyone, that is, except us, the officials.

It didn't bother me too much, because I was just happy to be there and be part of it all. But it was a good example of how officials are given more respect in Europe than in North America. Over there, they are highly respected and might have been the first people introduced at a banquet of that nature. After the conclusion of a game in Europe, and in international games, in most instances, the team captains go over and shake hands with the referee and linesmen.

We went up to the head table at the conclusion of the ceremonies, while people were leaving, and asked Al Eagleson, the Canada Cup head honcho, if he had forgotten about us. He said, "Oh damn, you guys were on the list there. I don't know what the hell happened that you never got introduced, but you know we were thinking of you."

During the course of that 1981 Canada Cup, Lou Nanne of the Minnesota North Stars who was general manager with team U.S.A., became upset with linesmen John D'Amico and

Ray Scapinello. He complained that they had called a game too strictly and that maybe they shouldn't be as tough on North American teams.

John and Ray were flabbergasted. There had been a couple of calls in the game — such as an icing being waved off — that could have gone either way but had ended up going against Lou's team. Lou doesn't hesitate to say what's on his mind. Things were hot and heavy for a while and it took a couple of days for him to settle down.

That game was proof that no matter which countries were playing, the officials were going to call the game the way they saw it. That's the way John and Ray have always done their job and that's why they were there to begin with.

One change that had been made since the previous Canada Cup, with the agreement of all the teams, was that the linesmen would all be from North America. This was for two reasons — their excellent abilities and the fact that they were already here. Selecting referees for games was not going to be quite as easy. Scotty Morrison, referee-in-chief of the NHL at the time, was responsible for the chore, with a mandate to keep in mind the neutrality factor as much as possible.

Some countries — including Sweden, Finland and the United States — consented to Canadian referees doing games in which Team Canada was playing, though it wasn't a policy that was readily instituted. For example, if Andy or I was allowed to work a game in which Team Canada played Sweden, then maybe the Russians would demand that their own referee be used in a game against some other team — and nobody could be sure of one of their officials.

The political jockeying was unbelievable. Selections were made to try to satisfy everyone and often involved assigning a referee for one game so that someone else could referee another game later on. Scotty didn't have a lot of fun with that job.

The setup for the tournament was much the same as for those in Europe. Two games were played on the same day — one in the afternoon and one in the evening. I enjoyed working the afternoon games. I could get up in the morning, have a late breakfast, go to the arena to work the game, be finished by four-thirty or five o'clock and then go up to the press lounge and have a bite to eat and a beer.

Linesman Leon Stickle and I worked the afternoon game one day and had dinner and a few beers while watching the next one. We were sitting up in the stands, enjoying ourselves, when one of the European officials got hurt. We both looked at each other and realized one of us might have to work. We weren't in the best condition to skate, let alone officiate, and were relieved that the injury was minor and the game could carry on. Whew!

The series came down to the final game in Montreal between the Soviet Union and Canada. I had reported to the NHL training camp by then, and watched on television as the Soviets trounced the Canadians, 8-1.

IN 1983 I WAS invited to go to Finland by the Finnish Ice Hockey Federation, to participate in an officiating seminar. I headed over in June of that year, along with Joanne — her first trip abroad.

We flew to Helsinki and the view from the plane was breathtaking. It was like a hidden city — you could hardly see it for the foliage. Kim Pihl and Esa-Tuomas Malinen came to the airport to meet us and escort us into the city. Both Kim and Esa had attended my refereeing school in previous years and it was great to see them again, as we had become good friends.

We stayed at Kim's apartment downtown, which turned out to be a wonderful arrangement because Helsinki is not very big and you can walk just about everywhere to take in all the sights. We had arrived a couple days early so we had a chance to do some sightseeing, with Esa our guide.

They have very strict liquor laws in Finland, as I found out right away. Esa, Kim and I were having a beer in a bar across the street from Kim's place and I told a joke that involved sliding off the bar stool a couple of times. On the next order for beers, the barmaid said something in Finnish and both Esa and Kim started laughing. She said she could not serve me because I was obviously drunk, falling off the stool and all. She wouldn't budge, either, and it took a lot of talking I didn't understand to get her to change her mind.

The seminar was set to run from Friday through Sunday and was held on the outskirts of Helsinki, at Verimaki, a beautiful, wooded setting that is used to develop Finland's

Olympic and international athletes. The pole-vaulters were there and so was the cross-country ski team, whose members were training with wheel-equipped skis. They would fly down the miles of paved pathways and we could hear them coming through the woods long before we saw them.

The seminar was attended by most of the senior officials in the Finnish Ice Hockey Federation. We spent a lot of time on the ice doing various routines and I was also able to show them some stretching exercises, the benefits of which were becoming more appreciated at the time. Stretching makes for less chance of a pulled muscle and improves a referee's agility for dodging pucks or getting out of the way of players.

Most of the officials on hand couldn't speak much English. When I was instructing a course in a classroom there would always be an interpreter there to translate the discussion. As well, the instructional films I had brought from Canada were well-received. The Finns were able to add a number of elements to their training program. It felt good to be able to offer something important to another group of officials, and especially to my friends in Finland.

MY NEXT TRIP to Europe was in December 1984, to referee in the Spengler Cup. This oldest hockey tournament in Europe is held in Davos, a beautiful city nestled in a Swiss mountain valley.

The tournament is very popular in Europe and is televised in three different languages in Switzerland alone. The top teams from each country don't participate, but usually a club team is sent as the representative. Canada's entry was made up of a number of Canadians playing professionally in Switzerland, along with some Canadian university students and a few minor pros. It's exciting hockey, played before packed houses.

I had been invited as part of their policy to have two guest officials join the Swiss officials at the tournament. Dag Olsen, the veteran from Sweden, was the other one.

All the officials stayed at the same hotel. When we arrived a meeting was called. Rene Fazel, in charge of the officials for the tournament, led us in a discussion of some rule interpretations and applications. Rene told us that the teams played good hockey and that we should let them play if they stuck to hockey. If they wanted to act up, then we should apply the rules and get them out of there.

I worked the first game of the tournament and everything went well. One incident involved a lot of pushing and shoving in front of the net, but based on our pre-tournament briefing I didn't feel it was that serious and didn't hand out penalties.

Rene explained to me later that Europeans expect penalties in situations like that. So I said that was fine with me and from then on I applied my usual standard and let the players know that kind of stuff was not acceptable.

The way they arranged the seating at the arena was amusing. Fans would be in place two hours before the game, packed in elbow to elbow on the bench seats according to which team they were cheering. For example, all the German fans were put in one section and all the Swiss in another. This allowed the fans to wave their banners, ring their bells, sing their songs and generally have a great time together in support of their team.

In one game the Swiss referee, Willie Voglin, got into a little hot water and brought the wrath of the people down on him. He had done okay, but he really hadn't taken charge the way he should have.

There was a meeting that night and I suggested that they put Willie right back in the next game to indicate that there was faith in his work. I had been scheduled to work that next game, but after all, I was going back to Canada so it wasn't going to matter how many games I worked. It was more important that the Swiss referee, who worked there full-time, not let his confidence or the confidence of the fans and teams deteriorate because of one questionable Spengler Cup game.

Rene agreed and it turned out to be the right decision, because Willie went out the next day with the support of his fellow tournament officials and was right on top of his game. That demonstrated he had the confidence and skills to do the job. The opportunity to play a part in restoring the confidence of a young man was very important to me because many times I had been in a similar position.

Rene Fazel is now the Swiss representative on the board of the International Ice Hockey Federation tournament and has been elected to the position of chairman of federation officials. His attitude and experience made him a natural choice. He has tremendous rapport with all the countries and certainly with all the officials. International officiating will rise as a result of his being there.

Canada ended up in the finals of the Spengler Cup that year and went on to win it. I wasn't able to officiate but I still enjoyed being there to watch the final game.

IN 1985 ALAN EAGLESON asked if I would like to officiate at the world championships in Prague. The answer was easy — of course I would. Al filled me in on the details, including that a seminar would be held for all the officials in the summer, in Germany. He told me not to worry about that, because I wouldn't need to attend. As it turned out, the dates of the camp would have conflicted with my annual referee school anyway.

Later I found out my name was on the roster of that camp and they were a little surprised that I didn't show, because a Canadian delegation had indicated I would be there.

I flew to Czechoslovakia at tournament time and was anxious to see how hospitable the people would be. I found out soon after arriving at the airport. As I was clearing customs and immigration I handed my passport to the guard who was standing in the inspection booth in his uniform. He looked at me solemn-faced and then at the passport, and then a big grin broke out on his face. He said, "Canada . . . welcome," and put out his hand.

That's how it was everywhere I went. As soon as they found out I was Canadian, they smiled and said hello. If they spoke a little English they tried to make conversation. They are wonderful people and their country is one of the most beautiful I have ever visited.

After leaving the airport I was taken directly to the arena. A meeting of all the officials concerning the rules and their interpretation was just ending when I got there and some of the officials were already leaving. I felt awfully conspicuous walking in but there were quite a few familiar faces so I went in and made the rounds. Andrei Starovoitov, the head of the officiating committee at the time, was there along with several officials with whom I would be working during the tournament. Most of them I knew from past tournaments — some had been to our training camps, some had been to my referee school and some I had worked with in the Canada Cup.

Each country had its own representative. There was Dr. Vladamir Subrt, a longtime friend from Czechoslovakia, Yuri Karandin from the Soviet Union, Perti Juhola of Finland, Josef Kompalla from Germany, Mark Faucette of the U.S.A. and Kjell Lind from Sweden.

Most of the linesmen were from Czechoslovakia, including Jan Taticek, Miroslav Lipina, Slavomir Caban and Josef Kriska. Lasse Vanhanen represented Finland, Rainer Kluge was from East Germany, Uwe van de Fenn from West Germany, Kjell Karlsson from Sweden and Igor Prusov from the Soviet Union.

It was also good to see Milan Jirka, an up-and-coming official from Czechoslovakia who had been to my referee school years before and who would eventually work in the 1988 Olympics in Calgary.

Bob Nadin represented Canada on the referees committee along with Ove Dahlberg from Sweden, Quido Adamec from Czechoslovakia, Willie Penz from Germany and of course, Andrei Starovoitov from the Soviet Union.

Starovoitov was an amazing man and an imposing figure in that room. He didn't speak any English — I don't think — and had an interpreter with him everywhere he went. He was like the godfather to all those officials in international hockey. When he said jump, they jumped.

It was often clear which country he owed his allegiance to. Sometimes this was evident in decisions he made in games involving two other countries, affecting his country.

Following the meeting I met with Bob Nadin and Mark Faucette. It was neat working with Mark. Many years before I had worked with his father when he had been an American Hockey League linesman in his hometown, Springfield, Massachusetts. Mark was a good young American prospect on the NHL staff and had been chosen to represent the U.S.A. in the World Championships. He worked his first games in the NHL during the 1987-88 season.

We stayed at the Tri Pstrosi Hotel, which translates as the Three Ostriches. It was a 400-year-old building only four stories high that actually looked like a big old house. It stood near the main part of town, in old Prague right next to Charles Bridge, which had been built in the fourteenth century.

The hotel contained eighteen rooms in a variety of different shapes and sizes. I lucked out — there was little doubt I got the best room in the whole place. It was so big that it was actually like a three-bedroom apartment. It had a refrigerator, table and chairs, a big bed, a chesterfield, a television and a startling view of that old bridge. My room was actually called "The Blue Room" in recognition of Labatt's Blue, one of the sponsors of Team Canada. It turned out to be a rather fitting name.

Labatt's had flown hundreds of cases of beer over from Canada and Doug Kelcher, who was the official Labatt's representative, gave me a dozen cases to share with the officials and other friends. He was staying at a different hotel, but we had cars supplied to us so I put the twelve cases in the back of mine and drove them over to our hotel. I stocked up the fridge and my room quickly became "the meeting place."

It was usually quite a scene because there wasn't a lot to do after the games were over. Officials from every country would sit around my room and have a gab session. While the majority could speak some English, there were some who couldn't, so if there were any jokes told there had to be someone interpreting. It's funny, though — after you have been around people long enough they seem to be able to understand what you are talking about. You become a pretty closely knit group when you have that common denominator — officiating hockey.

The ringleader of the officials was Josef Kompalla of West Germany. If there was anything going on, he was in the center of it. He was the type of guy you couldn't help but like. And he sure liked our Labatt's Blue.

As far as working games in the series, I didn't do any that involved Team Canada, of course. And because Canada was involved in games right through to the finals, I wasn't allowed to officiate any games that might affect the standings around them. The same rule generally applied when it came to using the American referee for Canada's games. They figured the officiating still would not be neutral, since he was from North America, too.

As neutral as the system was supposed to be, it seemed that Starovoitov, the head of the officiating committee, had attempted to take the American referee, Mark Faucette, under his wing. Mark was bothered by this because he felt that Starovoitov was trying to sway his thinking in calling a game.

After two games had been played in the tournament a meeting was called at our hotel. Starovoitov talked in Russian and I could sense that he wasn't very happy. I could see the heads of the officials who spoke or understood some Russian beginning to droop. Then the interpreter translated the speech to us. I couldn't believe what he was saying — that the quality of officiating had been terrible and that he was very upset. I was sitting at the end of the table across from Mark and he was just shaking his head.

I said to him, "I don't believe this."

After the speech I asked Starovoitov what the problem was exactly, but he never really got into detailing his complaints and didn't like my asking for his reasoning.

The consensus after the meeting was that Starovoitov was trying to intimidate the officials and particularly Mark, who — surprise — was working the next Soviet game.

Jim Proudfoot had this to say in his May 1, 1985, *Toronto Star* column:

OFFICIATING IN PRAGUE JUST ABSURD

PRAGUE — The World Hockey Championships are a big-time sport event, without a doubt, except for one thing: the officiating is totally, absurdly Mickey Mouse.

Evidence to support such a claim lies in the fact that Andrei Starovoitov, a superannuated zebra from the Soviet Union, is chief of the referees — the Scotty Morrison, that is, of the International Ice Hockey Federation.

This is the equivalent of a bank hiring a safecracker to set up its security system.

Comrade Starovoitov is probably a decent chap who doesn't beat his wife or kick small children. He seems like a nice enough guy. But his priorities are all wrong for the job he's got. His primary objective is victory for the Soviet side. It's got to be or he wouldn't be allowed past the Moscow city limits.

So a lot of the blame for an absolutely silly situation rests with the IIHF itself for appointing Starovoitov in the first place and for sticking with a setup that no longer makes sense. You could get two countries facing off here for the global title and the game would be refereed by a man the participants agreed upon. No kidding. That's the way it works. Each would have the right to veto an appointment. And so the poorest official here could end up handling the season's most important contest.

The opposite is what ought to happen, actually. The crucial matches should draw the best striped shirts, as selected by the person in charge. And his decision should stand, no matter what, above any nationalistic concerns.

The problem is nobody trusts Starovoitov to act objectively. Events here would seem to justify that point of view, all right. On the other hand nobody trusts anybody at these festivals of shinny.

Mark Faucette of the U.S. was assigned to Canada's confrontation with the Soviets last week. Beforehand, he and the other referees were lectured at length by Starovoitov. His point was that certain individuals in the room had been excessively lenient with rough play and that he wanted a clampdown.

"I worked in the National Hockey League for 21 years," reported Bruce Hood, the Canadian official here. "And I was never subjected to abuse like that."

Faucette chose to believe he was the specific target and that the evening's game was what Starovoitov was really talking about. Offended and defiant, he went out and acted as though he were in the NHL. That is to say he permitted plenty of physical contact. The Soviet players, 9-1 winners, didn't seem to mind. But Starovoitov was livid. He announced Faucette's suspension from the tournament.

IIHF bigwigs informed him he was out of line. In fact, Canada and the U.S. took Faucette for their Monday matchup—hardly a choice the Canadian coaches would have welcomed. Starovoitov tried to block them but couldn't. So he put out a press release emphasizing Faucette had been nominated over his objection.

"What he's really tried to do," fumed Thayer Tutt, head of the American Amateur Hockey Association, "is to intimidate all the referees in Russia's favor for the rest of the schedule. We'll have to wait and see if he's succeeded."

Kjell Lind of Sweden will do the Canada-Russia rematch tonight. Hood, a professional first and foremost, would be preferable in every way but the IIHF doesn't operate in that manner. Lind will be out there because he's the least offensive and not because he'll produce a good show.

Starovoitov is coming to the end of his term as a member of the IIHF's inner circle and the guessing is he won't be re-elected. Here's the opportunity to put a forceful, honorable, independent individual in that pivotal office. But don't expect it to happen. They're liable to go for Josef Kompalla. The Russians love Joe.

The highlight of the tournament was definitely the game between Czechoslovakia and the Soviet Union. The Soviets had been everybody's choice to win the championship, with Canada a likely second and the Czechs a close third. But in this game the Czechs came up big in front of their own fans and won the game. In its intensity it reminded me of the game I had seen in Montreal between the same teams during the 1976 Canada Cup, a game that put them into the finals against Canada.

The whole city of Prague went wild with happiness, as if it was a victory for the whole country rather than just for a hockey team.

The Czechs went on to defeat Canada in an exciting final game, which of course prompted more celebrations. I was involved with CBC radio during the tournament and helped with the commentary on that final game.

When that final day arrived and everything was wrapped up, it was time for the officials closing ceremonies. We had our regular get-together and then it was time for the special ceremony.

During the tournament, the skates I had worn for a long while as an NHL referee had finally fallen apart. We decided that to climax the tournament we would launch them off the Charles Bridge into the Vltava River. We made our way to the front steps of the hotel, where I put the skates on; it had been decided that it would be proper to wear them. There were about forty of us there at this stage, including some of the writers who had covered the championships, friends of the officials, and my son, Kevin, who had flown in a few days earlier to see Prague and enjoy the final few games. We proceeded up the cobblestoned street and onto the bridge, with cameras flashing and sparks flying from the blade contact on the stone.

The others raised glasses in a salute while I removed the skates and ceremoniously dropped them into the river, one at a time, to the sound of cheers from all the onlookers. It was quite a scene — a fitting farewell to my old pair of skates and a great way to wrap up a World Championship after a fantastic stay in Prague.

EXTRACURRICULAR
ACTIVITIES

*The officials dressed in a room downstairs from the main
level and sometimes the money would just be thrown
from the top of the stairs.*

T HE NHL SCHEDULE is a tough grind for a referee.
With all the games and travel, it seemed like whenever I got
back home during the season there was just enough time to
get the laundry done, arrange more airline tickets and discipline the children based on what had gone on during my
absence. By then it was time to rush off to the airport again.

As much as officials or players enjoy their work, the off-
season is a special time of year. By the end of the summer, of
course, everybody is anxious to get back into action. But
during those few months off, an official's time is his own, to
do with as he chooses, whether it's fishing, working at
another job or continuing his education. Everyone has his
own way to relax and revitalize himself.

For me, the best way to relax was to keep busy, and I was
fortunate enough to have a number of opportunities to do
just that.

A twist of fate, oddly enough involving the World Hockey
Association, led me to one activity that has turned out to be a
mainstay in my summer schedule for the past fifteen years.

Until 1972 I had worked in the summers as an instructor at
Vern Buffey's referee school in Haliburton. When the WHA
came into being that year, Vern moved over to that league as

its referee-in-chief. There was no love lost between the NHL and the WHA in those days, and it was strongly suggested by the NHL that we not be involved in any activities involving WHA officials. If not for this directive I would likely have been content to continue with Vern's school as an instructor.

I had enjoyed the work and had learned a lot about how to run a school like that so I figured, why not? — and Bruce Hood's International School of Refereeing was born.

Over the years it has been located in Haliburton, Bobcageon and Milton, and at the University of Guelph in conjunction with the CAN/AM elite hockey camp. The "international" part of the name has certainly rung true — each year half the students are Canadian, half are American. Officials have also come from around the world, from countries like Finland, Sweden, Czechoslovakia, Holland, England and Australia.

There are usually about eighty pupils at the school at a time, divided into four groups of twenty. Each school session runs from Sunday to Friday night, during which time we run as thorough and intense a program as possible.

Operating the school is a big responsibility and I am fortunate that my son Kevin and my daughter Marilyn have pretty much handled most of the administrative duties — registration, operating the pro shop, etc. — in recent years.

Certainly the other officials who instruct at the school are a major part of its success. John D'Amico, the veteran linesman who retired from the NHL in 1988, is an excellent example of that. John is one of the top instructors we have at the school; Ron Wicks, Leon Stickle and Bob Hodges are a few of the many who have been involved over the years. Each year we invite a number of NHL referees and linesmen, as well as representatives from other leagues, who cover all the rule variations.

A typical morning at the school starts out with a skating session featuring specialized power-skating training and exercises specifically designed for officials. After that it's on to some classroom sessions for discussion of, and instruction in, such topics as mental approach and situation handling. Before lunch there's a break for a stretching program, and after lunch it's either to the rink for more drills — positioning, signals, face-offs, and so on — or to the sports field for out-door activities. In the evening, the officials work actual games. These are videotaped. Following the game is a discussion period.

The school provides students with the opportunity to learn from qualified instructors, allows them to compare themselves with other officials and gives them the chance to be seen. Most have bettered themselves and moved up the ladder, some into the pro ranks. A couple of examples are Andy van Hellemond who attended Vern Buffey's National School of Refereeing, and linesman Leon Stickle, who showed, at my school, what he was capable of and subsequently went on to the NHL.

One of the students we had in our earlier years is unique in that he wears the black and white in two chosen fields. First and foremost Father Jim Armstrong is Catholic priest in the Pittsburgh area and chaplain of the NHL officiating staff, and second, he's a referee — not only in hockey, but also in football and basketball. On top of that he also umpires baseball and softball. He now attends the school every year, assisting with officiating instruction and counselling as a priest. He has also gotten to know many of the players in the NHL, and attends weddings and various events across Canada and the United States. He is one of the best public speakers I know, and I'm always amused at how he catches people off guard. When he gets up to the speak at one of the many functions he attends, people think they're in for a long, boring speech from a priest. By the end of it they're rolling in the aisles.

We get all kinds at the school, as young as fourteen and as old as sixty-one. Some have never been on skates before. Most of the students, though, are in their early twenties and come to the school full of energy and ambition. We've had women as well, and some of them have done extremely well for themselves.

The students work hard, but we also have time for some fun. We put on a talent show one of the evenings, with each class contributing some acts. For example, they might re-enact game situations, poking fun at how the referee makes his hand signals. It makes for some good innocent fun in a relaxed atmosphere, and let me tell you, some of the performances can get pretty bizarre.

I have often made it a point, when I'm visiting different parts of Canada and the United States, to call up people who have attended the camp. The friendships I've developed over the years with officials from all over the world is one of the most rewarding things about operating the school.

AT ONE TIME high-quality referee sweaters were unavailable in Canada. It seemed to me that a manufacturer in Canada would make sense, so I approached a company by the name of Tease Knit of Toronto (since been purchased by Saxon Athletic Manufacturing), and we began to work on one.

A referee sweater may just be a sweater to the fans but to an official it is more than that — it has to have the proper knit, cuff, waistband and collar. It has to be roomy and should be comfortable. After about four years of working on the sweater we finally came up with a design we were happy with. Then it was a matter of going out and proving its quality. That did not turn out to be a problem at all — each year the number of sweaters manufactured has doubled. They are now being sold all over North America and in parts of Europe. It is worn in the NHL and OHL, as well as in college hockey and, coast-to-coast, in many different leagues.

During the time the sweater was being developed I sustained an injury that made me think that more protection around the shinbone, kneecap and side of the knee would be a big help to officials. I went to Cooper Canada and worked with Norm Widdis, a specialist in pad development, on a new model of referee shin guard. After about three years and many prototypes, we worked out the kinks and put the new design on the market. The demand has been huge. The guard is worn by officials worldwide.

Elbow injuries are another problem. At one time there seemed to be so many that Scotty Morrison insisted that all officials wear elbow pads. But the kind hockey players use are too big. I worked again with Cooper Canada, this time with Ross Johnson, and we designed an elbow pad that wasn't too bulky, folded properly with the arm and provided good protection for the elbow and the bone structure around it. As with the shin guards it involved a lot of fiddling with the design. After finalization and testing, the pads hit the market and became very successful.

Another problem officials used to have was getting a standard referee pant. They used to be all different materials and shades of black. In the beginning we wore a black dress pant that had no give to it. After a while the legs looked like stovepipes. I was able to lend my knowledge of what officials like to Saxon Athletic Manufacturing, and help create a new design. A knit material solved many of the problems — it provided the flexibility we needed, looked good and had the crease sewn in to keep the legs looking neat.

DOUG MOORE WAS the chief engineer at Maple Leaf Gardens for almost forty years and knew a little about ice! When water freezes on the rink in the usual way, the impurities rise to the surface layer. What the players skate on can be soft and mushy, resulting in more snow buildup. Doug came up with a new water-treatment system he named "Jet Ice" and the best-quality ice became available in many more arenas. Doug's system puts the water through a de-mineralization process that removes the oxygen and other impurities from it, and then allows it to freeze properly. More and more NHL arenas are using Jet Ice, with excellent results.

I was involved with the world of ice-making right from the time the first artificial ice was installed in the old Milton arena. I also studied refrigeration and got my operator's certificate. So I was always fascinated by the subject. Before Doug and his innovation came along, the ice in many arenas around the NHL was poor. There could have been many reasons — too much heat in the arenas, incompetent arena workers, too many different events held in the arena, the ice damaged by being covered with boards or by being constantly put in and out. But as it turned out, the real culprit in most instances was the quality of the water.

I traveled with Doug and introduced him to the people responsible for the ice in NHL and other rinks. It was the least I could do for such a good cause.

Megnets are another innovation important to the game. Dennis Megs, whom I knew in connection with Doug Moore, invented the nets. After seeing them, I was convinced he had a timely idea.

The old Art Ross style of net had been used since 1927. That kind of net was held in place by six-inch, solid-steel posts and had no give. In the Megnet system, a magnet is installed in each post of the goal frame. The posts attach themselves firmly to tapered metal pieces that extend about one inch out of the floor. The result is a net that gives way much more easily when someone crashes into it, which prevents injuries. The goal frame has also been redesigned, to help keep the puck in the net as well as to remove the sharp center point that used to stick out from the bottom middle of the net, a point that caused a serious injury to Mark Howe.

I was more than willing to do anything I could to help Dennis. I arranged for Scotty Morrison to go to Waterloo, where the Megnets were in place in the college arena, so he could see the benefits. I also arranged for Dennis to present his idea at the NHL meetings in Montreal, and sent my VCR along for his demonstration. It wasn't difficult for Dennis to convince others of his net's advantages. Megnets are now compulsory in the NHL and many other leagues.

There are still some problems with the Megnet system, mostly stemming from improper installation in some buildings and the fact that certain teams or players will push them off their moorings to stop play when things get hot and heavy in their own end. Still, if they can save the career of one hockey player, then they are worth it.

Neil Degle, a hockey official from the Boston area who has worked at my referee school for many years, developed a device to measure hockey sticks for width, length of blade and curvature to determine whether they are legal or not. He asked me to help him finalize his invention, which I did, and then I arranged for him to present it to Scotty Morrison. It received a trial in the NHL and is now standard equipment in that and most other leagues.

IN THE MID-SEVENTIES I thought I'd better start looking for some work to do when I retired from the NHL. Real estate looked promising and I drew up a rough plan for my retirement days whereby I would sell real estate during the summer around my cottage in Wasaga Beach and then spend the cold winters in Florida or some other warm place.

During the summer of 1978 I attended school, obtained my real-estate license and went to work for a Milton real-estate company owned by a friend of mine, Gary Thomas. At the start it seemed like a pretty exciting world. I got some listings and made some sales and things seemed to be going along pretty well.

One Friday night Joanne and I had invited some friends to our home for a barbecue. At about five o'clock, just as I was getting ready to put the steaks on, I got a call from some people who wanted to look at a property right away. I realized right then that real estate was putting too much strain on my time: I'd be gone all winter and then be gone all summer. It wasn't fair to Joanne, especially, so I went back to operating my referee school and putting on seminars around the country.

I like to compare real estate with refereeing. I tell young referees that if they work hard and get the breaks, they'll succeed. They need the right tools, but as in real estate, a major part of any success comes from being in the right place at the right time to get the proper exposure.

I HAD TO GIVE UP some activities during my career because of time restrictions. The Lions Club in Milton, of which I was a charter member, was one. Another was playing bass drum in a militia pipe band, the Lorne Scots. I had been a member for about ten years, right up to 1967. We traveled around playing at many different events, and each year we used to welcome the Santa Claus parade to Milton by marching up and down the ice at the town arena. I enjoyed being in the band; probably the highlight of that experience was in 1959 when we flew to Scotland — my first overseas trip — to participate in the Edinburgh Festival.

Tennis is a favorite sport and is a great way to keep in shape. As president of the Milton Tennis Club on two occasions, I was able to help a lot of dedicated volunteers plan and create a new headquarters.

Community involvement and charity work have always been important to me. If using my name can do anything to help a particular cause, then I feel privileged to be able to help. Most athletes and officials realize how fortunate they are and try to give something back any way they can. And it certainly doesn't hurt to have a little fun at the same time. The Officials Association raises money for charities in a number of ways. For example, I used to play on a softball team in which the proceeds from our games went to charity.

I played in Wayne Gretzky's celebrity tennis tournament in Brantford for several years. I took a lot of kidding there — the proceeds went to the Canadian National Institute for the Blind. It has turned into a major event now, but in its early stages only a small group of people were involved. Wayne's younger brother, Keith, was very young and very shy at the beginning and didn't want to participate. I said to him, "Come on, you and I will go and play." He hadn't played much tennis, but it was just for fun and we had a good time. He went on to play every year after that, and Walter Gretzky, the boys' father, thought it was great that I had got Keith out to play and helped him over his shyness.

I got to know Rick Hansen at the tournament by sitting next to him at a banquet. He turned out to be a heck of a guy. When he came through Toronto on his famous trip around the world in a wheelchair, I was at the Toronto city hall to present him with an official Bruce Hood NHL sweater and whistle.

Another celebrity tennis tournament takes place annually and is taped for CBC, to be used as a weekly series each Saturday afternoon during the winter months. Entertainment, media and sports celebrities take part. I got to know John Ziegler, NHL president, through that tournament, and discovered he's really a fun-loving guy.

As one of the hosts of a golf tournament in Milton — held every year with the support of the *Canadian Champion*, a local newspaper — I have another opportunity to enjoy myself and raise some money for the local hospital at the same time. There's always a good turnout of local people. One of the favorite entertainers over the years has been John Allan Cameron, a popular Canadian entertainer, especially on his native east coast. He's always ready and willing to help us raise funds. This is one of many fund-raising golf tournaments that I attend along with other hockey players and retired and active officials. Many of the charity tournaments are played on the east coast with the help of Canadian Airlines International and Moosehead Breweries.

While officiating I also took some college business courses in marketing and business development. A Dale Carnegie course helped me deal with the different personalities in hockey: it helped me understand myself and my own hang-ups better, which in turn helped me accept those of other people. One portion of the course, entitled "How to Win Friends and Influence People," I thought was rather amusing and appropriate, considering my role as a referee.

Keeping in shape was always important during the summer and refereeing lacrosse fit the bill. I started out in the Ontario Lacrosse Association and worked games in both junior and senior lacrosse, in places around Ontario that weren't too far from home.

I didn't know a lot about the game at first, but it didn't take long to learn. I must have done a decent job because I moved up the ladder quickly. I had the pleasure of refereeing the Minto Cup for the junior championship of Canada, as well as the Mann Cup, the senior championship.

Following that I became referee-in-chief of the OLA, responsible — along with John McCauley, who is the current NHL supervisor of officials — for the lacrosse officials. John and I worked together to upgrade the quality of the officiating and implemented rule changes to improve the game.

One of the problems we faced in amateur lacrosse was the payment system. The officials were paid on a game-to-game basis, but paying them at the end of the game wasn't working out. A representative of the home team was responsible for doing it and if he wasn't happy with the officiating, he would pay them in a way that showed his team's displeasure. In Brooklyn, Ontario, the officials dressed in a room downstairs from the main level and sometimes the money would just be thrown from the top of the stairs. These and other incidents led us to change the rule so that officials were paid before the game.

In 1968 a professional indoor lacrosse league was formed— the Canadian Lacrosse Association. Terry Kelly, a lawyer from Oshawa, Ontario—known in Canada as "Superfan" because of all the major sporting events he attends around the world—was involved with the formation of that league. He asked me if I would set up the refereeing team.

My job involved drafting new rules in the CLA, which meant adjusting existing rules and implementing new ones to help speed up play and make it more appealing to the fans. For example, we did away with the time-consuming face-offs that used to occur every time the ball went out of play. The new rule gave the ball to a player on the team that wasn't responsible for the ball leaving the playing area. The player would be given the ball and, after the whistle blew, he could do anything with it except take a shot on net or carry it himself. That made a tremendous difference in the speed of the game. We also added a rule that required the official to carry an extra ball in his pocket. That way, he wouldn't have to go to the timer's bench when the ball went out of bounds. He could just toss the player the ball and within seconds play would be under way again. We also changed the play-off setup and made other minor changes to add excitement to the play.

There were four teams at the start: Detroit, owned by Bruce Norris, then the owner of the Red Wings; Toronto; Montreal, owned by Brian McFarlane of "Hockey Night in Canada" fame; and Peterborough, which is one of the biggest hotbeds of lacrosse anywhere.

Several other hockey people became involved in lacrosse, most notably John Ferguson, who played the game the same way he played hockey — tough and hard-nosed — but without the fighting.

A couple of years after it began operation, the pro league expanded to add teams in Rochester, Washington, Philadelphia, New York and Boston. Unfortunately the sport never caught on in a big way and the league folded. The main reason probably was that in many cities the fans did't like the idea of going inside an arena in the summertime to watch sports.

IN MY FINAL YEAR before retirement a group of us worked to put a new hockey league together. It was to be called the

Canadian Professional Hockey League. Teams were to be based in Toronto, Hamilton, Montreal, London, Windsor and Ottawa. Studies had shown that many pro players were finishing their NHL careers at the age of twenty-four or twenty-five. They had a lot of good hockey years ahead of them but nowhere near their homes to play. Some would go to the minors and some to Europe, but the idea of this new league was to allow them to keep playing hockey in the places where they had grown up. Many of them were at a loss as to what to do, and this league would instill in them that there was life after hockey. At the same time it would give them a chance to get involved in their community's business world. They could use their talents as players and their high profiles as businessmen.

I was asked to be the league's commissioner and I accepted. Many meetings took place in an attempt to get the league rolling but we needed a big budget to make it go. We had many minor sponsors on board but needed one major sponsor still. A number of times we were close to being ready to go, but it never did come to fruition. David Blair, a Toronto-area entrepreneur who was the catalyst for the new league, along with my son Kevin worked hard night and day for three years to try to get the league off the ground. I still believe it's a great idea and that some day it may still come into being.

My off-season activities didn't lead directly to my post-retirement activities, but they all, in some way, taught me skills I would use later.

Even though I kept busy during the summers, as soon as the air started to chill and the leaves began to change color, I was raring to go for another season of hockey.

REFEREES DON'T GET
HURT, DO THEY?

*"Don't worry," the doctor said. "I'm just putting your
nose back into place."*

MANY PEOPLE THINK it must be pretty hard
for a referee to get injured. He doesn't have to worry about
getting hammered against the boards by a big mean defenseman. He doesn't have to slug it out with a six-foot-four
winger who has had two goals all season, or block shots coming at ninety miles an hour.

Believe me, there are lots of ways for a referee to get hurt.
Officials don't wear as much equipment as players do — although that has been corrected to some degree in recent years
— and therefore don't have the same protection. What makes
it worse is that usually the official does not expect to get hit
by a puck, or bumped by a player, and so is not in a position
to protect himself.

When I was refereeing in the minor leagues, not only did I
have to deal with the possibility of getting hurt in the actual
game, but I also had to deal with arenas themselves. Some
were in terrible shape back then, and there was no glass
around the ice surface as there is now. They had wire mesh
instead.

The arena in Providence, when the city was part of the
American Hockey League, was one of the worst. It was a run-
down building. Nails were used to hold the boards in place

and the wire mesh to the boards, and although they were bent over, they still stuck out in places.

When jumping up on the boards to avoid the play, an official could easily tear his pants or sweater. One time I got the cuff of my sweater caught in the mesh and while the play continued on I tried desperately to get loose. Another time I jumped up on the boards and cut my hand on one of the nails. I got a couple of stitches — no big deal — but the real problem came a few days later when the hand got infected. I had to take special medication and get the injury drained when it swelled up. It certainly wasn't bad enough to keep me away from the game, but the throbbing pain was a nuisance.

Conditions improved over the years as far as arenas went, but at the same time the game got faster and the players' shots got harder. And in this era of the curved stick you can no longer be sure where the puck is going — few of the players know themselves.

It's difficult enough to get out of the way of a puck, and even harder if you don't know it's coming. I was refereeing a game between the Rangers and the Los Angeles Kings at the old Madison Square Garden in the first year of expansion when I called a penalty on New York. As usual, the fans let me know their opinion of the call. During the power play, I was standing to one side of the Rangers' goal as Dale Rolfe took a shot from the blue line. The last thing I remember is the puck heading directly for the net. In the next instant I felt something hit me in the face, and fell to the ice like I'd been shot.

My first thought was that one of the fans had thrown something and hit me. What really happened was that the shot from the point had deflected off the skate of a player in front of the net. The puck shot up and hit me right between the eyes, breaking my nose.

I was down on my hands and knees with blood pouring out of a cut between my eyes. When I put my hand up to the cut I discovered my nose was all over my face. The linesmen, Brent Casselman and Pat Shetler, helped me off the ice and into the first-aid room. I was very groggy, couldn't see because of a towel over my face and had no idea what was going on.

The Ranger team physician, Dr. Yanigisawa, laid me on the table and was mopping up all the blood when suddenly there was a clunk! And then a thud!

I said, "What's that?"

"Don't worry," the doctor said. "I'm just putting your nose back into place."

Then he stitched me up, and I wiped the blood off and went back on the ice to continue refereeing.

Most times when I got an injury, instead of leaving the ice, getting patched up and staying out of the game, I was always so wound up that I just wanted to get back out there if it was at all possible. Many times it would have been smarter to take the rest of the night off, but I felt like it was my duty not to miss part of a game, or any games, for that matter.

Other times I had ulterior motives for not missing an assignment. On one road trip during the second year of expansion in the 1968-69 season, I was scheduled to work a Saturday-afternoon game in Detroit and a Sunday-night game in Chicago, then head out to the west coast where I didn't have to work until Wednesday. I was looking forward to that beautiful weather in California after having spent a long time in the cold back east.

In the Detroit game the Red Wings were hosting the Flyers. During the second period Detroit had a power play and dumped the puck into the Flyers' zone. Ed Van Impe picked up the puck and slapped it along the boards to send it down the ice. I was skating into the zone at the same time when suddenly the puck ricocheted off the boards and headed right for my face. It happened so fast that I instinctively put my hands up to protect myself. Bang! It hit me on the right wrist and I could tell immediately from the severe, burning pain that something had broken. I figured I could still get by, so I kept right on going and finished up the period, despite the pain.

At intermission the doctor came into our dressing room and checked my wrist. He told me the chances were pretty good that it was broken and that I would need X-rays. I got him to wrap the arm so I could finish the game and afterwards I went to a Detroit hospital. Sure enough, the X-rays showed a break, and a cast was placed on my arm.

I was still determined to make that west coast trip and have my time in the sun, and that cast wasn't going to stop me. If I had been thinking clearly I would have gone to the airport and caught a flight home to Milton. Instead, even though I could hardly carry my garment bag and referee's equipment, I went on to my next stop in Chicago.

The pain kept me awake most of the night and I had to call Scotty Morrison the next day and tell him that I would not be able to referee the game in Chicago but that I would probably be all right after that. Lloyd Gilmour, who was in a nearby city, was called in to replace me and I went to the game just to watch.

The next morning the wrist felt a little better, so I thought what the heck and flew to Los Angeles.

I worked the Wednesday-night game with no problems, but when I had my arm checked by another doctor, it was determined that the cast had been put on incorrectly. I needed one that did not allow the arm to rotate. As it was, because the cast only went up to below my elbow, every time my arm turned it separated the break. The doctor in L.A. put on a different type of cast that solved the problem while allowing me to work the games.

Still, my arm wasn't much use to me. Anybody who has lost the use of their right arm knows the problems you face. I had to get one of the fellows I was working with to tie my tie and carry my luggage. Never mind that I am left-handed — most things in this world are made for right-handed people. On top of that I had a hell of a time with everyday things like shaving, brushing my teeth and doing up buttons and zippers.

In the games I could no longer raise my right arm to indicate a delayed penalty, as referees are supposed to do. I had to raise my left hand, then lower it to blow the whistle and point at the player. That was a little different, because normally I would still have my arm raised when I blew the whistle, to let everyone know a delayed penalty was being called. I had to learn how to drop the puck for face-offs with my left hand, which took a while getting used to, but since I was only required to do so at the start of a period or after a goal, it wasn't too bad.

Through it all I managed to miss only that one assignment in Chicago. Best of all, I was still able to sit by the pool in the California sunshine before heading back east to the cold and snow.

Getting hit with a puck happens fairly frequently to a referee, but most of the time it's just a bruise, if anything at all. I suffered a different, and more serious, injury in a game in New York. Carol Vadnais, the Ranger defenseman, went behind his net with the puck and came out on my side so that I was between him and the winger, a situation that occurs many times in a game. He wound up and slapped the puck along the boards to get it to that winger and I jumped up on the boards to get out of the way — again, a common occurrence. I saw the puck coming in plenty of time, but it kept rising. It came up and hit me right on the side of the ankle even though I was a foot off the ice. I thought as soon as it hit me that I was in trouble. When I lowered myself to the ice, I knew for sure.

I left the ice and had the doctors look at it. They thought it was broken, but once again I got it wrapped up and bandaged and went back out. This time, however, I couldn't skate and had to leave for the hospital, where they determined that my ankle was fractured in two places. Bryan Lewis was at the game watching with supervisor Frank Udvari, so he finished the game for me.

MY LAST SERIOUS puck injury happened in Philadelphia in my final year as a referee. The New York Islanders were on a power play and heading into Philadelphia's end. I was following the play at about the blue line when a pass was intercepted. The player tried to blast it down the ice but instead blasted it right into me. I had jumped in the air to avoid it, but it had an arcing curve and caught me in the shin.

Much to the delight of the Philadelphia crowd, I could not skate and fell down when I tried, and had to leave the ice. Even though I was going to retire soon, I got the doctors to wrap it up and back I went. Once again I made a valiant effort, but once again I just couldn't skate. The X-rays showed that the shin bone wasn't broken but that I'd taken a severe bone bruise, which can hurt almost as much as a break and last almost as long. Fittingly, I finished my career icing my shin down between periods and after each game, trying to work through an injury.

Not all injuries were so serious. One time in Vancouver, I was following the play along the boards behind the linesman, Ron Ego, when Hilliard Graves of the Canucks went inside his blue line to get the puck. He reached it and backhanded it out of his zone in one quick motion. It happened so fast that Ron, who was in front of me, had just enough time to duck. It missed him and hit me right in the forehead. I guess it must have looked pretty funny. It happened right in front of the Canuck bench and the players started to laugh. Even I had to laugh, and gave heck to Ron for ducking. Still, I had to get stitched up after the game.

Getting hit with a puck was bad enough. Getting hit by a player in full flight can be a lot worse. Once in St. Louis Chuck Lefley of the Blues was flying down the opposite side of the rink from me into the opposing team's end. He made a pass to the front of the net and circled around behind it, still at full speed.

We were both watching the play in front of the net when all of a sudden — bang! I could have sworn I had just run into a brick wall. Lefley's shoulder had collided square with the point of my jaw. I was down on my knees immediately. When I put my hand to my jaw I realized I had a problem because I couldn't feel it; there was only a numbness.

Chuck had also hit the ice. We had collided with so much force that he had to leave the game and have an ice pack put on his shoulder.

I left the game, too, and was checked over by the St. Louis team doctor, who was pretty sure the jaw was broken. Since I didn't feel any pain because of the numbness, I decided to go back out and finish the game. It would have been hard for me to blow the whistle, but I was still ready to go. The doctor strongly suggested otherwise and finally common sense prevailed and I agreed to go to the hospital. Will Norris, one of the linesmen, refereed the rest of the game.

At the hospital the doctors determined that not only was my jaw broken, it was broken in three places. It had to be wired shut. That involved the doctor putting wires between my teeth and shaping little hooks, over which elastic bands were placed to keep the jaw closed.

The next night I was scheduled to work in Kansas City and the jaw didn't feel too bad. I started the game, but couldn't finish it. The jaw started to throb so much that once again I had to hand the reins over to Will Norris. Really, I shouldn't have been there in the first place. If I had been in the east somewhere, where I knew another referee was close, I probably would have called Scotty and had him replace me, but since I was so far away from anywhere, getting a replacement would have been tough. Also, I was scheduled to work a game the following week between the Islanders and a Soviet Union team, and I didn't want to miss it.

The next day I headed back home for some time off. I found out I had a problem with my jaw similar to the one I had when I broke my wrist: there was still too much movement in it. I could take hold of my jaw with two hands and move it up and down on each side. Again I had to have it fixed up by other doctors. This time they wired the jaw completely shut.

That's the way I stayed for six weeks, during which time I got to know just about every recipe ever invented for blenders. I lived on milkshakes. In fact we burned out one blender and had to get a new one. I used to go crazy for mashed potatoes and when I got a craving, I would put the potatoes in the blender with milk, butter, salt and pepper and mix it up until it was really creamy. That was like heaven to me. I even put roast beef in the blender, along with just about everything else. Joanne never knew what a great cook she was until she came up with some of those concoctions.

About a week before the wires were supposed to come off I got back into action. The jaw had healed pretty well by that time and it was no problem working, though I had to carry a pair of wire cutters with me in case I became sick. If I started vomiting, the wires would have to be cut quickly so I didn't choke to death.

The first game I did when I came back was in Washington. Very seldom does it happen that a referee gets bumped from behind. I suppose the reason it happened then was that I had been off awhile and was still getting my positioning back. A player was coming out of the corner from behind me. I thought he was going to move to my left so I moved to my right. Wrong choice. He smacked into me, jarring just about every bone in my body, not to mention loosening all the wires in my mouth.

I was scared as heck. All I could think about was having my jaw wired shut for another six weeks. Luckily, though, it turned out not to be a problem.

Some of the players, when I had my jaw wired, found it rather amusing. They would come up to me with little grins on their faces and start a conversation. When I couldn't respond very well, they would say, "What's the matter, can't you talk?" I could still talk some, but I sounded like Burt Lancaster.

It was very difficult to breathe with the wires on. It is hard enough in normal circumstances to catch your breath during a game, but this was unbelievable. I was sucking in air so hard and fast that it felt like my whole body was going to cave in.

Even after the wires came out — I took them out myself — I would keep my jaw in place hours at a time, out of habit. Besides, I wanted to make darn sure it healed properly. I didn't want to go through that again.

MY MOST SERIOUS injury, and the one that caused me to miss a whole season, I didn't get from hockey but from that fierce contact sport known as badminton.

I opened the season in Minnesota in 1975, and the next night was home in Milton playing badminton in a league. I reached to my right with my left hand to hit the bird. My right foot was planted and didn't give, but my right knee did. I made what they call a pivot shift and tore the ligament right off the lower part of my leg.

When I had it checked by a doctor, he said it was in very bad shape. I had torn it so badly that they had to go in and cut about eight inches up the side of my leg, pull the ligament down and fasten it to the lower bone of the leg. Then they operated again a week later and removed the cartilage from my knee.

I was in a cast for six weeks, with my leg turned to the right and my knee bent. I had to have a special loop around my neck to hold the cast up so I could walk with crutches, which was just about impossible anyway. After about two weeks they removed the cast, turned my foot almost to normal position and put another cast on for the remaining four weeks. After the cast came off for good I thought I would be all right and just go about my business. Little did I know that my legs and muscles had got used to the new position and didn't want to change.

I had to have a tremendous amount of physiotherapy. Karl Elieff was the physiotherapist and he was located at Maple Leaf Gardens, where the Leafs used his services. I had to go for treatment after treatment. He would massage the leg and then get me up on the table and press on my knee to straighten it.

And he really pressed — the pain was unbelievable! When Karl first started treating me, I'd be in so much pain while he was pressing down that I would go to reach out for him. Karl would step back and say, "Don't touch me!" Then he would start pressing again. I wouldn't be able to stand it and would reach for him again. Finally he screamed, "Don't touch me! Don't you ever touch me!"

I got the message eventually. Whatever Karl's methods, he knew his job and if it wasn't for him, I would not have done as well as I did in rehabilitation.

Mert Prophet, the former trainer of the Toronto Argonauts, also worked with me in my rehabilitation program. Sometimes he had me run the length of the field at Exhibition Stadium, other times up and down the stairs in the grandstand.Mert was a source of inspiration because he knew it could be done and made me work hard to achieve my goal.

Dr. Charles Bull, who'd been in charge of my surgery, had said that they would leave the leg bent a little, about five percent, to protect it. He also said that he never thought I would be able to do the things I could do before the surgery. Thanks to the good surgery, Karl's physiotherapy and months of rehabilitation on my own after that, lifting weights and strengthening, the leg actually became stronger than my other one and I was able to do all the things I could do before.

ANOTHER PROBLEM for referees and one that I personally had a lot of trouble with was back injuries. Referees skate in an upright position, which puts strain on the back. Anyone with a swayback like mine has even more trouble.

I also think the back reacts to stress a lot more than people realize. There's no question that a referee's job involves a lot of stress and tension. As well, all the motion from the different flights, trains, buses, cars and taxis puts a strain on the lower back.

When I was about twenty-one years old I had some back problems, but nothing serious. Each year, I had a few more, but not enough to keep me away from the game. I wasn't doing the things I should have been doing, like conditioning and stretching, so the back wasn't as loose as it could or should have been.

It got worse, till after a while I could hardly work the games. I would leave directly after the game and go back to my hotel room, where I would put ice on my back or just lie down. One night on Long Island after an Islanders game I went straight back to the hotel and right to bed to rest my back. I had a game to work the next afternoon in Washington and then I was off for five days. I figured I'd just do the game and have enough time to rest my back later.

During the game I tried to do the best I could, but I had to adjust for the fact that I couldn't skate as far or as well, or position myself properly. As a consequence I got flattened by a player coming out of his zone. I felt like I couldn't go on, and I shouldn't have, but I did. I finished the game and, in extreme pain, made it to the airport. Every motion of the plane was excruciating, but I made it back to Milton.

The next morning I was standing in my kitchen about four feet away from the counter. The pain at that point was so severe that I couldn't move and couldn't even take a step to get to the counter. I was in pretty bad shape and called the doctors in Toronto. I went down there and they immediately hospitalized me.

I was in the hospital for two weeks while they ran all kinds of tests on me. It seems they were always around sticking pins in me. They wouldn't even let me out of bed to go to the bathroom, but I snuck out anyway when nobody was around. They gave me some drugs for the inflammation but I think it was the rest, more than anything, that was helping me feel better.

I spent quite a bit of time learning about back problems and all the various stretching exercises that can help. I applied a lot of what I learned and still am very careful to take care of my back. I never get out of bed in the morning without pulling my knees up and stretching each leg, one at a time, to loosen up the vertebrae in my lower back. If I don't do that I stiffen up like a board.

I was not alone. Former NHL referees Frank Udvari, Vern Buffey and Ron Wicks were known for their back problems, as are current referee Andy van Hellemond and linesman Bob Hodges, among others. In fact, while I was disabled with back problems, Andy and Ron were also off for the same thing.

The guys used to kid Vern that his difficulties seemed to get worse each year around Christmas, or when he wanted time off. I don't know whether that was true or not.

Most back problems can be greatly alleviated through rest and conditioning. NHL officials now have their own therapist and their own stretching program. Officials today have to be more agile because the speed of the game has increased so much and the traffic is trickier with more moving pass patterns all over the ice.

I had a number of other injuries along the way, including bruises on just about every part of my body, and all kinds of stitches. I was able to work through a lot of injuries, like pulled stomach muscles and cracked ribs, that players couldn't. That's because I didn't have to skate as hard, or start and stop as frequently, and because there wasn't as much contact throughout the games.

It was ironic that one of the reasons I got into officiating was that I wasn't supposed to play hockey anymore because of an injury I had received while playing for the Milton Intermediates.

Refereeing would be a heck of a lot safer . . . so I had thought.

LIFE AFTER HOCKEY

With a replay I was fine, but while the game was going on I was actually looking for infractions.

I RETIRED FROM THE GAME in the spring of 1984 at the age of forty-eight. In the final years of my officiating career I mentioned to Ralph Mellanby, the producer of "Hockey Night in Canada," that I was interested in getting involved in TV. He said it was a good idea, but that it was not as easy as it looked. It required a lot of hard work, he told me, just like officiating.

The Sports Network, the Canadian equivalent to ESPN in the United States, gave me my first on-air opportunity, which just happened to coincide with their own first broadcast. I had the honor of being there at twelve noon on September 1, 1984, when the button was pushed and TSN went on the air.

I went on the air later that afternoon, along with Roger Nielson, an assistant coach for the Blackhawks at the time, and Jim Van Horne and John Wells, who were the hosts. We took the feed in the studio for the Canada Cup games; my job was basically to comment on the officiating, although as the tournament went along I would talk about other things as well.

The same year I did a series for a Detroit TV station (WKBC) along with Mickey Redmond called, "You be the Ref." We would show an actual play and then invite the viewer to make the call. After a commercial break, Mickey and I would discuss the play and say why it was or wasn't a penalty. It turned out to be a very popular series. Later, in Buffalo, I would sometimes do a similar show, also with good results.

I had been contacted by parties in New York and Washington about the possibility of doing some television work and went to New York to meet with that group, but an offer from Buffalo Sabres Television Productions turned out to be the best deal. I could live at home, which was only an hour and a half away, and commute to the games by car. It meant the first winter in more than twenty-one years that I could pursue other winter activities, like skiing, without having to jump on a plane all the time.

I did the Buffalo games that year and was also in contact with Don Wallace of "Hockey Night in Canada," who asked if I would be interested in doing a few games with them. He had taken over from Ralph Mellanby when Ralph moved on to produce the Winter Olympics in Calgary, and he told me that he would give me a tryout. I was an analyst between periods for a game and neither did particularly well nor poorly. Wallace then sent me a two-page letter saying that because the Leafs were doing so poorly, he didn't think it was a good time to introduce new talent on the show. I suppose it was just a way of telling me they weren't interested.

During my second season of retirement I got a call from Winnipeg, asking to see if I would be interested in doing the color commentary for their games. I had bought my travel agency the previous March and was also doing the Sabres television work, which I was enjoying, but I thought why not?

I was just terrible in the beginning. It took me a long while to realize why I wasn't seeing some of the things that I should see — I was still watching the game as a referee. As a referee you have an overview of the whole game but don't really see all the individual plays — they run together as the game goes on and are forgotten unless the need to make a ruling appears, or something else happens that clicks your automatic into gear. With a replay I was fine, but while the game was going on I was actually looking for infractions. When it came to explaining what had happened — why the play broke down or why the winger didn't get the pass — I was out to lunch.

It was my first season broadcasting the Jets games for CKY TV and the people I worked with there were all class — from Bill Davis at the top, a director of both the Jets and the television station, to the play-by-play man, Curt Keilback, who is one of the best I've come across, to the host Rod Black, a real pro.

The Winnipeg station is an independent and is responsible for weeknight games — usually on Wednesdays — but the production was still handled by Hockey Night in Canada. They would send in a director to run the show, to make sure that the format was identical to that of their other mid-week productions. That way wherever in the country you were watching a game, it had the same look.

A few weeks after I started I was called into the Toronto office of Don Wallace. In Winnipeg we were still working out the bugs and learning our jobs so we knew we were not yet in the same class as cities that had been broadcasting for many years. Some constructive criticism would have been a great help, to me especially. Wallace played a videotape of one of our games and it wasn't long before I realized I wasn't going to be offered any assistance. He spent the whole time cutting up the broadcast, pointing out in general terms how bad he thought it was, and talking about the whole crew like we were a bunch of amateurs. It wasn't the kind of inspiration I was looking for and I left the session that night feeling really down.

I finished the season. The Jets had won only three of the seventeen games we had telecast, which didn't help get those "positive vibes" going. I learned a great deal as I went, mostly from watching other people and videos of our shows. The following season I was contacted by Winnipeg to see if I was interested in coming back, which I was, but I was sort of relieved when they told me later that they were being supplied commentators by Hockey Night in Canada and wouldn't need me.

I continued doing the Buffalo telecasts that season and have done them now for four years. Each year it's been a different format. John Gurtler, Danny Gare, Mike Robitaille and

Ted Darling made up the talent in the most recent season. My job as an analyst — videotaping and then going on air between periods — is fun and I can do almost anything I want. I can show the mistakes or the good plays, and have learned how to call them the way I saw them, not just from a referee's point of view. I show good passing plays or bad defensive lapses, and never hesitate to pass along an opinion as to a coaching move or anything else. I am also in a position to show a call by a referee or linesman and explain why it was made.

By the way, the officials are never wrong — they just see things from a different perspective than the rest of us! I always make sure to explain this.

I watch the game in the control center, which is in a truck parked outside the Auditorium. I have access to three video replays but generally use a video placed at one end of the rink that allows an overview of the players' positions on the ice.

Usually I mark three or four plays to use during the intermission. That part of the broadcast is presented from a studio inside the Auditorium. The replays are usually run in slow motion, to allow time to explain the play, and sometimes we stop the tape to make a point before going on to finish the segment. A video operator in the truck runs the video according to instructions I provide.

It has worked out well. I've gotten to know the people of Buffalo and have developed a pretty good following. One day a fan asked me, "How did you end up here? It seems so hard to believe — the fans used to boo you so much and now you're part of the organization and everybody likes you and the work you do!"

Most television watchers are familiar with the Lite Beer commercials that show retired athletes arguing over whether Lite Beer from Miller tastes great, or is less filling.

A referee, of course, would have to be impartial in a debate like that, and I was asked to take part in a commercial using the popular theme, with Eddie Shack, Bob Nevin, Billy Harris, Bill White, Bobby Baun and Pierre Pilote.

The commercial starts off with the group of us sitting around a table after coming off the golf course. We're sitting around, obviously having a good time, when Shack says, "Everybody asks, who had the harder shot — me or Bobby Hull." We all laugh. Then he says, "Everybody asks, who was the better skater — me or Gordie Howe." Again more laughter. Finally he says, "Well, we can't all agree on that, but we can all agree on Miller Lite." Then the debate starts. Nevin, Harris and White say it tastes great, and Baun and Pilote say it's less filling. I'm there in the background, and as the two groups start to come together, I blow my whistle and come between them. Shack speaks up and says, "I'm gonna keep my nose out of this one."

Twenty-five or thirty people were needed on the set to do the commercial and twenty-three takes were required before we got it just the way they wanted it. It's natural for a bunch of guys to sit around having a beer, but when you're forced to do it on cue it's pretty hard to look natural. The answer to that problem, we found, was to sip on the beer between takes.

The funniest line of the day was delivered by Eddie Shack, after we had been through about ten takes. Instead of saying what he was supposed to, when the camera rolled, he said, "Everybody asks, who got laid more — me or Bobby Hull." We all laughed, but this time it was for real. It broke the tension and helped get everybody relaxed.

Another thing I did for a few years was write a column for *The Hockey News* called "Ask the Referee." Readers were invited to send in questions concerning the officiating aspect of the game. I figured I'd seen just about everything that could happen in hockey, but not only had I not seen some of the hypothetical situations posed, but they also weren't covered in the rule book. One such question was what the penalties would be if two players on the same team got into a fight during a game. There's no specific rule for that unusual circumstance, but my reply was that it was a case in which the referee would have to excercise his discretion. I would throw them out of the game and give their team a delay-of-game penalty, but another referee might do it differently.

Some of the questions were challenging and thought-provoking, obviously sent in by knowledgeable hockey fans, and others were simple and straightforward. Either way, it was a fun job, and I was always glad to see how much interest there was in the rules of the game.

THE CONSTANT TRAVELING that goes with being a referee — 100,000 miles a year, sometimes seven flights a week — could be fatiguing at times, but I also found it intriguing, and even after all the miles I logged in my career I still enjoy traveling. Getting into the travel business seemed a logical step after retirement.

When I first started in the NHL, officials received a set amount of dollars to get from point A to point B. For example, if we had to go from Toronto to Montreal, the airfare at the time might have been thirty-five dollars, so that's what we would get no matter which means we took to get there. If I took the bus and it cost eighteen dollars, then the other seventeen was mine to keep. If I had a few days between assignments, I would often take the bus or the train, which not only saved me some money but also gave me a chance to see the countryside. In later years the league changed the system and paid exactly what the trip cost, with the officials reporting that amount on their expense sheets. That system had some problems: some officials were making too many stops in order to take advantage of the frequent-flyer programs, with the result that their travel costs escalated. To ensure that traveling was done by the most economical means, the league now uses a central agency that has all the tickets for officials delivered directly to their homes.

Before this system started I used to book all my own travel through Milton Travel Service, which at the time was one of the few travel agencies around. I stayed with them right through my whole career, except for a couple of years when the league changed its credit card system, so really, I grew up with that agency. It had opened business in 1961, just a year before my refereeing career started. I already had some business experience and wanted to buy a business in a field that I was already familiar with, as a sort of hobby that would go along with my hockey-related activities when I retired. I happened to mention to the owners, Bill and Ellen Casson, what my plans were and asked them about the travel business. It just so happened they were thinking of selling so we talked extensively and I ended up buying the agency from them. Bill helped me get settled for a few months and then they retired to Las Vegas.

I remember Carl Voss telling me that I should make use of my name. In sport your career doesn't go on forever, so you should take advantage of whatever credibility your name has. The first thing I did was rename the agency: Bruce Hood's Milton Travel.

I couldn't have been happier about the situation. I had a business right downtown in my hometown, and thought I would keep it as a backup to my other activities and, as I said, treat it as sort of a hobby. I figured I could spend a few hours a day there, travel during the winter months and do whatever else I wanted to do. Little did I know . . .

Not long after, I saw how the business demanded to be modernized and started working long hours — sometimes from seven in the morning to twelve midnight. The next thing I knew we were swamped with business. I expanded the offices and got them computerized, and within three years business had more than tripled. What with the demands of marketing, advertising and expansion, my "hobby" had quickly become a full-time job.

There's no doubt that my name opened a lot of doors, but in a service business, no matter what your name is, you won't last long if you don't provide service. My agency succeeded because I knew about the needs of the business traveler.

The business has developed to the point where I now have a manager running it, which has allowed me more time to explore other interests.

ONE OF THOSE things was politics. In 1987 Ontario's Liberal Party had tremendous popular support throughout the province and called an election in an attempt to win a majority in the provincial parliament. (A note for Americans: Canada has a vastly different political system than is found in the United States. In a provincial election, the party that elects the most members in the province's "ridings" — or electoral districts — forms the government, with the leader of that party becoming premier.)

When our local incumbent, Don Knight, decided not to seek reelection, I was approached by a number of people pressing me to run for his spot. I was also contacted by people offering their support, including a former riding member of the provincial parliament, Julian Reed, and several people in the local Liberal association.

I gave the idea a lot of thought, discussing the pros and cons with Joanne, and our son Kevin and daughter Marilyn, both of whom were active in politics. It seemed like an exciting thing to do and a new challenge, so I threw my hat in the ring.

The toughest hurdle in that election came not from the public, who were almost sure to elect a Liberal member, but from other Liberals in the riding. Before running, I had to be nominated as the riding's Liberal candidate. I was up against some tough competition — people who had been involved in politics for many, many years. Still, after the first ballot at the nomination meeting, I was ahead of the other candidates and only a few votes from a majority. The nomination process requires that the bottom vote-getter drop out after each ballot, until one person has a majority. As the other candidates dropped out, they threw their support to Walt Elliot, a longtime Liberal who had been involved in politics for twenty-five years. After three ballots, I had lost.

Walt had a pretty strong core of support, and I was like the outsider coming in and infringing on their territory. I respected that and was not bitter. I gave it a good shot and had a lot of fun, and most of all it was a great education. As a matter of fact, Walt Elliot has his riding office right next door to my travel agency in downtown Milton and I lend him my support in anything I can.

Politics, I have learned, is a business, and in many respects similar to a game or sport. You have to use a lot of strategy to win, and experience counts heavily. I didn't have that experience and consequently wasn't able to do as well. Politics, like hockey, requires a good team, good coaching and managing, preparation and strategy — experience provides much of that for you.

As far as running in politics again, I haven't ruled that out; maybe I'd do better next time as a non-rookie.

I KEPT UP AN interest in other hockey-realated activities besides broadcasting, and became more directly involved in
two. One of them was "Reach for the Stars," a fantasy camp
run by the CAN/AM hockey group and held in Lake Placid,
New York. The idea of the camp is for people to become involved in an NHL setup: they live, train and play with hockey
greats and Hall of Famers from the past. They do everything
a regular NHL team does — the morning practices, the team
meal at noon followed by a team meeting, the afternoon nap,
and a game each of the five nights, with the teams vying for
the "Stanley Cup." There were four teams and each of them
had former NHL stars. Gordie Howe, Stan Mikita, Dennis
Hull, Frank Mahovlich, Red Kelly, Bill Gadsby, Walt Tkaczuk,
Vic Hadfield, Johnny Bower, Eddie Shack, John McKenzie
and Wayne Cashman were some of the participants. They
even had Danny Gallivan there to call the play-by-play and
Stan Fischler as the reporter and analyst.

The two referees were Red Storey and myself and I really
enjoyed the atmosphere. One of the interesting things about
the camp was that I got a chance to meet up and chat with
some of the players who used to give me a rough time —
people like Wayne Cashman and Johnny McKenzie. But even
that was fun.

While I was at the camp, King Clancy — Hall of Famer and
former player, coach and referee — died in Toronto. The
CAN/AM group arranged a small plane to take Johnny Bower,
Red Kelly and myself back to Toronto to attend the funeral.
The weather conditions were far from ideal as we set out to
the airport in nearby Saranac Lake. The plane we were to
travel in wasn't in tip-top shape, either.

The problem with the plane was that a wire at the back that
was supposed to help stabilize the steering mechanism was
out of order. The pilot suggested that I lie down in the back of
the plane and hold onto the broken wires. He'd picked me
because I was tallest. There were only four of us; the other
three sat up front while there I was, lying on my stomach
facing into the tail of the plane, both while we took off and
again later when we came in for a landing. Johnny and Red
didn't seem too nervous about the plane, but it was a little
scary for me. We attended King Clancy's funeral and then

headed right back to Lake Placid on the same plane, as dark-
ness set in.

The other hockey-related project, "Relive the Dream," was
a Canada-Soviet series with the same two teams and players
from the memorable 1972 series. I hadn't refereed in the
original series — no pros were used.

In Canada just about everybody remembers where they
were and what they were doing when Paul Henderson
scored that historic goal to give Canada the victory in the
final game. I'd been with my son Kevin, watching in the
family room of our home. As soon as that puck went in the
net, we were up dancing in circles, arm-in-arm in the middle
of the room.

Paul Henderson became an instant hero, of course, and still
is in Canada. I recall refereeing the first game of the regular
season in Toronto after that series. Henderson wasn't there
because he wasn't mentally or physically prepared to play
yet after that big series.

Henderson was one of the people who played in the
"Relive the Dream" series, along with Bobby Clarke, Stan
Mikita, Pat Stapleton, Daniel Bouchard, Yvan Cournoyer,
Gary Smith, Darryl Sittler, Frank and Peter Maholvich, Bill
White, Serge Savard, Dale Tallon, Red Berenson, Bill
Goldsworthy, Steve Shutt, Mickey Redmond, Don Awrey,
Reggie Leach, Bill Barber, Rod Seiling, Jacques Lemaire, Gary
Bergman, Rod Gilbert and Brad Park. John Ferguson was be-
hind the bench as coach.

Three games were played, starting off with one in Hamilton and followed by games in Montreal and Ottawa. The
Hamilton game started off slowly but as the game went on,
the old competitiveness started to come back. By the second
game in Montreal the atmosphere was building and the
players were taking the games very seriously. There was
yapping from the bench and players started getting upset
when a penalty was called.

Bill White said to me after I had given him a penalty,
"Hoody, I'm forty-four years old — give me a break!"
Some things never change. He'd been looking for breaks
when he was twenty-four and was doing the same thing
now.

The two teams really went at it and were out there to win. Once a puck came along the boards and glanced off me. Jacques Lemaire, who had made the pass that had re-directed off me, was hollering at me to get out of the way. Bill Barber, known throughout his career as the master of the art of diving, was still diving, and Serge Savard was blocking shots just like he did during his NHL career. Bobby Clarke looked to me like he could still be playing in the NHL.

The players really put on a great show and received a standing ovation when it was all over. After the final game, the players exchanged sweaters and John Ferguson, not really known as a friend of the officials, came onto the ice and put on the sweater of Bill Friday, a referee!

Oh yes, and Canada won that series as well.

Retirement was hardly an apt word when I finished my NHL career — I became even busier. But that's the way I like it.

21

A BIG PUSH FOR FAIR PLAY

Between 1976 and 1983 forty-two players in Canada suffered spinal injuries. Of the forty-two, seventeen suffered full paralysis below the point where the backbone was injured. Most of the injuries were the result of players being "checked" from behind or hit into the boards.

IN 1986 WHEN Otto Jelinek, Canada's Minister of State for Fitness and Amateur Sport, announced he was going to establish the Commission for Fair Play in Sport, I volunteered my services. I believed there was too much violence in hockey and too many things happening that were unnecessary at all levels of the game. I felt it was time something was done to put the fun back into hockey and encourage fair play.

This program is not just directed at hockey — though that is my main interest in it — but at any sport in which the true meaning of competition has been lost and the win-at-all-costs mentality has taken over.

The commission is endeavoring to provide a "values framework for sport" that entails "demonstrating attitudes and behavior in sport consistent with the belief that sport is an ethical and humane pursuit."

The overall objective of the campaign is this: "to make athletes, all members of the sport community, parents and teachers aware that integrity, sportsmanship and honesty remain the most important ingredients of any sport."

To accomplish these goals, the commission has a number of projects under way: ad and poster campaigns, television advertising, material to be distributed to elementary schools across the country and awards for those demonstrating fair play — including a national honor called the Fair Play Award, given annually to the athlete, coach or team that demonstrates the true essence of fair play.

In 1987 the award was presented to Douglas Mitchell, the coach of the Port Elgin Bears Junior C hockey team, for his stand against on-ice violence. He showed the depth of his conviction by withdrawing his team from a play-off series. Although his actions caused a mixed reaction within the hockey community, Mitchell and his team showed just how serious an issue violence in hockey is becoming.

Because of the importance of hockey in Canada and its high profile, much of the Commission's emphasis is on that sport. It has been proven that many kids are staying away from the game because it's too rough and the chance of injury is too great.

The number of serious injuries hockey players have received over the years is a definite concern. Allan Fothering-ham reported in his column in *Maclean's* magazine that between 1976 and 1983, forty-two players in Canada suffered spinal injuries. Of the forty-two, seventeen suffered full paralysis below the point where the backbone was injured. Most of the injuries were the result of players being "checked" from behind or hit into the boards.

Some leagues in Canada have already instituted a penalty for checking another player from behind, and that is certainly a step in the right direction.

One of the posters distributed by the commission has a picture of an empty hockey rink with this headline — THE SCENE OF THE CRIME — printed in large letters at the top and a message at the bottom promoting good sportsmanship along with the motto: LET'S GET BACK IN THE GAME.

One such way of playing it fair was initiated in London, Ontario, on a trial basis. Two house-league hockey divisions — Atom and Pee Wee — are working under a new point system. Nine points are allotted for winning the game, while six points are given to each team at the beginning of the game for conduct. Throughout the game, a team will lose conduct points each time it incurs a minor, coaching or major penalty, thus providing incentive for the teams to play fairly.

The first Honorary Chairman of the commission was Wayne Gretzky. The members of the Commission for Fair Play in Sport Commission along with myself, are: Chairman, Gilles Neron, author of the Neron Report; Vice-Chairman, Tom Nease, a director of Cooper Canada Limited; Ed Chynoweth, president of the Western Hockey League and the Canadian Major Junior Hockey League; Murray Costello, president of the Canadian Amateur Hockey Association; Pam Gollish, chairman of the Athletes' Advisory Council of the Canadian Olympic Association; Dr. Geoff Gowan, president of the Coaching Association of Canada; George Gross, *Toronto Sun* columnist and corporate sports editor; Abby Hoffman, former Olympic athlete and director-general of Sport Canada; Russ Jackson, former Canadian Football League great; Diane Jones-Konihowski, retired Olympic athlete; Lyle Makosky, assistant deputy minister for Fitness and Amateur Sport; Ralph Mellanby, CTV executive producer for the 1988 Olympic Winter Games and former "Hockey Night in Canada" producer; Dr. Andrew Pipe, of the Civic Hospital's Heart Institute and the University of Ottawa's Sport Medicine Clinic; Dr. John C. Pooley, professor at the School of Recreation, Physical and Health Education at Dalhousie University in Halifax; Julian Pristanski, former minor-hockey referee and member of the Sault Major Hockey Association; Brian Ward, executive director of the Canadian Council on Children and Youth; and Joy Harrison, who is the Fair Play program coordinator.

I submitted a report to the commission after talking to as many sports people as I could on the subject including a number of professional and minor-league referees and linesmen, as well as several NHL players.

These were my findings, as reported to the commission:

1. The rules of hockey, although generally having a standard interpretation across the country, are not applied in a standard manner. Many varying levels of application in all areas of the game and of the country cause much frustration to players, coaches, officials and fans.
2. Players generally do not accept that body-checking is

part of the game, and a get-even attitude prevails within the player when he is checked — which is condoned by his coach, his manager, his peers and likely his parents.

3. Parents in particular, coaches and managers, fail to accept the ruling of the Officials, and set a poor example by berating and chastising the Official for a call, therefore setting an example for young players that "this is the way it is supposed to be." They then maintain that realm of thinking as they grow into becoming parents, coaches and managers.

4. There is a lack of a firm standard in the areas of hooking, holding, interferences — the restraining fouls; and this causes much frustration within the players, to the point of discouraging them from playing their best, or to reacting in a "violent" way — to cross-check, slash or charge, etc. or even fisticuffs. It is this type of play which causes the long games with the continual push and shove after the whistle to establish supremacy.

5. The "big brother" syndrome, or more often referred to as the "goon squad," is far too prevalent in the game — the attitude of "don't you check me or you-know-who will come onto the ice and get even on the next shift" has changed the structure of hockey. Again, the lack of rule application, the failure to accept that bodychecking is a part of the game, has led the sport into falsely believing that every team has to carry the "equalizer."

Some people have wrongly concluded that the idea of the campaign is to turn hockey into a "rinky-dink" sport. The intent, however, is not to take away the competitiveness or the intensity of the game but rather to convince people to play it fair.

Otto Jelinek has met with the NHL's president, John Ziegler, and made him aware of the commission and its intent, though it is not meant to affect the NHL directly. The NHL is already doing some things to alleviate the problem of violence—by changing some rules and giving larger fines and longer suspensions.

Our aim is to start with the kids and instill in them an attitude of fair play right from the start.

It is hoped that Canadians will react to the program like they did to the one that followed an earlier campaign aimed at improving physical fitness. This program, known as Participaction, was highly effective in helping people become aware of the benefits of better physical conditioning.

A good example of that is the number of old-timer hockey leagues now in operation. One league, which I play in, doesn't even keep track of the standings or leading scorers. And penalties are rare. The guys just want to play for the fun of it and because they see how important it is to keep active. But it's still very competitive.

In hockey and other sports it's not too late to make a change for the better. As the motto of the Commission for Fair Play in Sport suggests: LET'S GET BACK IN THE GAME.

PARTING SHOTS

The strangest thing about people who direct abuse at officials is that they think they are doing nothing wrong. They've been conditioned to think it's acceptable.

I WAS IN THE LOCAL Canadian Tire store one afternoon when the sports report came on over the store's sound system. In it Red Kelly, the Toronto Maple Leaf coach at the time, was quoted condemning my work and criticizing me severely for the previous night's game.

There was no escaping it — I was shopping, for crying out loud!

At times like that I had to wonder: What if a reporter had asked me how a coach had handled a particular game, and I'd said, "That man is clearly incompetent. He doesn't belong in this league, and his coaching methods are a joke to the profession."

What an uproar it would have created! Imagine a referee criticizing an NHL coach's competence. "He has no right," they would have said. "Who does he think he is?"

The brass would have been outraged and probably would have taken disciplinary measures against me. Still, maybe it wouldn't have been such a bad idea. A lot of coaches and general managers wouldn't be so quick with their comments if they'd known they might pick up a newspaper and read a referee's analysis of how the coach's strategic errors had cost his team a game.

231

A coach could say whatever he wanted about me and there was nothing I could do to defend myself. Officials are defenseless in that respect. We are expected to be above responding. As the authorities on the ice, we have to maintain our impartiality. So I had to forget about it when a coach blamed me for a loss by his team. I had to forget how he, without thinking twice about it, had got his own frustrations out by verbally abusing me. Staying cool was difficult, but I had no choice — it was my job.

We, the officials, had to show respect for the game — and rightfully so.

There were many incidents during my career that were unpleasant. The on-ice brawls; a cigarette lighter hitting me on the head; a lit cigarette hitting me in the face in Quebec; the "Hood Sucks" sign somebody held up in Long Island; a T-shirt made up with the same message, worn by a guy in Philadelphia; "Hood Milk" cartons from a Boston-area company, that a fan held up against the glass while giving the thumbs-down signal; the sign man in Philadelphia holding up derogatory comments about the officials; being hit with a toe rubber thrown from the stands in Montreal; being chastised in hotel lobbies.

But all of those memories are offset many times over by the thrill of being part of professional hockey, by the excitement of the games, and by the players and all the great people I met along the way.

People like Tom "The Bomb" Barnwell in New York, who is definitely one of a kind. His memory for games and the officials in them is remarkable — he can recall a particular game or incident at will. He's always available and appreciated for his friendship, by both officials and players. And he knows most of both. Other people were special as well. There was Dan McQueeny in Providence, who used to come to the AHL games in his area — another good friend of the officials.

Once I needed a ride from Hershey to Harrisburg to catch a midnight train, and a local fan came to the rescue. Another time a couple in a Springfield diner sat down with me for a bite to eat after a game and then drove me to the train station. And then there was a cab driver in New York who, when he realized who I was, told me how he had grown up around the old Madison Square Garden and how proud he was to have met me. And I won't forget the off-ice officials, or the many on-ice ones, whom I met through the referee schools and through international hockey.

These are just some of the great people I met in hockey, who made it all worthwhile. In numbers they far outweighed the other kind, both in and around the game.

Putting up with all the aggravations was a price I had to pay on the job, and sometimes the cost was excessive.

I don't mean to insinuate that referees should be put up on a pedestal. I made mistakes out on the ice, as do all officials. We're human, and expect to be criticized to a certain extent. We expect to be booed by the fans and expect people to question some of our decisions. But we don't expect to be held up to public ridicule.

The strangest thing about people who direct abuse at officials is that they think they are doing nothing wrong. They've been conditioned to think it's acceptable. Since there have been so few attempts to stop others, they see no reason why they shouldn't do it too.

For example, after the Don Koharski-Jim Schoenfeld incident in the 1987-88 play-off series between the New Jersey Devils and the Boston Bruins, Schoenfeld said he didn't see what the big deal was about confronting the referee in the hallway after the game. After all, Schoenfeld said, everybody else did it. But does that make it right? Of course not. And it's not Schoenfeld who should be blamed for that attitude. For as long as he's been in hockey he's seen it as acceptable behavior. He's not guilty — the system is. When the system changes, so will the attitudes of the people in it.

This incident may have been a blessing in disguise. People could finally see for themselves why referees should not be used as whipping boys. Schoenfeld was suspended for one game, a big step in the right direction on the league's part.

Unfortunately, much of the controversy surrounding the incident centered on the league's failure to grant a proper hearing. As a result a New Jersey court granted an injunction that allowed Schoenfeld to continue coaching.

Dave Newell, and the two linesmen, Ray Scapinello and Gord Broseker, refused to work the next game because they wanted protection when they learned Schoenfeld was not serving his one-game suspension. And they went one step further by emphasizing that the officials in the NHL have had enough. Their actions showed that it's well past time — for the good of the game — to ensure that officials are treated with respect.

People ask me if I would have done the same thing as Newell, Scapinello and Broseker if I'd been in their shoes. Given my frustrations over the years, I think I would have. Those who think that their stand hurt the integrity of the game are wrong. Newell and all the officials are fighting *for* the integrity of the game.

When I was out on the ice, all I wanted to do was work the game to the best of my abilities. Outside interference impeded me. It would cause me to get down on myself and I'd have to work hard to build back my confidence. When there was no interference I knew there was nothing in the game that I couldn't handle.

People don't realize that without a doubt NHL hockey is the toughest sport in the world to officiate. It's the fastest and roughest game, and it involves more split-second decisions, all of which directly affect the outcome, than any other game or sport. The referees and linesmen in the NHL earn their way there; they're the best in the world. To make it that far isn't easy, and to last for very long is even harder.

Refereeing is becoming increasingly difficult. It surprises me when I hear people say the game isn't as good as it used to be. Its speed alone is far greater than it was twenty-five years ago. On top of that the passing and playmaking are better, as is the conditioning of the players. Special teams are more in use. Through the use of video, coaching has become more sophisticated.

Because of all that, the officiating system will perhaps have to be changed. The physical demands on the referees who now must go end to end for the whole game could be reduced by implementing a two-referee, one-linesman system. That way, the responsibility for calling the infractions could be distributed between two people. Either referee could call a penalty, with one referee keeping an eye on the play when it's in his zone, and the other watching what's happening away from the play. This would also reduce penalties, because the players would have the two referees to sneak past.

Because this system would be less physically demanding, it would allow the league to keep officials on staff longer. The game would benefit from the extra talent and experience. It would also solve some problems in international hockey, because it would guarantee presence of the best-qualified officials for the most important games. As things now stand, referees who are used to working in top-level hockey are not allowed to work the important games because they usually come from the countries that are playing them. By using a referee from each country, much of the problem would be solved.

Referees are not likely to favor their home country — as some have been accused of in the past. Their work is too closely scrutinized, and with more games being televised now any favoritism would be conspicuous.

Communication is a key ingredient in improving the attitudes of players and coaches towards the officials. If a player or coach can ask a question in a proper manner, then the official should be able to give him a satisfactory answer. As it is now, many times the coach just wants to yell at the official to get his frustrations out. Of course the official is not interested in listening to that, and as a result, the lines of communication are cut off, even when he wants to pose a sensible question.

One way to improve those relations is to have a meeting before every game between the officials and the coaches and captains to discuss any questions about certain rule interpretations or other problems. Besides clearing up problems, it also serves to put the officials on better terms with the coaches. If they speak in a rational manner before the game, then they're more likely to respect each other and discuss problems that come up in the game in an intelligent manner.

I think changing the color of the officials' sweaters might be a good idea. The black-and-white jail bird stripes invoke a negative attitude. A solid color would get away from that, and perhaps change the image of the officials.

There are other changes that could be made to help the game. Play should be started more quickly and there should be fewer stoppages. The scrums that occur after whistles in front of the net or in the corner should be eliminated. These senseless get-togethers are ridiculous. They only happen because the players want to intimidate each other. Fighting, as I've said many times, has no place in hockey. When the games are decided solely by which team plays the game the best, that's when hockey will be at its ultimate.

Having officials on the ice during the warm-ups, to eliminate pre-game flare-ups, is being considered, and I find that very depressing. The teams' management and the players themselves have some responsibility to maintain control and show respect for the game. The officials are responsible for the game itself and that's where it should end. There's not a policeman on every corner to make sure each citizen upholds the law. There are certain rules and certain standards in life that have to be adhered to. Giving a man a hockey stick does not exempt him from them.

I was talking to a father once who told me how he had taken his two boys to a local Junior game, dropped them off and then gone back later to pick them up at the approximate time the game should have ended. When he drove up to the arena he saw flashing lights and police cars. There had been a brawl on the ice. He decided he didn't want his sons to be a part of it. Even the kids themselves were turned off.

The attitudes fostered in the NHL filter down to the juniors and the kids. If we're trying to teach our children the right values in life, then it's something we should be concerned about.

The game doesn't have to be like that. Hockey is the greatest game in the world without fighting and violence. The NHL seems genuinely concerned about its image. New rules and standards are gradually being implemented that will make the game of hockey better for everyone. The firm stand taken by the league against restraining fouls during the 1987-88 season proved that.

MY OTHER accomplishments in life have flowed directly out of my career as an NHL referee, and I have had a lot of success. I'm happy that I've been able to give something back to the sport through the referee schools, the Officials Association, equipment development and television analysis.

It may seem contradictory to say, on the one hand, how great a life officiating was, and on the other hand, how tough it was. But that's the life of an NHL referee.

My hope is that people who have read my story will know what it's like to wear the striped shirt, and have some insight into the world of officiating.

For me it was just one year at a time. The fact that the league wanted me back each successive season for more than twenty years was a reward in itself. I worked more than 1,000 games, which has given me a lifetime of memories.

When I was young I used to sit by the radio and listen to the Foster Hewitt broadcasts of the games from Maple Leaf Gardens on Saturday nights. It was as if that was another world. It was up in the sky somewhere — something to dream about. But my dream came true, and I was able to be a part of that world. For that I am eternally grateful.

APPENDIX

REFEREE'S WORK SHEET

GAME NO. _____

REFEREE _____

	EXCELLENT	GOOD	SATISFACTORY	FAIR	UNSATISFACTORY	EXCELLENT	GOOD	SATISFACTORY	FAIR	UNSATISFACTORY	EXCELLENT	GOOD	SATISFACTORY	FAIR	UNSATISFACTORY

1. OFFICIATING PRESENCE AND FITNESS

Appearance
Grooming
Weight Control
Skating
Keep up for Period/Game

2. SIGNALS

Signals
Use of delay
Arm erect on delay
Complete stop in assessing penalty
Clear signal at penalty box
Excessive wash-outs around goal area
Point to net on goal

3. POSITIONING - END ZONE

Work the goal line
Turn back on the play
In the players' way
Hit by puck
Always protect his net
Allow too much movement behind him

4. POSITIONING - PURSUIT OF PLAY

Is he too close
Anticipations
Use of boards
Turns back on play
Cheats too much
Check back on play

5 OFFICIATING POLICY

Goaltender moves puck
Player moves puck along boards
Hand signals on line changes
Use the differential
Correct 54(e) procedures
Too much talking
Correctly interpret hand pass
Correct procedure re disallowed/disputed goals
Use of wash-out signal

LINESMEN'S WORK SHEET

GAME NO. _____

LINESMAN _____

	EXCELLENT	GOOD	SATISFACTORY	FAIR	UNSATISFACTORY		EXCELLENT	GOOD	SATISFACTORY	FAIR	UNSATISFACTORY		EXCELLENT	GOOD	SATISFACTORY	FAIR	UNSATISFACTORY

1. OFFICIATING PRESENCE AND FITNESS

Appearance
Grooming
Weight control
Skating
Keep up for Period/Game
Strong in altercations

2. SIGNALS

Use of wash-out
Over signalling
Point with non-whistle hand
Signals to partner
Signals clear and concise

3. POSITIONING

Blue line to make call
Center line to make call
Good position to judge icings

4. FACE-OFF TECHNIQUE

Correct stance
Puck dropped flat
Advantage on face-off
Departure from end zone
Signal Partner to release line

5. FACE-OFF EXECUTION

Controlled the face-off
Removal of Players
Encroachment

6. OFFICIATING POLICY

Pre-game preparation
Supportive of referee
Preventive measures re altercations
Separation of players
Scoring of Goals
End of period/game
Change of ends/sides

7. JUDGEMENT

Accuracy-blue line
Use of the delay whistle
Accuracy-red line
Too technical on icings
Too technical on off-side passes
Respond to challenge
Attitude - players/bench

8. CONSISTENCY

Period/period
Throughout game
Follow a pattern in face-offs and icings

9. TEAM WORK

Cover for the referee when trapped
Cover for his partner when trapped
Communicate with partner

10. AWARENESS

Respond to altercations
Respond to penalty situations
Respond to feuding players lvg penalty box
Aware of face-off locations
Aware of game conditions
Aware of players leaving zone

INFRACTIONS NOT PENALIZED

P	T	#	PENALTY	TIME	R	COMMENTS

GOALS SCORED   0 - Power Play   ▭ = Man Short

P	T	GOAL #	ASSISTS	TIME

PENALTY EFFICIENCY

Penalties Called____ x3=_____

Infractions Missed____ x3=_____

Penalty Total_____ (a)   Total(b)_____

(a)_____
          x 100=_____%
(b)_____